JIM PURDY

THE JOKE'S ON ME

IMPROVE YOUR VOCABULARY AND ELEVATE YOUR LINGUISTICS
THROUGH HUMOR

iUniverse, Inc.
Bloomington

The Joke's on Me
Improve Your Vocabulary and Elevate Your Linguistics through Humor

Copyright © 2011 Jim Purdy

iUniverse books may be ordered through booksellers or by contacting:

iUniverse
1663 Liberty Drive
Bloomington, IN 47403
www.iuniverse.com
1-800-Authors (1-800-288-4677)

ISBN: 978-1-4502-9532-1 (pbk)
ISBN: 978-1-4502-9533-8 (cloth)
ISBN: 978-1-4502-9534-5 (ebk)

Printed in the United States of America

iUniverse rev. date: 2/23/2011

Respectfully dedicated to Ronald W. Reagan,
40th President of the United States.
In addition to everything else,
he had an incisive sense of wit and humor

Contents

Preface

The purpose of this book is twofold:
1. To teach an appreciation of the American/English sense of humor.
2. To improve your vocabulary and elevate your linguistics through humor.

Each joke is in three parts: The Joke, Analysis, and Vocabulary.
1. The Joke is pretty much self-explanatory.
2. Analysis is an explanation of the joke, its punch line, and why it's funny. It is also an attempt to answer the refrain: "I don't get it." It is the offering of an explanation for each joke which makes this book unique.
3. Vocabulary is an explanation of the words associated with the joke. It is my attempt to define the words which go with the joke. Inasmuch as this is a matter of judgment, this explains why the reader is advised to have four things handy as he or she starts.

The remainder of the book (Ode To Obama, Reid and Pelosi, Dirty Ditties, Short Takes, A Few Political Short Takes, Confucius Say, Quotes Worth Remembering, and One-Liners) is largely taken up with the author's eclecticism during his college years and his travels throughout Europe.

Since most jokes are based on sex, politics or religion, we have used a great deal of each of these in this work – sometimes we even use vulgarity to make a point. The purpose of this is not to titillate, but these factors are an integral part of the humor embodied in these jokes. In other words, most of these jokes are paraprosdokian – they depend on the unexpected. (But if the jokes titillate you, that's fine too.)

Like William Shakespeare, I believe that: "Brevity is the soul of wit." If some of the following jokes seem long-winded, let me assure you that some of them were longer to begin with. Where jokes have been lengthened, this has been for instructional purposes only.

The basis of all humor is incongruity. Expect the unexpected. Indeed, if you can predict the punch line of a joke, or you've heard it before, it's probably **not** funny. This probably gives rise to the saying: "A gentleman has never heard another gentleman's joke." There is no greater put-down than: "Oh, I've heard it before."

It has been our experience that sex education varies from state to state. Moreover, sex education varies widely between countries. As a result, many students are partially or completely ignorant about sex. The vocabulary is heavy on definitions of a sexual nature for this reason.

Similarly, many foreign students have studied formal English in school, but have little knowledge of spoken or colloquial English as it is utilized in everyday conversation (see appendix III). This present work is an attempt to fill this gap also.

We have always known that your entire life is denoted by your speech. Indeed, some linguistics scholars are good enough that they can even tell where you're from just by listening to a few sentences you utter. The minute you open your mouth, you betray yourself to others. Therefore, this present work is not a suggestion as to how you should speak. Rather, it stresses the importance of knowing about the "other side" of English. We hope that this knowledge will be useful to you as a serious student of the language.

Further, the present work is founded on the transition or morphing from separate French and Anglo-Saxon roots (and other sources) into Modern English.

In the following pages, we will fulfill both primary purposes of this book. We will also attempt to give the history of certain turning points such as the Battle of Hastings in England. After this battle, the ruling class of Norman knights spoke French and the subjugated Anglo-Saxons spoke a dialect of German. See the joke on "Par Excellence" for an up-close and personal view of the Battle of Hastings.

Sit back and enjoy yourself. Have fun!

Warning:

If an explicit reference to sex or sexual content offends you, please skip this book entirely. Similarly, no attempt has been made to avoid jokes which are based on ethnicity or male chauvinism. If such jokes offend you, please skip this book entirely.

Jim Purdy
June 27, 2010

Introduction

Before you get started, you may want to have the following four things handy:

1. An English Dictionary. We suggest some version of Webster's.
2. An English Thesaurus. We suggest some version of Roget's, but the student may prefer their own variation.
3. A dictionary which translates your native language into English and vice versa.
4. A Thesaurus written in your native language.

This last is purely optional and depends on how deeply you intend to study. The first is in case you run across a word you don't know, or I have forgotten to define.

Some Definitions to Start

Antonym – A word which means the opposite.

Battle of Hastings – The decisive battle in which William the Conqueror (Duke of Normandy) defeated the Anglo-Saxons under King Harold II (1066) and thus left England open for the Norman Conquest.

Betray – Reveal unintentionally.

Chauvinism – Fanatical patriotism. Prejudiced belief in the superiority of one's own gender, group, or kind. Named after Nicolas *Chauvin,* legendary French soldier under Napoleon, noted for his vociferous and unthinking patriotism.

Confucianism – The teachings of Confucius emphasize love for humanity. A high value is given to learning and to devotion to family (including ancestors). Peace and justice are also strongly emphasized.

Confucius – Chinese philosopher, whose ideas and sayings were collected after his death and became the basis of a philosophical doctrine known as Confucianism. He strongly influenced the traditional culture of China.

Dictionary – A reference book containing an alphabetical list of words with information about them.

Eclecticism – Selecting or employing individual elements from a variety of sources.

Elevate – Promote: give a promotion to or assign to a higher position. To make higher or enhanced.

Ethnicity – An ethnic quality or affiliation resulting from racial or cultural ties.

Linguistics – The scientific study of language.

Merriam – Clinton Hart Merriam (December 5, 1855-March 19, 1942) was an American zoologist, ornithologist, entomologist and ethnographer.

Norman Conquest – The invasion and settlement of England by the Normans following the battle of Hastings (1066).

Morphing – Morphing is a special affect in motion pictures and animations that changes (or morphs) one image into another through a seamless transition. An example would be: The ugly caterpillar morphs into the beautiful butterfly.

Obama – Barack Hussein Obama II (born August 4, 1961) is the 44th and current President of the United States.

Ode – A lyric poem of some length, usually of a serious or meditative nature and having an elevated style and formal stanzaic structure.

Paraprosdokian – A figure of speech in which the latter part of a sentence or phrase is surprising or unexpected in a way that causes the reader or listener to reframe or reinterpret the first part. It is frequently used for humorous or a dramatic effect, sometimes producing an anticlimax. For this reason, it is extremely popular among comedians and satirists.

Pelosi – Nancy Patricia D'Alesandro Pelosi (born March 26, 1940) is the 60th and current Speaker of the United States House of Representatives. She is the Democratic Leader, and a member of Congress elected from the state of California.

Put-down – A crushing remark.

Reid – **Harry Mason Reid** (born December 2, 1939) is the senior United States Senator from Nevada and a member of the Democratic Party, for which he serves as Majority or Minority (depending on who is in power) Leader.

Roget – Peter Mark Roget 1779-1869. British physician and scholar who compiled the Thesaurus of English Words and Phrases (1852).

Satire – Sarcasm: witty language used to convey insults or scorn.

Stanzaic – One of the divisions of a poem composed of two or more lines usually characterized by a common pattern of meter, rhyme, and number of lines.

Synonym – A word which means the same thing. The adjective form is synonymous.

Thesaurus – A dictionary of synonyms and antonyms. You look up a word, get its number, and go to that number to see words that have the same (and possibly opposite) meanings. The plural (Assuming you know Latin) is Thesauri – Thesauruses (If you don't know Latin).

Titillate – To excite (another) pleasurably, superficially or erotically.

Transition – Passage: the act of passing from one state or place to the next.

Vice Versa – With the order reversed.

Vulgarity – Crude, coarse, lacking refinement or cultivation or taste.

Webster – Daniel Webster (January 18, 1782 – October 24, 1852) was a leading American statesman during the nation's Antebellum Period. He gives his name (along with Clinton Hart Merriam) to the Merriam-Webster Dictionary.

William Shakespeare (1564-1616) – English poet and dramatist considered one of the greatest English writers. The above quotation about wit is taken from Lord Polonius' speech from Hamlet written in 1602.

About the Author

James Purdy graduated from Duke University in 1959 with a BA in English Literature. Specializing in eighteenth century English literature, Jim learned the hard way that Charles Dickens was paid for his novels by the word. He was active in the Duke Players and the musical society Hoof 'n' Horn.

He continued his post-graduate work, and obtained a Certificate in Programming and Systems Analysis from New York University's Management Institute in 1972.

A proud veteran, Jim spent three years in the U.S. Army Security Agency. During his stint in Germany, he was elected Soldier of the Month.

Throughout his frequent travels in Europe, Jim Purdy was expected to provide the joke of the day. Moreover, he learned that English had become the language of business and travel throughout the world. It occurred to him, after retirement in 2001, that there was a market for the present combined compendium of jokes, a tutorial based upon the jokes, and significant turning points in history.

In his previous life, before becoming an author, Jim was involved with the Food and Drug Industry as a consultant for about thirty years. Primarily as a part of Worldwide Chain Store Systems (WCSS), he was involved in a variety of consulting assignments in various parts of Europe.

He currently lives with his wife in Jacksonville, Florida where he splits his time between shopping, taking his wife to medical appointments, and reading other fiction and non-fiction authors. His favorite fiction author is John Grisham. His favorite non-fiction author is Dinesh D'Souza from India. See *A Few Political Short Takes* below.

Disraeli and Gladstone

The Joke:

Benjamin Disraeli and William Gladstone had just finished an acrimonious debate in the House of Commons, when they happened to chance on each other while waiting for an audience with the King.

Gladstone, still irate from the debate, says to Disraeli:

"You, Sir, are going to die either on the gallows or of venereal disease."

Disraeli replies:

"That, Sir, depends on whether I embrace your political principles or your mistress."

Analysis:

This joke depends on the dual meaning of the word 'embrace'. This word can either mean a hug, or accepting someone else's ideas or beliefs as your own. If Disraeli accepts Gladstone's political ideas, he will hang on the gallows for treason. If he hugs and sleeps with Gladstone's mistress, he will die of venereal disease. This joke is a classic use of the French term *double entendre*.

Vocabulary:

Acrimonious – Filled with dissension or anger. Nasty.

Audience – An interview with a person of higher rank. A good example of this is Gladstone and Disraeli both waiting for an audience with the King of England.

Debate – A process during which two or more opponents say different things about the same issue. A good example of this would be a discussion over pro-choice and pro-life between two opponents with differing views on the subject of abortion.

Double entendre – This expression is French, and means a saying which can be taken more than one way. The word 'embrace' is a good example.

Gallows – A place where someone is hanged by the neck until he is dead. The game of hang-man is a good example.

Hurled – Thrown.

Invective – Insult, name-calling. Vituperation: abusive or venomous language.

Irate – Angry or mad.

Nasty – Full of nastiness, sarcasm, and hurled invectives.

Sarcasm – Witty language used to convey insults or scorn.

Scorn – Contempt or disdain felt toward a person or object considered despicable or unworthy.

Venereal disease – A disease which you catch from having unprotected sex with a person who is already infected.

Lady Astor and Sir Winston Churchill

The Joke:

While debating Sir Winston on the House of Commons, Lady Astor gets a little carried away, and says:

"Sir Winston, if I were your wife, I should poison your tea."

To which Sir Winston replies:

"Madam, if I were your husband, I would drink it."

Analysis:

One-upmanship seems to be the name of the game here.

Vocabulary:

Carried Away – In this case, overly excited.

Churchill (1874-1965) – Sir Winston Leonard Spencer Churchill. Educated at Harrow and Sandhurst, he became (1894) an officer in the 4th Hussars. On leave in 1895, he saw his first military action in Cuba as a reporter for London's *Daily Graphic.* He served in India and in 1898 fought at Omdurman in Sudan under Kitchener. Having resigned his commission, he was sent (1899) to cover the South African War by the *Morning Post,* and his accounts of his capture and imprisonment by the Boers and his escape raised him to the forefront of English journalists.

Churchill was elected to Parliament as a Conservative in 1900, but he subsequently switched to the Liberal party and was appointed undersecretary for the colonies in the cabinet of Sir Henry Campbell-Bannerman. Under Asquith, he was initially (1908–10) president of the Board of Trade, then home secretary (1910–11), and championed innovative labor exchange and old-age pension acts. As first lord of the admiralty (1911), he presided over the naval expansion that preceded World War I.

Discredited by the failure of the Dardanelles expedition, which he had championed, Churchill lost (1915) his admiralty post and served on the front lines in France. Returning to office under Lloyd George, he served as minister of munitions (1917) and secretary of state for war and for air (1918–21). As colonial secretary (1921–22), he helped negotiate the treaty that set up the Irish Free State.

After two defeats at the polls he returned to the House of Commons, as a Constitutionalist, and became (1924–29) Chancellor of the Exchequer in Stanley Baldwin's Conservative government. As an advocate of laissez-faire economics, he was strongly criticized by John Maynard Keynes.

Churchill was not a financial innovator; he basically followed conventional advice from his colleagues. Nevertheless, Churchill's decision to return the country to the prewar gold standard increased unemployment and was a cause of the general strike of 1926. He advocated aggressive action to end the strike, and thus earned the lasting distrust of the labor movement.

Out of office from 1929 to 1939, Churchill wrote and remained in the public eye with his support for Edward VIII. He was involved in the abdication crisis of 1936 and with his vehement opposition to the Indian nationalist movement. He also issued warnings of the threat from Nazi Germany that went unheeded, in part because of his past political and military misjudgments. When World War II broke out (September, 1939), Neville Chamberlain appointed him first lord of the admiralty. The following May, when Chamberlain was forced to resign, Churchill became prime minister.

Churchill was one of the truly great orators; his energy and his stubborn public refusal to make peace until Adolf Hitler was crushed were crucial in rallying and maintaining British resistance to Germany during the grim years from 1940 to 1942. He met President Franklin Roosevelt at sea before the entry of the United States into the war, twice addressed the U.S. Congress (Dec., 1941; May, 1942), twice went to Moscow (Aug., 1942; May, 1944), visited battle fronts, and attended a long series of international conferences.

The British nation supported the vigorous program of Churchill's coalition cabinet until after the surrender of Germany. Then in July, 1945, Britain's desire for rapid social reform led to a Labour electoral victory, and Churchill became leader of the opposition. In 1946, on a visit to the United States, he made a controversial speech at Fulton, Mo., in which he warned of the expansive tendencies of the USSR (he had distrusted the Soviet government since its inception, when he had been a leading advocate of Western intervention to overthrow it) and coined the expression "Iron Curtain."

As prime minister again from 1951 until his resignation in 1955, he ended nationalization of the steel and auto industries but maintained most other socialist measures instituted by the Labour government. In 1953 Churchill was knighted, and awarded the 1953 Nobel Prize in Literature for his writing and oratory. He retained a seat in Parliament until 1964. He refused a peerage, but his widow, Clementine Ogilvy Hozier (married 1908), accepted one in 1965 for her charitable work.

Lady Astor (1879-1964) – Nancy Witcher Astor, Viscountess Astor, HC, was the first woman to sit as a Member of Parliament (MP) in the British House of Commons. Nancy Astor represented the Conservative Party and was the wife of Waldorf Astor, 2nd Viscount Astor. Lady Astor was born Nancy Witcher Langhorne in Danville, Virginia, in the United States. Her second husband, Waldorf Astor, was born in the United States but his father had moved the family to England when Waldorf was twelve and raised his children as English aristocrats.

Several elements of Lady Astor's life to this point influenced her first campaign, but the main reason she became a candidate in the first place was her husband's situation. He had enjoyed a promising career for several years before World War I in the House of Commons, but then he succeeded to his father's peerage as the 2nd Viscount Astor. This meant that he automatically became a member of the House of Lords and forfeited his seat of Plymouth Sutton in the House of Commons. So Lady Astor decided to contest the vacant parliamentary seat.

Vocabulary:
Poison – A substance that causes injury, illness, or death, especially by chemical means. To use such a substance.

Sir Winston and the Labour M.P.

The Joke:
While Sir Winston is at a party during the evening, a Labour Member of Parliament approaches him and says:

"Sir Winston, you're drunk."

Sir Winston peers more closely at his assailant, and replies:

"And you, Madam, are very ugly – but tomorrow I shall be sober."

Analysis:
Sir Winston is saying that there is a cure for his drunkenness, but there is no cure for ugliness. Tomorrow, he will be sober, but she will still be ugly.

Vocabulary:
Assailant – Someone who confronts someone else. Usually with something he or she considers to be a defect.

Churchill – See above for a full description of Sir Winston Leonard Spencer Churchill.

Labour – A political party in England. Sir Winston is a member of the Conservative Party. Therefore, he and the lady are on opposite sides.

Peers – Looks at, or sees.

Churchill and Attlee

The Joke:

Sir Winston arrived at a London hotel for a function when he decided to stop by the men's room. No sooner did he find a position to relieve himself than who should enter the men's room but his old political rival Clement Attlee. To Churchill's surprise, Attlee came and stood right next to him. So, Churchill nervously moved a few places away.

"My, my, Winston," Attlee exclaimed. "Are we being modest?"

Winston replied, "Not at all, Clement. It's just that every time you see something that is large, privately owned, and working well, you want to nationalize it."

Analysis:

Clement Attlee was Prime Minister of the Labour Party in England. His party was responsible for nationalizing large parts of the British economy.

Vocabulary:

Churchill – See above for a full description of Sir Winston Leonard Spencer Churchill.

Function – In this case, an official ceremony or a formal social occasion.

Par Excellence

The Joke:

An elementary school teacher says:

"OK, children, we are going to study sex education. As your first homework assignment, go home and find out what a penis is."

Little Johnnie hurries home, and finds his father watching TV in the living room. He asks:

"Dad, what is a penis?"

His father says:

"I can see it's time for your sex education to begin. Follow me."

He leads little Johnnie to the bathroom, drops his trousers and his underpants, and says:

"Now this, son, is a penis. As a matter of fact, this is a penis par excellence."

The next day, little Johnnie is on his way to school with Mary. She asks:

"Did you find out what a penis is?"

Johnnie answers in the affirmative, so she says:

"Tell me."

Johnnie says:

"I can't tell you, but I can show you."

She answers in the affirmative, so he says:

"OK, come with me behind the bushes."

She comes with him, and he drops his trousers and underpants. He says:

"Now this, Mary, is a penis. And if it were two inches shorter, it would be *par excellence*."

Analysis:

Par excellence is actually borrowed from the French, and literally means by preeminence. English has many cognates with both French and German.

A little history is in order here. After the Romans abandoned England in 410 A.D., the Saxons and then the Angles invaded various parts of England, killing innocent women and children as they went. The Angles and the Saxons were two Germanic tribes, and even today the English are sometimes referred to as the Anglo-Saxons. Eventually, the Angles and the Saxons conquered all of England, displacing the Celtic and Gaelic populations that were already there.

As an aside, Celtic and Gaelic languages are still spoken in Ireland, Scotland and Wales today.

In 1066, William the Conqueror invaded the South of England, and defeated King Harold at the Battle of Hastings. William was Duke of Normandy in France, and invaded from there. The French got very lucky during the Battle of Hastings. A cross-bow bolt flew through the air and struck King Harold between the visor and the rest of the helmet, striking him in the eye. Although he did not die immediately, his command of the Housecarls and the Anglo-Saxon forces was seriously impaired. The French won the battle. To this day, no one knows exactly where King Harold is buried, because William was afraid his body would be used as a rallying point for his opposition. He refused the request of Harold's mother for the body for this reason.

Thus, English can be considered basically a German language with an overlay of French. Over the years, the two languages merged to form modern English.

Vocabulary:

Aetheling – A prince who was eligible to become king.

Affirmative – Yes. Used by the military to prevent confusion in communications. See *negative* below.

Amateur – Unpaid. Not professional.

Angles – A Germanic tribe which invaded England.

Anglo-Saxon – An earlier version of the English language. The name is taken from the two Germanic tribes which used the language.

Battle of Hastings – This battle is considered a turning point in the history of England, since after the battle the Norman French ruled and the subjugated Anglo-Saxons were politically powerless. The battle actually took place primarily on Senlac Hill, approximately 6 miles to the Northwest of Hastings. The Anglo-Saxons occupied the top of the ridge or hill, going on the defensive against the invading Norman French and their allies. They had only infantry. Even those who rode to the battle dismounted and fought on foot. The Anglo-Saxon army was composed of Housecarls (See Housecarls below) and people from the landed gentry who were charged with providing their own armor and arms. While the Housecarls were professional soldiers, the members of the landed gentry were part-time amateurs.

In contrast to the Anglo-Saxons, the Norman French employed archers (both longbow men and crossbow men), cavalry, and infantry. Moreover, the Normans were a polyglot force. In addition to the half of Normans, they

9

included soldiers from Brittany and Flanders, other parts of France, and even as far away as southern Italy. They were at a disadvantage, moreover, because they had to charge uphill to reach the Anglo-Saxons. At first, the battle did not go well for the Normans. The barrages of arrows shot at the Anglo-Saxons stuck in their shield wall. The Norman infantry were decimated by the stones, javelins, and maces thrown by the Anglo-Saxons. As a result, the Normans committed their cavalry much sooner than they had planned. After about an hour of fighting, the division on the Norman left from Brittany retreated in a rout. Unable to resist the temptation, the Anglo-Saxons chased after the fleeing Bretons. The two brothers of Harold, Leofwyne and Gyrthe, were killed in a Norman cavalry counter-attack. This was a double misfortune for the Anglo-Saxons. Not only did they lose these two tactical commanders, but they were also deprived of any experienced successor in the event that King Harold II was killed.

A horse was killed beneath the leader of the Normans. It was not until William stood up and threw off his helmet that his men were convinced that he was not dead after all, and the Normans stopped their retreat.

About this time, the bolt from a crossbow struck King Harold in the eye, and William discovered that the shield-wall was broken. The French went on to win the battle.

Battle of Stamford Bridge – Although this was a great victory for King Harold II and the Anglo-Saxons, it may have contributed to the Anglo-Saxon defeat at the Battle of Hastings. Both Tostig Godwinson and King Harald Hardrada of Norway were killed in this battle.

Battleaxe – An axe used in hand-to-hand combat. Also used to designate a very unpleasant woman. Calling a woman an old battleaxe is not a compliment.

Bolt – An arrow without feathers. Used in conjunction with the cross-bow. It is placed in the groove in front of the string on the cross-bow.

Breton – Some one who comes from Brittany.

Brittany – A region in the north-west of France.

Cavalry – Mounted horsemen. Nowadays, they have been replaced by tanks as armored cavalry in the modern army.

Celtic – A language spoken in ancient England. Spoken by the Celts at the time of the Romans.

Chain Mail – Made from metal rings sewn into a garment. Since this was expensive in both time and money, ordinary foot soldiers were rarely wearing it.

Cognate – A word which is the same in two different languages. The spelling may be different. An example would be house in English and haus in German. They are spelled differently, but they both mean house.

Conical – Shaped like a cone or a paper coffee filter.

Cross-bow – A bow which is fired like a rifle. The string is pulled back until it engages the trigger. The first known instance of its use in England was at the Battle of Hastings. See bolt above for a description of the arrow used by the cross-bow.

Dalliance – A romantic affair. A flirtation. Also, and perhaps more usually, a waste of time.

Danish – Pertaining to Denmark.

Danish Two-handed Battleaxe – From Denmark originally, this was a single-edged axe which required two hands to wield effectively in a battle.

Decimated – Partially wiped out.

Dismount – To get off a horse. Mounting a horse means to get up on his back.

Edgar The Aetheling – Since Harold's two brothers had been killed at the Battle of Hastings, Edgar was considered the only viable candidate for the throne. He ruled for only eight weeks, and was deposed. He submitted to William the Conqueror. Edgar was only fifteen when he was appointed King by the Witan. The term 'aetheling' meant he was a prince who was eligible to become King (See Aetheling above). Although appointed King of England, he was never crowned. Shortly thereafter, he had to swear fealty to William the Conqueror, formerly Duke of Normandy.

Edward III – Also known as Edward the Confessor. He was the immediate predecessor of Harold II. He ruled England from 8 June 1042 to 5 January 1066. He conquered the Danes, thus beginning his reign. His father was Aethelred the Unready and his mother was Emma of Normandy. He named Harold Godwinson his heir in his will as successor to the throne of England. If he promised fealty to William the Conqueror, he reneged on this promise and named Harold Godwinson to be his successor instead. William certainly thought he had promised fealty to him, and considered that he had been betrayed. Harold Godwinson had promised him fealty, but claimed this was overridden by the decision of the Witan confirming Edward's will.

Flanders – A region located in present-day France, Belgium, and Holland. The language and the people are Flemish; the language is a dialect of Dutch. It is sometimes referred to as Nederlands.

Flirtation – Making romantic overtures to someone of the opposite sex. Flirting with someone.

Gaelic – A kind of Celtic language spoken in southern Ireland and parts of Scotland.

Godwinson – One of the most prominent families in England, particularly at the time of election by the Witan of Harold Godwinson to be King of England.

Gyrthe Godwinson – One of two loyal brothers of King Harold II, he was killed at the Battle of Hastings.

Harald Hardrada – King Harald III of Norway. He was killed at the Battle of Stamford Bridge.

Harold II – Also known as Harold Godwinson. He was the last Anglo-Saxon King of England, killed at the Battle of Hastings. Although he had sworn an oath of fealty on sacred relics to his cousin William of Normandy, he had been elected King of England by the Witan. His reply to William stated that his oath of fealty to him was superseded by the decision of the Witan. The Witan had considered four candidates for King of England including Duke William of Normandy, and chosen Harold to be King. Duke William was outraged, and considered this to be a declaration of war. He immediately started to make plans to invade England, offering land and titles to anyone who would join him in his invasion.

His father had five sons: Sweyn, Harold, Tostig, Gyrthe, and Leofwyne.

His oldest son, Sweyn, was exiled in 1051 for life by Harold II's predecessor, King Edward the Confessor.

Early on, Harold had become Earl of East Anglia in 1045, because his father's sister was married to King Edward the Confessor. Upon his father's death in 1053, he inherited and became Earl of Essex. This earldom encompassed about one third of England, and was located in the South. Later, he also became Earl of Hereford in 1058. Thus, his power was second only to the King in England.

He gained glory in a series of campaigns (1062–63) against Gruffydd ap Llyweln of Gwynedd, the ruler of Wales. This conflict ended with Gruffydd's defeat, and death at the hands of his own troops, in 1063.

In 1064, Harold was shipwrecked in Ponthieu on the Norman coast of France. There is general agreement that he left from Bosham, and was blown off course, landing on the coast of Ponthieu, where he was held hostage by Count Guy. Duke William arrived soon after and ordered Guy to turn Harold over to him. Harold then apparently accompanied William to battle against William's enemy, Conan II, Duke of Brittany.

They pursued Conan from Dol de Bretagne to Rennes, and finally to Dinan, where he surrendered the fortress's keys on the point of a lance. William presented Harold with weapons and arms, knighting him. Harold swore an oath on sacred relics to William to support his claim to the English throne. After Harold's death, the Normans were quick to point out that in accepting the crown of England; Harold had perjured himself of this alleged oath.

Tostig was the younger brother of Harold, and became Earl of Northumbria in 1055. Due to an unjust doubling of taxation instituted by Tostig in 1065 that threatened to plunge England into civil war, Harold supported Northumbrian rebels against his younger brother, Tostig, and replaced him with Morcar. This strengthened his acceptability as Edward's successor, but fatally divided his own family, driving Tostig into alliance with King Harald Hardrada ('Hard Reign') of Norway.

Hauberk – A shirt made of chain mail extending down to at least mid-thigh. It is normally put on over the head.

Helmet – A covering over the head made of metal, usually for protection of the head.

Homework – An assignment from school to be performed at home, and brought back to class. Doing your homework has also come to mean preparation. Not doing your homework has come to mean unprepared.

Housecarls – English infantry with a devotion to King Harold. These were full-time professional soldiers. They were armed with a conical helmet, a chain mail hauberk, and a kite-shaped shield. Their primary weapon was the two-handed Danish battleaxe, though each man would have carried a sword as well. They were killed to the last man at the Battle of Hastings.

Javelin – A light spear, usually thrown by hand.

Leofwyne Godwinson – One of two loyal brothers of King Harold II, he was killed at the Battle of Hastings.

Mace – A hand-held club with a chain having a head with spikes.

Merged – Came together.

Misfortune – Not fortunate. A happening which is not lucky.

Negative – No. Used by the military to prevent confusion in communications. See *affirmative* above.

Norman – From the Normandy region on the coast of France.

Pevensey – The place on the coast of Sussex in England where William the Conqueror landed to start his invasion of England. In September 1066 there were no defenders at Pevensey, and the still-existing bay provided a safe haven for the invading fleet. The bay is located a few miles to the west of Hastings. Thence William moved to Hastings, a few miles to the east, where he built a prefabricated wooden castle for a base of operations. From there, he ravaged the hinterland and waited for Harold's return from the north.

Polyglot – Composed of several languages. Although most spoke French, several different dialects of French were used. If used to refer to a person, a skilled linguist speaking several languages is implied.

Rallying Point – A person, place or thing which can be used as a symbol to support a political idea.

Reneged – Went back on his word. Changed his mind later after giving his word.

Saxons – A Germanic tribe which invaded England.

Shield Wall – A wall made of locking shields.

Siege – To surround and cut off the target city. To lay siege to a city is an attempt to starve the occupants out.

Spear – A weapon with a pointed head made of metal, and a shaft made of wood.

Spike – A sharp raised point.

Subordinate – Some one who is inferior to some one else.

Subjugate – Defeat. Make subordinate to.

Successor – Some one who takes over from some one else. To succeed to the throne means to become King or Queen.

Sweyn Godwinson – The oldest son of the Earl of Essex and an older brother of Harold. He was exiled for life by Harold's immediate predecessor, King Edward the Confessor.

Tanner – Some one who cures hides of animals for a living.

Tostig Godwinson – The third son of the Earl of Essex and younger brother of Harold Godwinson, but he was a traitor. He was killed along with his ally the King of Norway, Harald Hardrada, at the Battle of Stamford Bridge on September 25th. Fewer than 20 ships out of an invasion fleet of 300 returned to Norway with survivors. Although this was a great victory for Harold II and the Anglo-Saxons, the army was greatly weakened and it may have led directly to their defeat at the Battle of Hastings some three weeks later.

Trousers – Male terminology for the outer garment worn below the waist. The female equivalent is pants.

Underpants – Foundation garment worn under the trousers next to the skin. The female equivalent is panties.

Visor – In this case, the part of the helmet which can be lifted to allow the eyes to see. Alternately, the word can be used to designate any covering for the eyes, such as sunglasses.

Wield Effectively – Use efficiently.

William The Conqueror – After the Battle of Hastings and after his coronation, he became King William I of England. Before this, he was also known as *William the Bastard*. This name was due to a dalliance with a tanner's daughter by his father, Duke Robert I of Normandy. As his only son, William was named his only heir at the age of seven in 1035. Thanks largely to the patronage of King Henry I of France (Later, King Henry would have second thoughts about his ward, because Henry thought William was becoming too powerful due to his marriage with a noble woman, Matilda of Flanders in 1053. Henry tried to invade Normandy twice in 1054 and 1057, but failed on both attempts).

William's illegitimacy strongly affected his early life. As a child, his life was in constant danger from his kinsmen who thought that they had a more legitimate right to rule. They derided him as the illegitimate offspring of a tanner's daughter. During his siege of Alencon in Normandy, they even hung tanned hides from the city walls (As revenge, William had the hands cut off from many of the townspeople of Alencon after the siege was over).

William was a cousin of Harold II, whom he defeated at the Battle of Hastings. Long after he became King William I of England, he realized that he was dying in 1087, and distributed his considerable wealth to the church and the poor.

Witan – The most important council in Anglo-Saxon England and was empowered to select the next king. It consisted normally of about sixty of the most prominent nobles and clergymen of England. Among four candidates, they chose Harold Godwinson to be King of England. The four candidates were: Harold, Edgar the Aetheling, Harald Hardrada and Duke William of Normandy.

An American Tourist in London

The Joke:

An American is touring London in England. He is lost and disoriented. He spots an English passerby and asks him:

"Excuse me, sir; is this the Tower of London I am standing beside?"

The Englishman informs the American that it is not proper to end a sentence with a preposition. But if he will rephrase the question, the Englishman will answer it.

The American responds:

"Excuse me, sir; is this the Tower of London I am standing beside, asshole?"

Analysis:

The American is annoyed to be accused of using improper English. So he responds by adding a rude expletive to the end of the sentence. As a matter of fact, it is not proper to end an English sentence with a preposition.

Vocabulary:

Asshole – A derogatory term used against someone disliked. The correct term is 'anal orifice.'

Disoriented – Not oriented – confused: having lost your bearings; confused as to time or place or personal identity.

Expletive – Curse: profane or obscene expression usually of surprise or anger.

Improper – Not proper – not suitable or right or appropriate.

Passerby – A person who passes by casually or by chance.

Preposition – A word that indicates the relationship between a noun or pronoun and other words in a sentence.

Rude – In England, this means vulgar or obscene. See appendix II.

Tower of London – A fortress in London on the Thames; used as a palace and a state prison and now as a museum containing the crown jewels. It is a big tourist attraction.

How to Get To Heaven

The Joke:

A 3rd grade teacher in the United States is attempting to find out how her students intend to get to Heaven. She is getting the usual responses – e.g., she asks little Mary and she responds:

"I would pray every night."

The teacher says:

"Could you give us an example?"

Little Mary says:

"Sure. 'Now I lay me down to sleep

I pray the Lord my soul to keep

If I should die before I wake

I pray the Lord my soul to take.'"

The teacher responds with:

"Very good, Mary."

Finally, the teacher reaches little Johnnie, and says:

"And how would you get to Heaven, Johnnie?"

Johnnie replies:

"I would just tell Him that I'm coming."

The teacher replies:

"Why do you say that, Johnnie?"

Johnnie responds:

"Because I was passing the master bedroom door, and I heard Mommy say: 'Oh my God, I'm coming – I'm coming!

My God, I'm coming – I'm coming!'

And if Dad hadn't been on top of her holding her back, I think she would have made it too."

Analysis:

Little Johnnie has witnessed his parents making love. When a woman climaxes during sexual intercourse, she will typically exclaim that she is coming. Little Johnnie's father is using the so-called missionary position, which explains why he is on top of his wife during the sexual encounter.

Vocabulary:

Atone – To make amends for. To compensate for.

Climax -Having an orgasm during sexual intercourse.

Cock – See penis below.

Coming – See orgasm below. Alternate spelling is Cuming.

Dick – See penis below.

Fornication – See sexual intercourse below.

Fuck – See sexual intercourse below.

Heaven – A serene and happy place where people go if they have been good in this life. If people have been bad in this life, they go to purgatory or Hell.

Hell – A violent and unpleasant place where people go if they have been bad in this life.

Missionary position – A position used during sexual intercourse with the man on the top and the woman beneath him with her legs spread apart.

Orgasm – May be achieved during vaginal sexual intercourse. This pertains to release through ejaculation. A slang term is coming.

Purgatory – A place only slightly above Hell, where people go if they have been bad in this life. Here, they can atone for their sins and hope to attain Heaven one day in the future.

Penis – The part of the male anatomy used during sexual intercourse. The adjective form is penile (not penal which has to do with the prison system). Slang terms are cock and dick.

Pussy – See vagina below.

Screw – See sexual intercourse below.

Serene – Quiet and happy.

Sexual intercourse – The physical making of love, normally between a male and a female. Another term is fornication. The slang terms are fuck and screw.

Vagina – A part of the female anatomy used during sexual intercourse. The adjective form is vaginal. A slang term is pussy.

Witness – To see something. The past tense is witnessed.

The Lone Ranger

The Joke:

The American Indians finally capture the Lone Ranger. They decide that since he has been such a gallant adversary, they will grant him three final wishes. They inform him of their decision.

The Lone Ranger says:

"Well, call Silver over here."

Silver comes trotting over, and the Lone Ranger whispers something in his ear. A few hours later, Silver comes trotting back with a beautiful brunette on his back. The brunette doesn't have a stitch on, so the Chief says:

"I suppose you need the use of my wigwam for about forty-five minutes."

When the Lone Ranger emerges, the Indians ask him what he wants for his second wish.

Again, the Lone Ranger says:

"Well, call Silver over here."

Silver again comes trotting over, and again the Lone Ranger whispers something in Silver's ear. In about four hours, Silver returns. This time, he has a beautiful blonde on his back – again without a stitch on. Again, the Chief offers the use of his wigwam for about forty-five minutes.

When the Lone Ranger emerges, the Indians ask him what he wants for his third and final wish.

Again, he says:

"Well, call Silver over here."

When Silver arrives, the Lone Ranger grabs him by the ear and says:

"I said, posse!"

Analysis:

Silver is obviously confused between posse and pussy. He was supposed to return with a posse. Instead, he returns with a beautiful woman because he thinks the Lone Ranger wants to sleep with a woman as his final wish. Like many jokes, this one depends on two words sounding similar. In other words, the joke may not work in another language.

Vocabulary:

Posse – A body of armed men. They are typically in search of a man wanted for bank robbery. In this case, they are supposed to rescue the Lone Ranger from the Indians.

Pussy – Slang for vagina.

The Pope's Car

The Joke:

A man dies and goes to Heaven. He notices that Saint Peter is giving out transportation according to what kind of life you've lived. A few people are getting cars, but many more are getting only a ten-speed bicycle, a skate board or even roller skates. Then he notices that he is about fifteen places behind the Pope, who has just passed away. He is really curious to see what kind of transportation the Pope will get. Finally, it becomes the Pope's turn.

Saint Peter talks to him about fifteen minutes, and calls him up a Mercedes. The Pope drives off. Saint Peter begins to speak to a man about three places behind the Pope. He continues to speak to him for about forty-five minutes.

Finally, he calls him up a Rolls Royce Silver Arrow and the man drives off.

It becomes our hero's turn and Saint Peter talks to him for about three minutes before calling him up a little Ford. Our hero says:

"Before I drive off, could I ask you a question?"

Saint Peter says:

"Yes, of course."

Our hero continues:

"I notice that you gave the Pope a very good car – you gave him that Mercedes. But you gave a much better car to the fellow about three places behind him. Who was that guy?"

Saint Peter replies:

"Oh, he was a lawyer."

Our hero responds:

"I don't understand"

Saint Peter says:

"Let me put it this way. We have a hundred and seventy-nine Popes up here, but that's the first lawyer we've ever seen."

Analysis:

Do not worry; the Borgia Popes are probably not among the Popes in Heaven. Neither is the Pope who had a palace built for his mistress in the middle of the Vatican.

Saint Peter is implying that all lawyers (except this one) are in Hell.

Vocabulary:

Attorney – Another name for a lawyer.

Saint Peter – According to Christian belief, St. Peter is the saint in charge of admission through the pearly gates into Heaven.

Vatican – The headquarters of the Catholic Church. It is located in Rome, Italy.

The Man Who Attained Heaven

The Joke:

A man passes away and is sent to Heaven. He is checked out with the usual standard equipment – namely a white robe, a halo and a harp. He is wandering around trying to learn how to play this instrument that he has just been issued. Suddenly, he spots his old next door neighbor sitting on a cloud, with a gigantic bottle of booze on one knee and a gorgeous blonde on the other. He goes hot-footing it back to Saint Peter.

"What kind of justice is this? Look, I lived a good life – gave my tithe to the church, went every Sunday, raised two kids, paid my taxes, and did everything I should. My next door neighbor never did an honest day's work in his life, drank, cursed, cheated on his wife, beat her, and did everything rotten you can possibly think of – he comes up here and gets checked out with this giant bottle of whiskey and this gorgeous blonde while I get checked out with this costume, halo and instrument I don't even know how to play. What kind of justice is this?"

St. Peter responds with:

"Not so fast. You have to realize that your old next door neighbor is in Hell."

"What do you mean, he's in Hell?" responds the fellow.

Says St. Peter:

"You have to realize that Heaven and Hell are not two separate places. They are simply different states of mind."

The fellow responds:

"I still don't understand."

St, Peter says:

"Let me put it this way – the bottle of booze has a hole in the bottom, and the blonde doesn't."

Analysis:

Heaven and Hell are indeed separate states of mind in this story. The next door neighbor has a bottle of whiskey with a hole in it, and a girl with no vagina at all. If that's not Hell, then I don't know what is.

Vocabulary:

Angel – In the Christian Religion, an angel is a creature with wings whose place is in Heaven. Except for the wings, he or she is usually portrayed as a human being.

Halo – A band of gold which appears above the head – used in the Christian Religion to denote a person or angel of religious significance.

Harp – A musical instrument with strings. In the Christian Religion, this is the instrument played by the angels and by humans who have gone to Heaven.

Hot-footing – Hurrying.

The Nun and the Liquor Store

The Joke:

A religious sister goes to a liquor store and purchases a bottle of brandy. She pays for it, and is about to leave when the proprietor stops her and asks:

"Excuse me. Sister, but could I ask you a question?"

The nun replies:

"Of course."

The owner continues:

"I don't want to appear nosy, but I thought that the members of your Order were absolutely forbidden to drink."

The nun replies:

"Oh yes, this bottle of brandy is for the Mother Superior's constipation."

Five o'clock rolls around. The owner closes his liquor store, and starts driving home. Who should he spot lying on a park bench, drunk out of her mind, but this nun?

He pulls over his car to the curb, approaches the nun on the bench, and says:

"Sister, I'm surprised at you. You lied to me. You told me that bottle of brandy was for the Mother Superior's constipation."

The nun props herself up on one elbow, and says:

"It is, it is – man, you think she ain't gonna shit when she sees this?"

Analysis:

The nun didn't lie. The Mother Superior is probably going to shit when she catches sight of the nun drunk.

Vocabulary:

Ain't gonna – Incorrect English for "isn't going to".

Constipation – Unable to have a bowel movement. The slang term is unable to take a shit.

Defecation – To have a bowel movement.

Mother Superior – In the Catholic Church, the head of an institution of holy sisters or nuns.

Proprietor – The owner, normally of a business.

Shit – A slang term associated with vulgarity. To have a bowel movement. To defecate.

Vulgar – Crude, coarse, lacking refinement or cultivation or taste.

Eighty

The Joke:
A professor of the course in marriage and family relations is giving a lecture, and says:

"So far, we have stayed away from one important subject during this course.

But it is an important part of any marriage, and I propose that we jump right in.

Does anyone know how many different positions there are for sexual intercourse?"

He hears a response from the back of the room of seventy-nine, but ignores it.

He continues:

"No one actually knows exactly how many positions there are, but the most typical position is the so-called missionary position with the man on the top and the woman beneath him with her legs spread."

Again comes the response from the back of the room:

"Eighty, eighty!"

Analysis:
The student at the back of the room apparently thinks that there are seventy-nine positions for sexual intercourse. When the professor mentions the missionary position, he or she revises his or her estimate, and exclaims:

"Eighty"

Vocabulary:
None. See the previous joke: *How to Get to Heaven* for definitions.

A Boy and His Goose

The Joke:
A little boy lived all alone with his grandmother. They were very poor. About the only possession they had was a pet goose. Finally, the grandmother says to the boy:

"I know that you could never stand to slaughter the goose, because he's a family pet. But our situation is desperate – we must have money to buy more food. So I want you to go down to the marketplace and sell the goose so we can buy some more food."

The boy goes to the marketplace, and spends all day trying to sell the goose.

He's not having any luck selling the goose. It's getting dark, so the boy decides to try selling the goose door-to-door. Again, he's not having any luck, but he encounters a front door which is partially ajar. He goes in. He is unable to find anyone on the ground floor, so he climbs the stairs and looks into one of the bedrooms. He is surprised to see a man and a woman in bed. The man looks up and exclaims:

"Hey, kid, get the hell out of here!"

The boy turns and is about to leave, when suddenly the downstairs door slams and a loud voice says:

"Hi, honey, I'm home."

"Oh my God, it's my husband!" exclaims the woman in bed.

"Quick, kid, come here," says the man, and he grabs his clothes off the end of the bed and they all three hide in the closet. The boy says:

"Say mister, I've got to sell this here goose."

Replies the man:

"Shhhhh. I'll give you a hundred and fifty dollars for the goose."

The boy doesn't think the goose is worth that much, and says;

"But mister this goose isn't …"

The man interrupts with:

"Shhhhh. I'll give you two hundred dollars for the goose."

The boy suddenly realizes that he has a good thing going, and says:

"Say mister, this goose has always been a family pet, and I wouldn't like to think that she's going somewhere where she won't be fed properly or taken care of right."

The man says;

"All right, two hundred and fifty dollars and you can keep the goose. That's my final offer. Now, shut up kid!"

They wait for the other man and his wife to fall asleep, and then they sneak out.

The boy goes running home to his grandmother, and exclaims:

"Look Ma, I got two hundred and fifty dollars, and I got to keep the goose too. I..."

The grandmother interrupts the boy with:

"You must have done something wrong, because you have the money and the goose too. Tomorrow, you go to mass and confess."

The boy says:

"But Ma, I didn't ..."

The grandmother interrupts him again:

"Tomorrow – mass – confess!"

The next day, the boy attends mass. He goes to the confessional box afterwards, pulls the curtain, and says:

"Father, you see I've got this here goose and ..."

The priest interrupts him with:

"Son, if you mention that goose to me one more time..."

Analysis:

It was the priest who was the first man in the bed. He was committing adultery with the woman in the bed when he was interrupted by the boy.

Vocabulary:

Abattoir – See slaughter below.

Adultery – The act of having sex with a person who is not your husband or your wife. This act takes place inside a marriage, but involves a different partner. The prevalent theory is that priests and nuns are married to the Catholic Church.

Celibacy – In the Catholic Religion, every priest takes a vow of chastity.

He is not supposed to even touch a woman, much less sleep with her. He is supposed to be celibate from the time he ordains as a priest.

Confess – Admitting your sins to a priest.

Mass – In the Catholic Religion, the sermon is delivered as part of the service. Formerly given only in Latin, it is now given in the native language of the country.

Slaughter – To kill. The place where animals are killed is called an abattoir.

The 12-point Buck Deer

The Joke:

A third grade teacher is trying to teach her students how to identify animals. To this end, she has arranged for an overhead projector and is displaying slides of different animals on the wall. She displays a rabbit. Little Mary raises her hand, and says:

"I know. That's a bunny rabbit."

The teacher says:

"That's absolutely correct. Very good, Mary!"

Next, the teacher displays a picture of a brown bear. Little Johnnie raises his hand, and says:

"I know. It's a bear."

Once again, the teacher says:

"Absolutely correct. Very good, Johnnie!"

Then, she displays a picture of a 12-point buck deer. No one says a word. Wanting to give her students a hint, the teacher says:

"Let me give you a hint. What does your mother call your father?"

Again silence. Finally, one little girl says;

"I know. I know. It's a horny bastard."

Analysis:

Sometimes when you think your child is somewhere else in the house, he or she is just around the corner, eavesdropping on every word you say. This is the case in the instance of the little girl. A man and his wife are probably just joking around when she calls him a horny bastard. But their little daughter doesn't know this, and assumes her mother is serious.

Vocabulary:

Bastard – Of birth outside of wedlock. A synonym is illegitimate. Also used as a term of derision about another human being.

Buck – Male. A female deer is called a doe.

Doe – Female. A male deer is called a buck.

Eavesdrop – To listen in without the conversationalist knowing that you are listening.

Horny – Slang for ready to have sex.

Overhead projector – An electrical device which will display slides against a screen or against a wall.

Point – A prong on the antlers of a deer.

A Small Plane Is Lost

The Joke:

A small airplane is lost in a fog somewhere near Heathrow airport in England. Half of the instruments are out in the small aircraft. Suddenly, the pilot spots a tall building with someone in the top floor. He turns to his passenger and says:

"You get that fellow's attention and ask him where we are."

They get the fellow's attention, and the passenger asks:

"Where are we?"

The fellow in the building answers:

"You're in an airplane."

The pilot immediately turns due south, travels for about three miles, and comes in for a perfect landing at Heathrow.

"My God" says the passenger: "How did you do that?"

"Very simple" says the pilot: "We asked that fellow a very logical question. His answer was 100% correct – and 100% worthless. So I knew that it had to be IBM, Cheswick which is directly three miles north of the airport."

Analysis:

A tall building is something of a rarity in England. Most buildings are no more than twelve to fourteen stories. If you doubt this, take a look of the skyline in London.

Vocabulary:

Heathrow – An airport in England which is very close to London.

Married For the Third Time

The Joke:

A man is completely surprised on their wedding night when his new bride says:

"I hope you will be patient with me. I haven't had any experience."

The groom says:

"But I thought you had been married three times before."

She replies:

"That's true, but the first time I was sixteen and he was eighteen, and our parents caught it and had it annulled before anything could happen.

The second time was to a homosexual, and he was just using me to further his business career.

The third time was to an IBM salesman, and he sat on the edge of the bed for two years telling me how great it was going to be."

Analysis:

IBM salesmen have quite a reputation everywhere.

Vocabulary:

Annulled – Canceled. Made null and void.

Homosexual – A male who is gay. Someone who doesn't like girls, but prefers other men as sexual partners.

Who Has the Smartest Dog

The Joke:

Three men are having diner. One is a medical doctor. The second is an engineer. The third is an IBM salesman. Soon, the conversation turns to who has the most intelligent dog. The doctor's dog builds a perfect skeleton from dog biscuits. The engineer's dog tops that by building a perfect suspension bridge. The IBMer's dog scoops up all the biscuits into a bag, buries the bag in the back yard, and comes back and screws the other two dogs.

Analysis:

Again, IBM salesmen seem to have the same reputation throughout the world.

Vocabulary:

Screws – Has sexual intercourse with.

The Violation

The Joke:

A novice goes to her Mother Superior and says:

"Mother Superior, I have a confession to make."

The Mother Superior replies:

"My child, what is it?"

The novice says:

"I'm afraid I violated my vow of chastity."

The Mother Superior says:

"I want you to go to the kitchen, ask the cook to cut a lemon in half, and go upstairs to your room and suck on that lemon for forty-five minutes."

The novice asks:

"Oh, will that keep me from getting pregnant?"

The Mother Superior says:

"No, but it will wipe that silly grin off your face."

Analysis:

Its one thing to admit committing adultery, but it's quite another to admit it with a grin still on your face.

Vocabulary:

Chastity – Being chaste. Not allowed to touch or have sex with another human being.

Grin – Like a smile, but with your teeth showing.

Novice – In the Catholic Church, a novice is considered a trainee nun. She wears white until she is ordained, entitled to wear a black habit and a wedding band. The wedding band signifies that she is married to the Catholic Church.

Pregnant – Going to have a child.

Calling a Spade a Spade

The Joke:

A novice goes to her Mother Superior, and says:

"Mother Superior, you must do something about the language used by the workmen just outside my window."

The Mother Superior replies:

"My child, you must realize that these are not gentlemen, but ordinary blue collar working men. Such men are likely going to call a spade a spade."

The novice answers:

"Oh no, Mother Superior, they call it a fucking shovel."

Analysis:

Profanity is normal for working men.

Vocabulary:

Novice – In the Catholic Church, a novice is considered a trainee nun. She wears white until she is ordained, entitled to wear a black habit and a wedding band. The wedding band signifies that she is married to the Catholic Church.

The Three Bulls

The Joke:

A farmer has decided to buy a fourth bull. Somehow, the other three find out about it. The largest bull says:

"This newcomer, he's not getting any of my one hundred cows."

The second largest bull says:

"He's not getting any of my fifty either."

And the smallest bull says:

"Well, you can bet he's not touching any of my three."

Three weeks pass. The three bulls are watching from the top of a hill when a truck makes a stop inside the corral below. No sooner does the truck stop than the tailgate goes flying end-over-end about fifteen feet from the truck. A huge, black, Brahman Bull emerges from the truck. Just as he does so, one whole side of the truck collapses inward. This new bull then proceeds to take out three sections of the corral fence.

Up on the hill, the three bulls have been watching this spectacle, and the largest one says:

"Hmmm, maybe I was a bit hasty about those hundred cows. Maybe, I could use some help after all."

The second bull says:

"Yeah, I could probably use some help with my fifty too. I'm not as young as I used to be."

They look over at the smallest bull. He's throwing dirt with his hoof, and pointing at this new bull. They cry in unison:

"Hey! What are you doing? He'll kill you!"

"Listen" says the smallest bull. "The way that dude is carrying on; I just want to make damn sure he knows I'm a bull."

Analysis:

The smallest bull wants to be sure that he is not mistaken for a cow. When a bull wants to fight another bull, he points at the other bull and starts to throw dirt with his hoof.

Vocabulary:

Bovine – In addition to cattle, this can also mean an ox or a buffalo.

Brahman Bull – The **Brahman** or Brahma is a breed of Zebu cattle (Bos primigenius indicus), later exported from India to the rest of the world.

Bull – A male bovine.

Calf – A baby bovine.

Corral – An enclosed area with a fence, usually used to contain livestock.

Cow – A female bovine.

Tailgate – The rear end of a truck. It can be let down to allow cargo to be unloaded. When driving, it has a second meaning – it means to follow another car too closely.

Twenty-four Hours to Live

The Joke:
A medical doctor is talking to a patient. He says:
"I have some good news and some bad news for you."
The patient replies:
"Give me the good news first."
The doctor says:
"You have about twenty-four hours to live."
The patient says:
"Oh my God, that's the good news?"
The doctor says:
"Yes."
The patient says:
"Oh my God, what's the bad news?"
The doctor replies:
"We've been trying to reach you since yesterday."

Analysis:
With good news like that, you don't need any bad news.

Vocabulary:
None.

The Vasectomy

The Joke:

Back in the days when a vasectomy was an inpatient procedure, a surgeon was making his post-op rounds in a hospital. He stopped at the bed of a patient, and said:

"We have some bad news and some good news for you."

The patient says:

"Give me the bad news first."

The doctor says:

"I'm afraid that during the operation, the scalpel slipped and we accidentally amputated your penis."

"Oh, my Lord!" exclaimed the patient. Then he asked: "What's the good news?"

"Well, it wasn't malignant," replied the doctor.

Analysis:

Again, with good news like that, you don't need any bad news.

Vocabulary:

Balls – Slang for testicles. See testicles below.

Benign – Harmless, the opposite of malignant.

Malignant – Bad, cancerous. The opposite of benign.

Penis – The part of the male anatomy which is used during sexual intercourse.

Sterile – Not capable of having a baby.

Sterilize – To make someone incapable of producing a baby.

Testicles – The term literally means 'little witnesses'. The orbs on a male right below the penis. It is the function of the testicles to manufacture sperm cells and the hormone testosterone. A slang term is balls.

Urethra – The tube extending down the length between the bladder and the tip of the penis. Its functions are the elimination of urine and a conduit for the human sperm generated by the testicles.

Vas Deferens – The chord or tube between the testicles and the urethra.

Vasectomy – An operation performed only to sterilize a male human being.

During the operation, the chord between the testicles and the urethra is cut. The male remains potent, but is now sterile. It is nowadays performed as outpatient surgery.

The Virgin Birth

The Joke:

A young lady goes to the doctor for a routine check up. The doctor calls her into his office and informs her that she is pregnant. She responds with:

"Doctor, that's not possible."

The doctor replies that it is possible, and he's not anticipating any problems with the delivery. She's a fine healthy young woman.

The young woman again says:

"You don't understand, doctor. It's really not possible."

The doctor replies:

"You mean you haven't..."

"Absolutely not."

"And you haven't been playing around or ...'

"Absolutely not."

The doctor turns around, draws the venetian blinds and is looking out the window.

"What is it, doctor? What are you doing?"

The doctor replies:

"The last time this happened there was a star in the East and I don't want to miss it."

Analysis:

Obviously, the doctor doesn't believe this young lady.

Vocabulary:

Blind – A window blind – a specific type of window covering which is made with slats of fabric, wood, plastic or metal that adjust by rotating from an open position to a closed position by allowing slats to overlap.

Pregnant – Going to have a child.

Star In The East – According to Christian legend, the three wise men were following this star. The three kings or wise men later gave the baby Jesus gold, frankincense and myrrh in the manger in Jerusalem. More specifically, this is the star which led the three wise men to the baby Jesus.

Venetian Blinds – A window *blind* consisting of a number of thin horizontal adjustable slats that overlap when closed.

Three Doctors

The Joke:
Three doctors are guests at a conference of medical doctors in Europe.
The German doctor says:
"In Germany, surgery is very simple. We have a grid system. We match the system on the human body with the corresponding system on the grid, and this makes surgery very simple."
The Japanese doctor answers:
"In Japan, surgery is also very simple. We have a color system. We match the system on the human body with the same system on the colored chart. This makes surgery very simple."
The Australian doctor says:
"In Australia, surgery is even simpler than that. There's only two moving parts – the mouth and the asshole, and they're both interchangeable."

Analysis:
This is an anti-Australian joke, just in case you haven't guessed as much.

Vocabulary:
Asshole – A derogatory term used against someone disliked. The correct term is 'anal orifice.'
Interchangeable – Can be changed for each other without noticing any difference.

The Dutch Air Ace

The Joke:

A Dutch flyer escapes to England at the beginning of World War II. He was immediately assigned to one of the foreign squadrons in the Royal Air Force. He succeeds in downing eight enemy aircraft and is a qualified air ace. This is now 1940, and the United States has not officially joined the war yet. The RAF needs someone to go over to the States and convince the people in the States to contribute to the British war effort. Since he speaks with an accent which is a natural attention getter, and is an air ace, the RAF settles on this guy to go over to the States. He is giving his speech at Bryn Mawr University (One of the seven sisters). At the lectern, he says:

"I was flying along about five thousand feet, when I spot these two fokkers closing in on me. So, I bank to the left and I spot three more fokkers closing in from the left. Then, I dove and I spot two more fokkers climbing towards me. So then I climb and I encounter four more fokkers diving on me. So there I am in the air completely surrounded by all these fokkers."

The girls in the audience are really cracking up. The Dean of Women gets up, goes to the lectern and says:

"Girls, there is nothing funny about this. The German Luftwaffe flies an aircraft called the Focke-Wulf and the allied pilots call them fokkers. Isn't that right, Major?"

And the Major replies:

"As a matter of fact, these fokkers were flying Messerschmitts."

Analysis:

Both the Focke-Wulf and the Messerschmitt were main fighter planes for the German Luftwaffe during WWII. WWII actually began in 1939, but the United States did not join the war until it was attacked by the forces of Japan in its raid on the U.S. Naval Base at Pearl Harbor on December 7, 1941. Until the U.S. officially joined the war, American pilots were also assigned to one of the foreign squadrons.

Vocabulary:

Fucker – A term of derision directed at someone you dislike. The Dutch Major is using this term to describe the German aircraft.

Lectern – A stand usually located at the front center of the speaker's platform. There is space for notes or a book on the top of the lectern.

The Vicar and the Little Girl

The Joke:

A Vicar in the English Anglican Church has just been reassigned to a new parish. He is wandering around trying to get to know his new parishioners when he spots a twelve-year-old girl out walking her dog. He meanders on over to the little girl, introduces himself and says:

"Pray tell, what might your name be?"

The little girl replies:

"Angela, your Grace." And she does a little curtsey.

"I'll bet I know why your name is Angela. It's because you have such beautiful blue eyes and such gorgeous blonde hair."

"Oh, thank you, your grace," responds the young girl, and she does another curtsey.

"And pray tell, what might the dog's name be?" Inquires the Vicar.

"Porky," replies the little girl.

The Vicar takes a little closer look at the dog, and says:

"I'll bet I know why he's called Porky. It's because he's a trifle on the chubby side, right?"

"Nope, fucks pigs," replies the girl.

Analysis:

Perhaps a little bit of history is in order here. The Anglican Church was started in England by King Henry VIII when the Pope refused to give him a ninth divorce. He converted the Catholic Church to the Anglican Church, and established its headquarters at Canterbury. That is why the head of the Anglican Church is called the Archbishop of Canterbury. Henry VIII converted some of the lands and monasteries to the Anglican Church, but he also gave some of the land and buildings to his nobles.

Vocabulary:

Chubby – Fat, obese.

Curtsey – A bow to a superior person executed by a woman or girl. This is executed by bowing from the waist while placing one foot in front of the other. This is replaced in the male by genuflecting. This is done by getting down on one knee. In the case of the Pope, this is accompanied by kissing his ring.

Meander – To wander aimlessly, not necessarily in a straight line. In this case, the Vicar doesn't want to alarm the little girl by approaching her directly.

Monastery – A home for monks.

Monk – A member of a religious order. They normally take a vow of chastity, or a vow not to touch anything female.

Noble – Of noble blood. Related to the king or nobility – e.g., an earl, count, or duke. A member of the aristocracy.

Obese – Excessively fat.

Parish – A geographical unit. This is normally serviced by a parish church.

Trifle – Little bit. A thing of no particular significance.

Vicar – Title given to some parish priests in the Anglican Church.

Outdoor Plumbing

The Joke:

A young lad takes the same route to school every day. He lives on a farm way out in the middle of nowhere. The farm has outdoor plumbing, and the outhouse is located a few yards from the farmhouse. The outhouse has been built so that two stilts locate it over a creek. Beside the outhouse is a woodpile with an axe imbedded in one of the logs. Every morning, the boy looks at the axe and at the two stilts and keeps going. One morning, the temptation becomes too great. He seizes the axe and chops down the outhouse into the creek. That afternoon, he delays going home by helping the teacher erase the blackboard, sweeping the floor, etc. But finally he has to go home.

When he reaches the house everyone is seated around the diner table. He says:

"Hi everyone, I'm home."

No one says a word. He looks at his father and realizes that he knows. Remembering the lesson he learned recently in school, the boy says:

"Like George Washington, I cannot tell a lie. This morning, I chopped down the outhouse into the creek."

His father takes off his belt, stands and says:

"OK, son, let's you and I step outside to the woodshed, and we'll settle this right now."

The boy protests:

"But Dad, when George Washington told his father the truth about cutting down the cherry tree, his father didn't beat him!"

His father responds:

"That's true, son, but George Washington's father wasn't sitting in that Cherry tree."

Analysis:

Almost every school child in America knows the story about George Washington and the Cherry tree. The story is probably not true, but is symbolic of the many legends which have grown up around the founding father of his country.

Vocabulary:

Outdoor Plumbing – Before the days of running water in houses, an outdoor toilet called an outhouse was very common in America.

Outhouse – See outdoor plumbing above.

Stilts – Poles, posts or pillars used to allow a person or structure to stand at a distance above the ground.

The Specimen

The Joke:

A lady in Ireland returns home from the doctor. Arriving home, she finds her husband watching TV in the living room. She says:

"Pat, me luv, what might a specimen be?"

Her husband replies:

"I dunno, luv, why do you ask?"

She says:

"The doctor said I should come back next week and to bring him a specimen."

"I don't know, but Mrs. O'Reilly next door will probably know. She's a great lady, and has traveled around the world several times."

His wife, as suggested, goes next door. A few minutes later, he hears the sounds of a big donnybrook coming from next door. A minute later, his wife comes back in the living room with her hat askew and a small trickle of blood coming from her nose. He exclaims:

"Good Lord, luv, what happened to you?"

"You and your Mrs. O'Reilly. Fine lady, indeed!"

Again, Pat asks:

"What happened?"

His wife answers:

"I went next door and knocked very politely. Mrs. O'Reilly came to the door, and I asked very politely: 'Mrs. O'Reilly, what might a specimen be?'

And you know what she had the nerve to say to me? She said: 'Piss in a bottle.' And I said: 'Shit in your hat."

And the fight was on.

Analysis:

The doctor means a urine specimen, which is why Mrs. O'Reilly says to *piss in a bottle* when asked.

48

Vocabulary:

Askew – Not straight, on crooked.

Donnybrook – A fight, usually accompanied by loud and aggressive noises.

This is a common expression in Ireland.

Luv – Love. Me luv means my love. Again, this is a common expression in Ireland.

Specimen – Normally a urine specimen, which is given by urinating in a bottle. A specimen is a sample of something.

Trickle – A small stream.

Urination – Making water as human waste. Slang terms are pee and piss.

Father Clancy's Sermon

The Joke:

An Irish Catholic Priest is fond of blaming everything wrong on the British. It's the dirty Brits this, the lousy English that, the rotten king this, the horrendous English military, etc. Since this is all taking place during the Black and Tan rebellion, his audience is in total agreement with him. Finally, the Bishop calls him in and says:

"Its not that we disagree with what you have to say, but your sermons are getting us into serious difficulties with the English authorities. So from now on, you are not to mention any term such as king, limey, Union Jack, Brit or British by name in any of your sermons. Have I made myself clear?"

"Yes, your Grace," replies Father Clancy.

The next Sunday, Father Clancy's sermon is on the Last Supper. He says, emulating Jesus:

"One of you will betray me."

Peter asks: "Is it I, Lord?"

"No Peter, it is not you," says Jesus.

John asks: "Is it I, Lord?"

"No John, it is not you," replies Jesus.

And so on around the table, until all had asked except Judas Iscariot.

Finally, after a long pause, Judas asks:

"Is it I, Lord?"

"Yes Judas, you!" replies Jesus.

"Oh, I don't know about that, Guv'nor."

Analysis:

By having Judas respond with "Guv'nor," Father Clancy is clearly indicating that he is English. Only an Englishman would respond with that term. Perhaps a little bit of history is in order here. The Back and Tan Rebellion lasted from 1920 until 1922. According to the Irish, the Royal Irish Constabulary released Irish criminals from jail, dressed them in black and tan uniforms, and allowed them to supervise Irish civilians. In actual practice, the Black and Tans were mostly WWI English veterans, and were paid to join the RIC and suppress the IRA. Nonetheless, the Black and Tans were well known for their brutal treatment of Irish civilians.

Vocabulary:

Black and Tan – The color of the uniform belonging to the oppressors of Irish civilians.

Constabulary – The police. They are normally housed in a barracks.

Emulating – Imitating, pretending to be someone else.

Guv'nor – An abbreviated form of Governor. This is an English term used when addressing a superior.

Judas Iscariot – According to the Christian religion, Judas Iscariot is the disciple who betrayed Jesus Christ for thirty pieces of silver to the High Priest Caiaphas who later turned over Jesus to Pontius Pilot and the Romans. He later hanged himself, when he realized what he had done. To this day, Judas is synonymous with betrayal.

Last Supper – In the Christian gospels, the final supper enjoyed by Jesus Christ with all of his apostles before his death at the hands of the Romans. This has been a motif for paintings by Leonardo da Vinci, etc.

Leonardo da Vinci – Italian painter, engineer, musician, and scientist. The most versatile genius of the Renaissance, Leonardo filled notebooks with engineering and scientific observations that were in some cases centuries ahead of their time. As a painter Leonardo is best known for *The Last Supper* (c. 1495) and *Mona Lisa* (c. 1503).

Limey – This is a term from the British Navy. In order to combat scurvy, English sailors were told to eat lemons or limes.

Scurvy – A disease caused by deficiency of vitamin C, characterized by spongy and bleeding gums, bleeding under the skin, and extreme weakness.

Sermon – A speech given during a religious ceremony.

Union Jack – The flag flown by Great Britain.

The Houses on the Street

The Joke:

A pair of Irish ditch diggers has broken for lunch. They are located in a rather poor section of Dublin, where the houses are denoted by a little red light in the front window. As they are consuming their beer and sandwiches, an Anglican minister goes into one of the houses. Pat says to Mike:

"Did you see that?"

Mike replies;

"Faith and Begorrah, I sure did. Can you imagine a man of the cloth setting foot in a house like that? True, not of the true faith, but a man of the cloth nonetheless."

They continue to drink their beer and eat their sandwiches. About fifteen minutes later, a rabbi goes into the same house. Mike says:

"Can you imagine? Two men of the cloth going into the same house within fifteen minutes of each other."

Pat replies:

"Yeah, the world's sure going to hell in a hand basket when you can see something like that."

About twenty minutes later, an Irish Catholic Priest goes into the same house.

Pat says:

"Did you see that?"

Mike replies:

"I sure did. Which one of them other two fellas do you suppose it was that went and died?"

Analysis:

The only reason that an Irish Catholic Priest could be going into the same house is to give the Last Rites to someone.

Vocabulary:

Anglican Minister – In any of the protestant religions, a minister is a priest who is ordained, and entitled to perform weddings, etc. Ordinarily, they are allowed to marry.

Faith and Begorrah – An Irish Christian term, used to signify surprise. It probably comes from an amalgam of 'By my faith' and 'By God.'

Fellas – Fellows.

Houses – Brothels, identified by a red light in the front window. Places where prostitutes entertain their clients. In some cities, the district where these houses are located is called the red light district.

Last Rites – In the Catholic religion, this is a final blessing given by a priest to someone who has just passed away, or is about to pass away.

Man of the Cloth – A priest or minister.

Ordained – A priest or monk who has gone through a formal ceremony, ordaining him into the church or temple.

Rabbi – In the Jewish religion, a priest who is entitled to perform weddings, give sermons, and provide counsel to his congregation.

The Price Is Right

The Joke:

A man walks into a bar, and orders a beer. Then he orders a club sandwich. When he is finished eating the sandwich, he asks the bartender how much he owes him, and is informed that the beer will be five cents and the sandwich will be ten cents for a grand total of fifteen cents. Impressed by the low prices, he asks:

"Where is the owner of this establishment?"

The bartender tells him:

"He's upstairs with my wife."

The patron asks:

"What is he doing upstairs with your wife?"

The bartender says:

"The same thing I'm doing down here to his business."

Analysis:

The bartender obviously knows exactly what is going on upstairs. He is revenging himself by deliberately charging low prices in the bar.

Vocabulary:

Bartender – A man who serves drinks in a bar or other establishment.

Club Sandwich – A sandwich composed of Turkey, bacon, tomato and egg. It is normally served on Rye bread with bar sticks – toothpicks with ribbon on the top.

Note: The sandwich was invented by the Earl of Sandwich, whence the name. It was invented so that he could eat the sandwich with one hand while gambling with the other hand.

Establishment – Place of business, as distinguished from a private home.

Patron – Customer, someone who patronizes a particular establishment.

The 12-inch Pianist

The Joke:

A man walks into a bar and notices a twelve inch tall pianist playing the piano in the corner. The pianist plays very well, so the man asks the bartender about the origin of the piano player. The bartender indicates an elf sitting at the other end of the bar. The man says:

"Do you mind if I try it?"

"No, go right ahead." Replies the bartender.

The man approaches the elf and asks for a million bucks. Suddenly, the bar is filled with ducks everywhere.

"What happened?" inquires the man.

"You don't really think that I asked for a twelve inch pianist, do you?"

Analysis:

The bartender obviously asked for a twelve inch penis.

Vocabulary:

Bucks – Dollars. This is a slang term for U.S. Dollars.

Elf – A short man dressed all in green. According to legend, elves are endowed with magical powers. The origin is in German mythology, but they were borrowed by the English romanticists – particularly by J.R.R. Tolkien.

Pianist – A man or woman who plays the piano.

The Quickie

The Joke:
A Roman Catholic Priest has a job lecturing at a college located across town. Every weekday, he drives across town, delivers his lecture, and returns to his monastery by car. One evening the car won't start, so he has to walk back through the center of the town. As he is walking along, a girl leaps out from a doorway, and says:

"How about a quickie, Father, only ten dollars?"

"No, no – get away," replies the priest.

He travels a few more blocks, and is again accosted by a young woman who offers him a quickie for ten dollars. Again, he declines her offer and says to get away from him. All night, this bothers him and he cannot sleep.

The monastery is co-located with a Convent, and the following morning he spots the Mother Superior out for a walk in the garden. He approaches the Mother Superior, and asks:

"Holy Mother, what's a quickie?"

The Mother Superior replies:

"Oh, ten dollars – the same as downtown."

Analysis:
This is a vulgar joke, saying that a Mother Superior knows all about the goings on downtown. Worse, it implies that sex is available for a fee right in the convent.

Vocabulary:
Accosted – Confronted. A face-to-face meeting between two people. In this case, for the purpose of propositioning the priest.

Convent – A place of dwelling for nuns. It is similar to a monastery for priests and monks. It is normally headed by a Mother Superior.

Downtown – Downtown and uptown are relative terms used to distinguish the center of town from the suburbs, where the monastery and convent are probably located.

Propositioning – A proposal to have sex with someone. For example, he propositioned her, with a suggestion that they do it in his bed.

Quickie – Quick sex. Sex which lasts only a few seconds or minutes.

Roman – An indication that the Catholic religious headquarters is in Rome, Italy. Catholics are sometimes referred to as Roman Catholics.

The Psychiatrist

The Joke:
   A psychiatrist is examining one of his new patients. He draws a circle on a piece of paper.
   "What does that remind you of?"
   "Sex," responds the patient.
   The psychiatrist next draws a square on another piece of paper.
   "What does that remind you of?"
   "Sex," responds the patient.
   The psychiatrist tries drawing a line on another piece of paper.
   "What does that remind you of?"
   "Sex," responds the patient.
   Finally, the psychiatrist draws a dot on another piece of paper.
   "What does that remind you of?"
   "Sex," responds the patient.
   In exasperation, the psychiatrist exclaims:
   "You've got the dirtiest mind I've ever seen."
   The patient replies:
   "Me? You're the one drawing all the dirty pictures, Doc."

Analysis:
   The psychiatrist is drawing innocuous pictures, which could be taken for anything. The patient is falsely accusing him of drawing salacious pictures.

Vocabulary:
   Psychiatrist – A medical doctor who has received advanced training in the field of psychiatry. Slang term is a shrink. This slang term is taken from South American natives (headhunters), who shrink their opponent's heads after killing them.
   Salacious – Arousing or appealing to sexual desire or imagination: lascivious.

The Turn Signal

The Joke:

Two Carabinieri are riding in their patrol car when the passenger says he doesn't think the turn signal is working. The driver feels that this is very serious, so he suggests they pull the patrol car over to the side of the road. The passenger will go in back of the car. The driver will turn on the turn signal, and the passenger will tell him whether it's working or not. They proceed to do what the driver has suggested.

The passenger says:

"OK, it's working."

"Oh, now it's not working."

"Oh, now it's working again."

"Oh, now it's not working again."

Analysis:

The turn signal is blinking normally. This is a standard stupidity joke. In Italy, almost all of the stupidity jokes involve the Carabinieri. They are named after the weapon first used by them – a carbine. They also used to wear three-cornered hats. The Carabinieri work very closely with the State Police even though they report through different channels to the Ministry of Defense. The State Police report to the Interior Ministry. They were established by Victor Emanule I, while he was King of Sardinia before he became the first king of a united Italy. The selection of the Carabinieri as the butt of stupidity jokes is unique to Italy. In most other countries, the butt of the stupidity jokes is some ethnic group such as the Poles or Italians in America, the Irish in England, the Belgians in France, etc.

Those interested in a more detailed history of Italy should read about Garibaldi and the various city states.

Vocabulary:

Carabinieri – See the analysis above.

Giuseppe Garibaldi – 1807-1882. The military genius who united all of Italy around 1861. He is a national hero in Italy, and the object of the Sons of Garibaldi in the American Civil War.

Call the Elevator

The Joke:

Emerging from his office, a Carabinieri Colonel asks the sentry stationed outside his door to call the elevator.

The sentry calls out: "Elevator, elevator."

The colonel says:

"No, stupid. With the button."

The sentry grabs the button on his tunic, and again says:

"Elevator, elevator."

Analysis:

The colonel means to call the elevator by pressing the button beside the elevator. The sentry is so stupid that he thinks he can call the elevator verbally.

Vocabulary:

Sentry – A soldier placed on guard.

Tunic – The upper part of a uniform. A military jacket.

The Carabinieri Payroll

The Joke:

In olden times, the Carabinieri had to physically report once a month for their pay. A clerk is calling the roll. When he reaches the end, he sings out:

"Totale, totale."

Finally, he turns to his Lieutenant and says:

"Lieutenant, I don't understand. This fellow totale earns more than all the others and he's never here."

Analysis:

Totale in Italian means total in English.

Vocabulary:

None.

The Gay Couple

The Joke:

A gay couple is on the way to a Gay Liberation Meeting. They stop their Volkswagen for a traffic light. An 18-wheeler comes along, and he can't quite stop on time. He slightly bumps the Volkswagen in the rear. The driver of the Volkswagen gets out, and walks back to the truck. He says:

"You naughty fellow. You have struck our vehicle."

The driver of the truck looks down and says:

"Oh, kiss my ass."

The driver of the Volkswagen turns around, and calls out to his buddy:

"George, George, come quick. He wants to settle out of court."

Analysis:

The driver of the truck obviously thinks he is saying something insulting, but the driver of the Volkswagen takes it another way.

Vocabulary:

18-wheeler – Another name for a truck. A large truck, like the one in this story, has eighteen wheels.

Out of Court – Without going before a judge or jury. To settle out of court means to reach an agreement without going to a court or being subject to a jury.

Vehicle – Another name for a car or truck. Car registrations are normally given out by the States in a vehicle's name.

The Guest on the TV Show

The Joke:

Groucho Marx used to have a TV show called *You Bet Your Life*. One evening, he is interviewing a guy and asks:

"Tell me, Sir, are you married?"

The guest indicates that he is married.

"How long have you been married?" asks Groucho.

"About sixteen years," responds the guest.

"Do you have any children?" asks Groucho.

The guest says he does.

"How many children do you have?" asks Groucho.

"Fourteen," answers the guest.

"You've had fourteen children in sixteen years of marriage. How do you account for that?"

"I love my wife," responds the guest.

Groucho says: "I love my cigar too, but I take it out of my mouth every once in a while."

Analysis:

They cut Groucho off the air. This was before the days of the ten second delay. To this day, this incident is listed as one of Groucho's bloopers. Groucho, Harpo and Firpo were brothers, and formed one of the most famous acts in Vaudeville.

Vocabulary:

Blooper – A mistake, which in this case, caused Groucho to be cut off.

Variety Show – A type of show which included magic, singing, comedy, ventriloquism, etc.

Vaudeville – A theatrical variety show popular from 1880-1930.

Ventriloquism – An act during which the ventriloquist throws his voice into a dummy or other person, making it appear that the dummy or other person is doing the talking.

How the Angel Got Atop the Christmas Tree

The Joke:

At the North Pole, Santa Claus had been having a bad day. When he went to inspect his team of reindeer, he found that one deer was pregnant and he found a broken trace in the harness. Returning to the cabin, he thought that he would have a cup of coffee. After he brewed the coffee, the handle broke as he was carrying it to the table, spilling the coffee all over the floor. About this time, there was a knock at the door. Answering it, Santa encountered this Angel carrying a newly cut fir Christmas tree, who said:

"Hi Santa, what do you want me to do with this tree?"

Analysis:

Since Santa was having such a bad day, he probably told the Angel to take the Christmas tree and shove it. I leave it to your fertile imagination to determine where.

Actually, the Angel symbolizes the host of Heavenly Angels attendant on the nativity. The practice probably originated in Germany where the celebration of Yule was supplanted by the Christian tradition of Christmas.

Although the practice is sometimes associated with Saint Nicholas (born in modern day Turkey), the tradition is probably more associated with Germany in America. Indeed, the reindeer which pull Santa's sleigh even have German names such as Donner and Blitzen (Thunder and Lightning in English). With the addition of Rudolph, the red-nosed reindeer, the reindeer are now nine in number.

According to legend, every Christmas evening, Santa Claus hitches up his flying reindeer to his sleigh and circles the globe. He gives presents and goodies to people who have been good, and he gives coal or switches to people who have been bad. In the U.S., he is portrayed as a chubby white man with a beard. He wears a red suit, with white fur trimmed around it. He also wears a fur-lined cap and a large black belt, with a gold buckle.

An interesting anecdote is told about Saint Nicolas, who was renowned for giving generous gifts. He knew a farmer who had three daughters, but no dowry for any of them. He visited the family one evening, but found them all asleep. He spied the three stockings left by the daughters on the fireplace. He divided the gold coins he had brought into three equal shares, and stuffed each of the stockings. The girls each now had a dowry, and were able to get married.

Vocabulary:

Atop – On top of.

Blitzen – German for lightning. See *Donner* below for a fuller description.

Christmas Tree – An evergreen tree, decorated by Christmas lights, ornaments and tinsel, usually associated with the Christian tradition of the Christmas Holidays terminating on the 25th of December. This celebration is of the birth of Jesus Christ.

Chubby – Fat, usually associated with a jolly nature.

Donner – German for thunder. You can tell how far away a thunder storm is by counting the seconds between when you see the lightning and hear the thunder – e.g., three seconds means the thunder storm is approximately three miles away.

Dowry – In olden times, a gift from the family of the bride to the new family of the groom. It was considered compensation to the groom's family for taking the girl off the hands of her family. Hence, the statement: "The uglier the bride, the bigger the dowry."

Globe – The Earth.

Harness – In this case, the leather harness which connects the reindeer to the sleigh.

Nativity – In the Christian religion, a scene of the birth of Jesus Christ in a manger in Bethlehem.

Reindeer – In this case, flying deer which pull Santa's sleigh.

Renowned – Famous.

Santa Claus – Also known as Father Christmas, Saint Nick, Kris Kringle and Sinterklaas. This last name is the origin of the name in the U.S.

Shove – Push.

Switch – A flexible piece of wood, used for beating someone.

Trace – A piece of leather in the breast harness.

Yule – A celebration of the Norse God Odin, which preceded the tradition of Christmas in Christianity. The celebration, which preceded the Christian tradition of Christmas, lives on in the Yule log, and the expression *Yuletide Greetings*.

Can't Get Back Up the Chimney

The Joke:

Santa Claus has just delivered presents. He is about to leave, when the lady of the house comes down the stairs dressed only in a filmy negligee. She says:

"Santa, won't you stay for some milk and cookies?"

Santa answers:

"Ho, ho! Got to go. Lots of boys and girls waiting in the snow."

Slipping her negligee down over one shoulder, the lady says:

"Santa, are you sure?"

Santa replies:

"Hey, hey! Have to stay. Can't get back up the chimney this way."

Analysis:

Santa has an erection. This explains why he is unable to get back up the chimney.

Vocabulary:

Chimney – A vertical flue that provides a path through which smoke from a fire is carried away through the wall or roof of a building. A path from the fireplace to the roof in a house – normally lined with brick or stone.

Diaphanous – Characterized by such fineness of texture as to permit seeing through.

Erection – In this case, an erect penis. A vulgar slang term for this condition is known colloquially as having a hard on.

Filmy – Diaphanous: so thin as to transmit light.

Negligee – A woman's loose dressing gown, often of soft, delicate fabric.

Santa Claus – According to tradition, he comes down the chimney to deliver presents every night before Christmas. He leaves back through the chimney when his work is done (after consuming the milk and cookies which have left for him). See the joke just above for a full description of Santa Claus.

He Ignores Her Until ...

The Joke:
Mary is looking for Harry. She finds him at his usual haunt, sipping on a Martini at the bar. She says:

"All right, Harry, you've really done it this time. You've put me in a family way, and now you've got to marry me!"

Harry ignores her, continuing to sip his Martini.

Mary continues:

"Harry, you've knocked me up, and now you've got to make an honest woman out of me."

Harry continues to ignore her, again sipping on his Martini.

"Harry, are you listening to me? I said you've made me pregnant, and now you have to marry me."

Harry still ignores her, so she says:

"Listen Harry, if you don't marry me, I'm going to walk out on that bridge, jump, and drown myself!"

Harry turns towards her, extends his hand and says:

"Mary, that's what I like about you. Not only are you a great lay, but you're a damn good sport about it too!"

Analysis:
Harry means that Mary will be a good sport, and go drown herself.

Vocabulary:
Gin – Alcohol made from juniper berries.

Haunt – Place habitually visited by a patron.

Honest Woman – A bride who has been living in sin – particularly if she is pregnant at the time of the wedding.

In A Family Way – Pregnant.

Knocked Up – Slang for made pregnant.

Martini – Alcoholic drink, normally made from gin and vermouth, and garnished with an olive. Also, the maker of the vermouth wine used for a Martini.

Vermouth – A dry white wine. Used as a mixer for a Martini.

The Hasidic Jew

The Joke:

In NYC, a hit-and-run driver rounds a corner, bowling over a Hasidic Jew into the gutter. The cop on the beat hurries over, and sees that the fellow in the gutter is dying. The officer asks whether the fellow wants him to call a rabbi. He is astonished when the fellow wants him to call a Catholic priest instead.

He hurries into the parish house in the same block, and rouses Father O'Reilly from a sound sleep. Father O'Reilly rushes to the street to see which one of his flock has been struck down. Looking at the fellow in the gutter, he exclaims that there must be some mistake. The Jew in the gutter says that there is no mistake.

Father O'Reilly asks:

"Let me understand. You want *me* to give *you* the Last Rites of the Holy Roman Catholic Church?"

The Jew nods affirmatively.

"Why?" says the priest.

"Because if you give me the Last Rites, I die a Catholic, right?"

The priest confirms this.

"Better one of *you* than one of *us*." says the Jew.

Analysis:

The Hasidic Jew is right. By accepting the Last Rites, he will become a Catholic before he passes away. Therefore, it will be a Catholic who passes away, and not a Jew.

Vocabulary:

Ancient – Old.

Flock – A group of sheep assigned to a particular shepherd. Used in this instance to indicate one of the priest's parishioners.

Hit-And-Run – A driver who does not stop after causing or witnessing an accident.

Hasidic Jew – Since they wear black with a hat, and have a beard and long sideburns, they are very obviously Jewish. The plural is Hasidim. The term is taken from old Hebrew, and means piety.

Hebrew – The ancient language of the Jews, and of modern-day Israel. To modernize Hebrew, many new words had to be added – e.g., words for million and billion. Ancient Jews could not conceive of a number that high.

Judiasm – The religion practiced by the Jews. The factions are known as Reform, Conservative, Reconstructionist, and Orthodox.

The Composer

The Joke:

A man walks into a bar and has several drinks. The bartender strikes up a conversation. The man states that he is a songwriter. He says that he has been unable to sell anything that he has written for the past twenty-eight years. He is really depressed. He indicates to the bartender that he is going to have a few more drinks. Then, he intends to walk out on the adjacent bridge, jump in, and drown himself, ending it all.

The bartender says that this is a show business hangout, with all kinds of actors, producers, directors, publishers, musicians and composers right here. He suggests that the man sit at the piano and play something that he wrote. He even offers the man a drink.

Reluctantly, the man sits down and begins to play.

By the end of his performance, the entire bar is in tears and gives him a standing ovation. It is the most beautiful song they've ever heard.

The bartender comes over, congratulates him and says:

"That's the most beautiful thing I ever heard. I don't understand how you were never able to sell anything in twenty-eight years. By the way, what's the name of that tune?"

"I Want to Fuck You So Much That I Could Just Shit," says the man.

Analysis:

By giving his songs such profane titles, the songwriter made sure that no one would buy any of his songs.

Vocabulary:

Adjacent – nearest in space or position; immediately adjoining without intervening space.

Depressed – Really down, in a low mood. Unable to function properly.

Hangout – Place where people come together.

The Difference between Heaven and Hell

The Joke:
The following is a story told around Europe:

In Heaven –	All the chefs are French,
	All the police are English,
	All the mechanics are German,
	All the lovers are Italian,
	And it is all organized by the Swiss.
In Hell –	All the chefs are English,
	All the police are German,
	All the mechanics are French,
	All the lovers are Swiss,
	And it is all organized by the Italians.

Analysis:

This story pertains to the national reputations of the various European countries:

The French are reputed to be great chefs, but lousy mechanics.

The English have a formidable reputation as policemen, but a lousy reputation as cooks or chefs.

The Germans are great mechanics, but are over-bearing and arrogant as policemen.

Italians have a great reputation for individual endeavors such as lovers, but a bad reputation for anything which requires cooperation or organization, such as government.

The Swiss (and the Germans) enjoy a good reputation for organization, but are considered too cold to be great lovers.

Vocabulary:

Chef – The overall manager of a kitchen. They also have a great reputation as cooks and food preparers. However, if you wish to insult a Chef, just call him a cook.

The Funeral Cortege

The Joke:
A bystander is watching a funeral procession pass by. He notices that, as usual, the funeral procession is headed by a hearse, but behind it he observes a man walking a huge Rottweiler on a leash. Then, he notices that strung out behind the man is a line of men extending for several blocks. Assuming the man walking the dog is the head mourner; the bystander approaches him and says:

"Excuse me, Sir, I don't want to intrude during your time of grief, but I want to understand what is going on."

The mourner explains that his dog attacked his mother-in–law and killed her. It is her body lying in the casket in the hearse.

"Oh, I'm sorry to hear of your loss. But, let me ask you if I could borrow your dog?"

"Of course, get in line," responds the mourner, pointing over his shoulder.

Analysis:
The mourner is not the only one who wants to get rid of his mother-in-law. The line extends for several blocks.

Vocabulary:
Casket – An enclosure for containing a human body. Once sealed, it is designed to preserve the human body.

Cortege – Procession.

Deceased – Dead person.

Gravesite – Place where someone is buried.

Hearse – A car which opens at the rear, used to carry the casket and the deceased from the funeral parlor to the gravesite before it is interred. It is longer than an ordinary car.

Infamous – Famous in a bad way. For example, Hitler would be considered infamous while Roosevelt would be considered famous.

Interred –Buried in a grave, or placed in a mausoleum above ground.

Mourner – Someone who is sad for the loss of a dead person.

Propensity – Capability plus intent.

Rottweiler – A breed of dog infamous for its bad temper, and its propensity for attacking other animals and humans.

The Double Negative

The Joke:

A grade-school teacher has received a gift of a box of chocolates. She wants to share the box of candy with her class. Everything is going fine until she reaches little Johnnie and offers him some candy. Johnnie says:

"I don't want none of your fucking candy."

Outraged, the teacher sends Johnnie to the principal.

The principal says:

"When your teacher offered you some candy, what did you say?"

Johnnie repeats himself:

"I don't want none of your fucking candy."

The principal indicates that he is going to call Johnnie's mother.

When she arrives, the principal asks Johnnie to repeat his response when he was offered some candy by his teacher. He does so.

"There, what do you think of that?" says the principal.

"Fuck him, don't give him none," says Johnnie's mother.

Analysis:

The mother appears to be as illiterate and uncouth as her son.

Vocabulary:

Double negative – The proper English usage is "Don't give him **any**."

Illiterate – Uneducated. Literally, the term means unable to read, or able to read only partially at a very low level.

Uncouth – Given to foul language. A culturally deficient person. Someone unaccustomed to proper behavior in the presence of others.

The Rattlesnake in the Desert

The Joke:
Since it is cold in the desert at night, a diamondback rattlesnake crawls into the same sleeping bag with a man and falls asleep. The following morning, the snake is startled by the man awakening and bites him on the head of his penis. Really awake now, the man calls out to his buddy:

"Joe, Joe, this rattlesnake has bitten me right on the head of my cock. What should I do?"

Joe says that he saw a pay phone up on the highway, and will phone an M.D.

He does so, and asks the doctor:

"A rattlesnake has bitten my friend here in the middle of the desert. What should I do?"

The doctor asks if he has a snake bite kit. Hearing that Joe doesn't have one, the doctor says:

"Here's what I want you to do. Cut an x-marked incision over the wound, suck out the blood and venom and spit it on the ground."

Joe says: "Is that the only way, doc?"

The doctor indicates that it is.

When he gets back to the campsite, his friend inquires:

"What did the doc say, Joe?"

"The doctor says that you're going to die!" responds his buddy.

Analysis:
Joe would rather that his friend dies than give him what appears to be oral sex in the middle of the desert.

Vocabulary:
Cock – A slang name for a penis.

Diamondback – A rattlesnake common to the South and West of the U.S. The name comes from the pattern of markings on the snake's back.

Incision – A cut, normally delivered by a doctor.

Oral sex – Sex by mouth. Slang terms are *blow job* and *eating her pussy*.

Snake Bite Kit – A device used to suck blood and venom from a wound inflicted by a snake. It is sold in almost any camping store.

Venom – The poison from a snake's bite. Also used to indicate the poisonous nature of a person's speech. The adjective form is venomous.

The Potato in the Bathing Suit

The Joke:

A Polish guy is walking along a beach in France. He wants to meet women, but is getting nowhere. In a bar on the beach, he spots a Frenchman with honeys crawling all over him. He waits for the guy to go to the bathroom, and intercepts him on the way back. He says:

"Excuse me, but I couldn't help noticing that you are a great success with women. Perhaps you can help me. I am not doing too well."

The Frenchman looks more closely at the Polish guy, and says:

"I think it's because of the Mother Hubbard style bathing suit. Nobody wears them any more. I want you to go down to the marketplace and buy one of the abbreviated Bikini style bathing suits."

The Polish guy does so, and the next day, he tries it out on the beach. Again, he has no luck with the ladies. So, he decides to search for his French friend. He finds him in the same bar, and employs the same strategy. As his friend emerges from the bathroom, he explains that he has had no luck on the beach that day. His friend says:

"I think I see the problem. I want you to go down to the marketplace again, buy a potato and stick it in the bathing suit."

Again, the Polish guy does as he is told. Again, he goes out on the beach and doesn't have any success. In fact, women seem to be avoiding him wherever he goes. He spots his French friend lying on the beach surrounded by honeys. As he approaches, the girls all split and walk away.

"Oh, no, I meant to put the potato in the *front* of the bathing suit," says the Frenchman.

Analysis:

Obviously, the Polish guy has placed the potato in the back of his bathing suit. No wonder women are avoiding him like the plague.

Vocabulary:

Bikini – An atoll in the Pacific, which has given its name to a very brief bathing suit. Primarily for women, the bottom is also worn by men.

Honey – Slang term for a beautiful young woman.

Mother Hubbard Bathing Suit – One-piece bathing suit with a tank top on the top and pants extending to the knees. It's considered old-fashioned now, but at one time in the past it was standard bathing gear.

Plague – A widespread affliction or calamity, especially one seen as divine retribution.

Split – Slang for *go away*.

The Newlyweds

The Joke:

A newly married couple is undressing on their first night. The husband tosses his trousers to his new bride, indicating that he wants her to try to wear them. She tries, but is unable to wear them. She says:

"I can't wear these. They're too big."

"That's right, I wear the pants in this family and don't you forget it," says the husband.

Tossing her panties to her husband, she indicates that she wants hum to try them on. He tries, but is unable to get into them. He is unable to get them past his thighs. He says:

"I can't get into these. They're too small."

"That's right, and you're not going to until you change your attitude," she says.

Analysis:

Since *getting into her pants* is a euphemism for having sex with a woman, the bride is indicating that the groom will not enjoy any sex until he changes his attitude.

Vocabulary:

Euphemism – Calling something by a more acceptable name. For example, referring to a *janitor* as a *sanitary engineer*.

Newlyweds – A newly married couple.

An Interfaith Conference

The Joke:
Three ministers are invited to speak at an interfaith conference. While the Protestant Minister is up speaking, the Catholic Priest turns to the Rabbi on the platform, and whispers:
"Have you ever tasted pork?"
The Rabbi confesses that he has tasted pork.
"I thought so," says the Priest with a smug look on his face.
The Protestant Minister is continuing to speak, so the Rabbi whispers to the Priest:
"Have you ever had sex with a woman?"
The priest admits that he has.
The Rabbi whispers:
"Hell of a lot better than pork, wasn't it?"

Analysis:
We believe that sex beats pork every time. In fact, we're sure of it.

Vocabulary:
Interfaith Conference – A meeting of Christians and Jews, usually with an aim towards promoting greater understanding between the faiths.
Pork – Meat from a pig. Jews are forbidden to eat pork as a part of their religion.
Protestant – Although Christian, Protestant religions in the U.S. are usually derived from the Anglican Church of England and King Henry VIII. Only the Lutherans and a few small Christian sects claim a more European origin.
Rabbi – In the Jewish religion, a person trained in Jewish law, ritual, and tradition and ordained for leadership of a Jewish congregation, especially one serving as chief religious official of a synagogue.
Smug – Overly confident. Self contented. Exhibiting or feeling great or offensive satisfaction with oneself or with one's situation; self-righteously complacent.

The Camel Train

The Joke:
A camel train is making its way across the desert, when it is stopped for an inspection by Saudi customs. The inspector is delighted when he discovers two bricks. He assumes the bricks are actually gold, and the camel train is caught smuggling. He tries to scrape off the red paint, but the bricks are real. He calls the head camel driver over, and demands an explanation.

He is told that the bricks are used to castrate camels. He asks how this is done. He is told:

"You sneak up behind the camel with a brick in each hand and POW!"

"Oh my God, doesn't that hurt?" asks the Inspector.

"Not really – unless you get your thumbs caught between the bricks," replies the camel driver.

Analysis:
When the inspector asks whether it hurts, he means the camel. The camel driver thinks he means the person doing the castrating.

Vocabulary:
Castrate – To remove the testicles. In this case, to pulverize the testicles.
Pulverize – To reduce to a powder.
Saudi – Short for Saudi Arabia.

The Naughty Parrot

The Joke:
    A lady buys a parrot from a pet shop. The next day, she comes back and complains about the language this parrot is using. Asked for an example, the lady turns to the parrot, and says:
    "All right, Mary Lou, give the man an example."
    Mary Lou responds:
    "My name is Mary Lou,
    and I love to screw."
    The owner of the pet shop says that he has a couple of parrots in the back room, and they'll reform her.
    They all three proceed to the back room. They find the two parrots at their prayers. One is reciting Ave Marias and using a Rosary. The other is wearing a Yarmulke and reading from the Torah. They toss Mary Lou into the same cage. She says:
    "My name is Mary Lou,
    and I love to screw."
    The Jewish parrot says:
    "Throw away those beads, Sam. This is what we've been praying for!"

Analysis:
    Mary Lou knows what she is doing.

Vocabulary:
    Ave Maria – A prayer recited by Catholics, praising the Holy Mother of God.
    Rosary – A set of beads used during prayer by a Catholic, and some other religions such as Buddhism.
    Screw – Slang for have sexual intercourse.
    Torah – The first five books of the Old Testament in the Bible, considered holy by the Jews.
    Yarmulke – A small round cap, worn by Jews when they pray and on certain other occasions such as weddings.

Adultery Confession

The Joke:
Pat decides to go to confession, so he goes to a Catholic church. He admits that it has been a long time since he confessed to a priest. The priest gives him assurances that it will be all right, quoting scripture from the Bible to prove his point. He says, quoting from Romans, Chapter 3, and Verse 23:

"For all have sinned and fallen short of the glory of God."

Thus assured, Pat confesses to committing adultery. The priest asks who this was with. Pat says:

"Oh no, father, I promised this lass that I wouldn't breathe her name to another living soul."

The priest indicates that he cannot grant absolution until Pat confesses fully and completely. He asks:

"Now tell me, it was Maureen O'Shaunessy, wasn't it?"

Pat indicates that it was not Maureen, and again reiterates his pledge to not give her name to another living soul. The priest again says that he cannot grant forgiveness until Pat confesses completely. He asks:

"Now tell me, son, it was Mary O'Toole, wasn't it?"

Pat says that it wasn't Mary, and again repeats his pledge to the other party.

The priest says that he cannot grant Pat absolution unless he confesses completely. Again, he asks:

"Tell me, son, it was Eileen O'Malley, wasn't it?"

Pat says it wasn't Eileen either, and again repeats his promise to the other party.

In exasperation, the priest exclaims:

"Well look, son, I don't have all day to hear your confession. When you're ready to confess completely, I'll gladly hear your confession. Twixt now and then, I don't want to see hide nor hair of Ye. Now, please leave so that others can confess their sins."

As Pat is leaving the church, he encounters his good friend Mike coming up the steps. His friend asks:

"How's it going, Pat?"

"Not too good, I had to confess to adultery," says Pat.

"Oh, did you get absolution?" asks his friend.

"No, but I got three hot tips!" replies Pat.

Analysis:
The priest has given Pat three names (Maureen, Mary and Eileen), which he thinks would be receptive to a proposition of adultery. These are the three hot tips he's referring to.

Vocabulary:
Absolution – Forgiveness. In the Catholic Church, this is given by a priest after an act is confessed to him.

Hide Nor Hair – Any part of. In this case, the priest says he doesn't want to see him.

Lass and lad – In Ireland, this means young woman and young man respectively.

Reiterates – Says again, states again.

Twixt – Between.

Ye – Older version of you.

What Do You Want To Be When You Grow Up

The Joke:

A nun wants to know what her students want to be when they are grown. She is getting the usual responses from her students – doctor, lawyer, fireman, religious sister like you, teacher, etc. She reaches little Josephine, and asks:

"And what do you want to be when you grow up, Josephine?"

Josephine answers:

"I want to be a prostitute."

Sister faints. One of her students runs for the Mother Superior. The Mother Superior finally succeeds in bringing the sister around, using smelling salts.

She says:

"What is it, Sister? What's going on?"

The nun responds:

"The most terrible thing you could imagine. Absolutely, unbelievable. Josephine, tell the Mother Superior what you want to be when you grow up."

Josephine repeats:

"I want to be a prostitute."

The nun says:

"Oh, thank Heaven – I thought you said Protestant."

Analysis:

Sister would rather her student become a prostitute than convert to Protestantism.

Vocabulary:

Mother Superior – In the Catholic religion, a woman in charge of a religious community of women.

Protestant – A non-Catholic. A member of a Western Christian church whose faith and practice are founded on the principles of the Reformation, especially in the acceptance of the Bible as the sole source of revelation, in justification by faith alone, and in the universal priesthood of all the believers.

Prostitute – One who solicits and accepts payment for sex acts.

Smelling salts – Salts smelling of ammonia, used to bring people around after fainting.

On A Train between London and Manchester

The Joke:

An American Air Force Colonel is traveling from London to Manchester. In the same compartment with him are two young Englishmen. The Colonel says:

"I was here during the War, you know."

One of the young Englishmen, who is hard of hearing, asks his brother: "What did he say?"

"Says he was here during the War."

The Colonel continues:

"When I was here during the War, I met an Englishwoman named Lady Ashmore. She was the best lover I ever had. She was absolutely fantastic in bed. Lord Ashmore would go out of town, and she and I would be alone for a whole week-end. It was utterly fantastic."

"What did he say?" asks the deaf brother.

"Says he knew Mother," replies the other Englishman.

Analysis:

The American Colonel obviously did not know that the two young Englishmen are the sons of Lady Ashmore.

Vocabulary:

Manchester – A city in the North of England, known for its rainy weather.

War – World War II is what the Colonel is referring to.

Now That I'm Eighty Years Old

The Joke:

A young man is admiring himself in the mirror. He has a beautiful suntan, but he notices that one part of his anatomy has no tan. He decides to remedy this situation. He finds what he believes to be a secluded area of the beach. He buries himself completely in the sand – except for this one area which he wants tanned.

About thirty minutes go by. Two old ladies decide to take a short cut through this section of the beach. Suddenly, one of them exclaims:

"Mabel, would you look at that? You know, when I was 20, I was curious about it; when I was 30, I enjoyed it; when I was 40, I asked for it; when I was 50, I paid for it; when I was 60, I prayed for it; when I was 70, I kind of forgot about it. Now that I'm 80 years old, the damn things are growing wild!"

Analysis:

The young man is getting his penis suntanned. Normally secluded, a shortcut taken by the two ladies takes them right to it.

Vocabulary:

Secluded – Lonely, without any people.

When I Was 50, I Paid For It – A man who is paid to service a woman is called a *gigolo*.

The Mermaid

The Joke:
A man rescues what he believes is a woman from a shark. Once he gets her to the beach, he realizes that he has rescued a mermaid. About that time, the mermaid comes to. Since he has rescued her from the shark, he is offered anything he wants. He decides that he wants to make love to her, but is informed that that is not possible, since she is a fish from the waist down.

So the man says, "All right, then how about a little head?"

Immediately, he feels his head shrink to about the size of an apple.

Analysis:
The man wants the mermaid to perform oral sex on him. She takes him literally, however, and gives him a small head.

Vocabulary:
Head – A slang term for giving a guy a blow job. To give head is to perform oral sex on someone.

The Married Woman

The Joke:

A man is making love to a married woman, when her husband arrives home unexpectedly. "Quick, jump out the window!" she says.

Completely naked, the man does as he is told. As luck would have it, a marathon is being run just outside the window. The man falls into the middle of the pack. As they are running, the man running next to him asks whether he always runs naked. He replies affirmatively. The man next asks him if he always wears a condom.

"Only if it looks like rain," replies the man.

Analysis:

Caught out without his clothes, the man has no choice but to join the marathon. Thinking fast, he answers the man next to him that he always wears a condom when it looks like rain.

Vocabulary:

Condom – A sheath worn over the penis, normally made of latex rubber. Used for birth control, and to prevent venereal disease. A slang term is rubber, in the U.S.

Marathon – A race of slightly over twenty-six miles. The name is taken from the Battle of Marathon, where the Greeks defeated the Persians. The Greek soldier, Pheidippides, supposedly ran the 26 miles as a messenger to announce the victory. He ran from the Battle of Marathon to the city of Athens in Greece.

The Priest and the Rabbi

The Joke:
A Catholic Priest and a Jewish Orthodox Rabbi have become very good friends over the years. The priest invites the rabbi to hear confession with him. At first, the rabbi is reluctant. But, upon being assured that it is dark back there and no one will know that he is there, the rabbi agrees.

The next Sunday, the two men are sitting together in the confessional booth.

A young lady confesses to committing adultery twice this week. The priest tells her to say three Ave Maria's and put five dollars in the collection plate, and God will forgive her. The parishioner thanks him and leaves. Several other parishioners confess their sins and the Priest grants them absolution. Then, another young lady comes in and confesses to committing adultery twice this week. Again, the priest advises her to recite three Ave Maria's and to put five dollars in the collection plate, and God will grant her absolution.

Several other parishioners confess to various sins, and the priest grants them all absolution. Suddenly, the priest says that he has to visit the men's room. He asks the rabbi to take over for him, saying that he now knows the routine. The rabbi is sitting by himself when a young lady comes in and says:

"Oh father, I've done something terrible. I've committed adultery this week."

The Rabbi inquires about how many times she's committed adultery this week. Upon hearing that it's only once, he says:

"Well, young lady, I want you to go do it again. This week, we have a special – two for five dollars."

Analysis:
The rabbi doesn't know what to do with a parishioner who has only committed adultery once this week. All of his experience is based on doing it twice per week.

Vocabulary:

Booth – An enclosed area within a larger complex. In this case, with a roof and a curtain to provide privacy. The parishioner speaks to the priest through an opening covered by a grill.

Orthodox – The most prevalent school of Judaism. This involves maintaining completely separate sets of dishes – one for meat, and the other for milk and dairy products.

The American Wrestler

The Joke:

An American wrestling coach is prepping his boy for the Olympics. He is to avoid the Russian pretzel hold at all costs. No one has ever broken that hold, and it's considered to be the *Kiss Of Death*. His wrestler promises to be careful. On the day of the match during the second fall, the American wrestler finds himself upside down, ass end over tea kettle, on the mat. The Russian is all over him like a blanket. Thinking that it is all over, the American coach starts to walk back up the aisle.

Halfway up the aisle, he is shocked to hear the Star Spangled Banner. Looking back, he sees the referee raise his boy's hand in victory.

Getting his boy back to the locker room, the coach asks:

"How'd you do that? No one has ever broken the Russian pretzel hold before."

The American replies:

"Well coach, there I was, ass end over tea kettle, upside down on the mat, Russian all over me like a blanket when I see this pair of testicles. So, I bit them. Let me tell you, coach, you don't know your own Goddamn strength when you bite yourself in the balls!"

Analysis:

The only way the American wrestler could break the Russian pretzel hold was to bite himself in the testicles.

Vocabulary:

Balls – Slang name for testicles.

Goddamn – Strong curse word. It literally means God condemn it. It is also known as *taking the Lord's name in vain*.

Kiss Of Death – Fatal, leading to the ultimate defeat.

Locker Room – Place where each team changes from street clothes to sporting gear and uniforms. There are lockers to hold each player's uniform and clothes.

Mat – A thick pillow. In this case, a wrestling mat.

Prepping – Short for preparing. A prep school is one that prepares a student for college. The most exclusive Prep Schools in the U.S. are Choate and Eaton

Star Spangled Banner –The national anthem of the Americans. The name is taken from the flag of the Americans.

Pretzel – A piece of dough which has been cooked. It is normally crooked, and sprinkled with salt. It lends its name to the wrestling hold because the opponent is twisted around like a pretzel.

Referee – Some one who ensures that each opponent plays by the rules. Sometimes, he is referred to as the *ref*.

Tea Kettle – Slang for a person's head.

The Car Stopped

The Joke:

An American is driving his English car along a dirt road in England when the car suddenly stops for no apparent reason. The man has the hood up and is looking at the engine, when he hears a voice behind him say:

"It's your carburetor. If you clean it, the car will start."

He looks around, but there is not a soul in sight in either direction. Then, he notices a white horse with its head over the pasture fence next to the road. Staring directly at the horse, he says:

"Excuse me, what did you say?"

Repeating himself, the horse says:

"It's your carburetor. Clean it and the car will start."

The man does as he is told. He unscrews the wing-nut, takes out the carburetor and knocks it against his foot. Sure enough, a little dirt rolls out and falls into the middle of the road. He gets back into the car, and it starts immediately as soon as he turns the key in the ignition. He rolls down the window, and says to the horse:

"Thank you."

"Oh, you're very welcome," replies the horse.

The American lead foots it down the dirt road, until he reaches the first pub he can find. He gets out, goes to the bar, and starts downing drinks one after the other. Overcome with curiosity, the publican finally comes over and asks the American if anything is wrong.

"Yeah, but you'd never believe me if I told you," responds the American.

"Try me," says the publican.

"Well, my car stopped out on this road. I had the hood up, and I was trying to figure out what was wrong, when suddenly I heard this voice behind me telling me that the carburetor was dirty. I looked up and down the road, but there was no one in sight. Then, I noticed a white horse with his head over the fence. It turned out that the horse was actually doing the speaking. Darndest thing I've ever seen."

"Tell me, did you happen to see a black horse?" asks the publican.

"Well, come to think of it, there was a black horse further up in the pasture," replies the American.

"You was lucky then 'cause 'e don't know fuck-all about cars," responds the publican.

Analysis:

The American is amazed that the horse can speak. The publican, however, is more surprised at the luck of the American who has found the right horse (the white horse) to tell him about his problem with his car. The wrong horse (the black horse) is completely ignorant about cars.

Vocabulary:

'cause – Slang for because.

'e – Slang for he.

Accelerator The gas pedal in a car. Stepping on it makes the car go faster.

Amazed – Surprised.

Carburetor – The part of a car which distributes gas to the cylinders.

Cylinder – The round part of an engine where the fuel is burned or combusted.

Darndest – Mild curse word.

Fuck-all – Slang for anything at all.

Gas – This is known as petrol in England.

Graze – Eat, normally grass. Sometimes refers to customer's habits of eating while in a supermarket.

Hood – The front part of a car. In England, this is known as the bonnet.

Ignition – The part of the car which causes it to start. It is normally operated by a key. In this case, by the car key.

Ignorant – Uneducated. Does not know anything.

Lead foots it – Speeds. The expression literally means with a heavy or leaden foot on the accelerator.

Not a soul – No person.

Pasture – A place where animals graze or eat. The ground is normally covered with grass.

Pub – In England, a place to have a drink or beer and relax. It is otherwise known as *your local*.

Publican – In England, the owner of a pub.

Staring – Looking at someone or something without blinking or averting the eyes.

Wing-nut – Nut atop the carburetor in some cars. A nut with wings that provide a grip for the thumb and finger.

The Conversion

The Joke:

The Pope is on a worldwide tour. When he stops in Los Angeles in the U.S., he converts Frank Sinatra. An aide explains that Frank was Catholic before, and this will not make any difference. The Pope returns to the Vatican in Italy, and succeeds in converting Gina Lollobrigida. The same aide explains that Gina was also Catholic before, and that this won't make any difference either.

The Pope says:

"You've got to get someone in here who's famous."

The aide replies that he did have an inquiry from the Seven Dwarfs. The Pope responds:

"Yes, yes, get them in here."

The seven dwarfs arrive, and are shown in immediately to the Pope.

The Pope makes a long speech about the advantages of Catholicism. When he is finished, he asks:

"Now, do you gentlemen have any questions?"

Grumpy answers:

"Yes, your holiness, we would like to know if the Church has any convents at the North Pole."

"I don't know, but I'll find out,." says the Pope. Turning to one of his aides, he asks him to go find out if they have any convents at the North Pole. A few minutes later the aide returns and tells the Pope that they have no convents at the North Pole.

"OK, your holiness, we'll let you know," says Grumpy.

As the dwarves are leaving the audience chamber, the Pope can hear them start to chant:

"Dopey did a penguin,

Dopey did a penguin."

Analysis:

Since the Catholic Church has no convents at the North Pole, Dopey must have been making love to a penguin.

Vocabulary:

Aide – Assistant.

Audience chamber – A place where someone of high rank (like the Pope) receives people for an interview, or some other purpose.

Catholicism – The Roman Catholic religion.

Convent – Place where nuns live.

Grumpy – One of the Seven Dwarfs. The others are called Dopey, Doc, Happy, Bashful, Sneezey and Sleepy.

North Pole – The traditional home of Santa Claus and all dwarves.

Pope – The head of the Catholic Church. His residence is at the Vatican in Rome, Italy. He is sometimes referred to as *The Holy Father*.

The Good Golf Game

The Joke:

Playing his usual bad game of golf, a young man hits a wicked slice off his sixth tee. Seeing the ball go into a thick wood, the young man goes to retrieve it. Combing through the woods, the man stumbles upon a witch stirring a steaming brew in a big cauldron. Transfixed, the man stares at the witch and the cauldron. Finally, he asks:

"What is that in the cauldron?"

The witch cackles:

"It's a magic potion. One swallow of this brew will improve your golf game to near perfection, but you will have a very bad sex life."

Taking a cup of the brew, the man drinks it completely. He goes on to win a tournament at his club. No one can defeat him, so he goes on to win the PGA and several other large tournaments over the following year.

On a whim, he decides to see if the witch is still there. He visits his old club, proceeds to the sixth tee and walks into the woods. He finds the witch just as he remembers her, and asks if she remembers him. She responds that of course she remembers him, and asks him how his golf game is going. He replies that his golf game is fantastic now and he has won all sorts of tournaments since he met her. She then asks how many times he got laid since he met her, and he replies:

"Six or seven times."

"Six or seven times," she scoffs, and reminds him that she warned him that his sex life would be lousy.

"Actually, I don't think that's too bad for a priest with a small congregation," responds the man.

Analysis:

A priest in the Catholic Church is not supposed to have sex with any woman.

Vocabulary:

Cackles – Speaks with a cackling noise or laugh, like an old person.

Caddy – Someone who accompanies each golfer, carries his golf bag full of clubs, tees and balls, and keeps score on a scorecard.

Capricious – Not serious, according to whim or fancy.

Cauldron – Large pot, usually with feet and a handle. It is normally black.

Choir – That part of the congregation behind the minister or priest which sings, normally hymns in praise of some holy object.

Club – In golf, the instrument used to hit the ball. These are numbered, and have a head which is either wood or metal. For instance, a four wood is a number four club tipped with wood; a number five iron is a number five club tipped with metal.

Combing – Searching. For example, a man who searches the beaches is called a beachcomber.

Congregation – In almost any religion, the crowd which gathers every Sabbath to hear a sermon.

Hook – See slice below.

Hymn – Religious song.

Laid – Slang for having sex.

Lousy – Bad.

Par – In golf, par means the number of strokes for this hole. Par five means this hole is rated at five strokes.

Potion – Mixture of fluids.

Preaching To The Choir – Slang for talking to people who are already convinced that you are right.

Sabbath – The seventh day, observed in Christianity as a special day reserved to worship the Lord. For a Christian, this is normally Sunday. Jews observe Friday night and Saturday. Seventh Day Adventists also observe Saturdays as their holy day.

Scoffs – Makes fun of, ridicules.

Slice – In golf, a hit to the right. A hit to the left is called a hook.

Tee – In golf, the place where a new hole begins. The place where the golfers tee off to begin a new hole. Par five means that normally it takes five strokes to complete this hole.

Transfixed – Held in place. Fascinated.

Whim – A sudden or capricious idea. A fancy.

Wicked – Bad.

The Lost Golf Ball

The Joke:

A foursome is playing golf when one golfer hits a bad slice and it goes into a pasture. A lady golfer is searching the same pasture for her ball. After searching the pasture for about fifteen minutes, he tells the other three in his party to go ahead. He says he'll meet them for drinks at the nineteenth hole. About an hour later, he joins his golfing buddies for a drink at the clubhouse.

His buddies ask him how it went, and he answers them in a hoarse voice:

"Not too good."

"Good Lord, what happened to you?" they exclaim.

The man explained hoarsely:

"Well, I searched for my ball a long time. This lady was searching for her ball, too. Just as I was about to give up, I noticed that every time this cow moved her tail I could see something white. So, I decided to investigate. Sure enough, there was a golf ball stuck in there. But, it's not mine because I only use Titleist, and this was a Spaulding. I turned to this woman, and said: 'Hey Lady, this looks like yours!' And ZAP, she got me in the throat with her putter!"

Analysis:

The lady golfer thinks that the man is referring to her kazoo, rather than to a golf ball. See the previous joke for a fuller description of golfing terms.

Vocabulary:

Euphemism – Calling something a different name. For example, calling a janitor a sanitary engineer.

Foursome – Party of four. In this case, four people who are playing golf together.

Hoarse – In a lower voice. Normally, the speaker is sick with a sore throat.

Kazoo – A slang term for a lady's vagina.

Nineteenth Hole – Since golf only has eighteen holes, this is a euphemism for the clubhouse.

Pasture – An enclosed space where animals eat, normally covered in grass and weeds.

Putter – In golf, a metal club used for short distances to sink putts.

Spaulding – In golf, the brand name of a golf ball.

Titleist – In golf, the brand name of a golf ball.

Arnold Palmer

The Joke:

A newly married man is on his way to the honeymoon in the Hawaiian Islands. He turns to his new bride and asks:

"Listen, I have to know. Was there anyone else before me?"

The new wife gets very embarrassed, and blushes. At last, she speaks: "Yes."

That chews on him for about ten minutes. Then, he says:

"Listen, I have to know who it was."

She replies: "Well, if you must know, it was Arnold Palmer."

That bothers him for a while, and then he says:

"Well, I can understand how a young girl's head might be turned by a guy like Arnold Palmer. I guess I can live with that."

They reach Hawaii and check in. After tipping the bellhop, the man and his wife make it in the bed. Afterwards, he goes for the telephone. She says:

"What are you doing?"

He replies: "I'm phoning down for champagne to celebrate the consummation of our wedding."

She says: "That's not what Arnold did."

He asks: "Oh no – what did he do?"

She replies: "He just went in and took a quick shower. Then, he came back and did it again."

Putting down the receiver, he says:

"Oh, yeah."

He goes in, takes a shower and comes back and makes love to her again. He goes over to the phone again.

She asks: "What are you doing?"

He replies: "I'm phoning down for that champagne."

Again, she says: "That's not what Arnold did."

He replies: Oh no, what did he do?"

Again, she says: "He just went and took a quick shower, came back and did it again."

Putting the receiver down again, he goes and takes a quick shower, comes back and makes love to her again. He then heads for the phone.

"Are you phoning down for that champagne?" She asks.

"No, I'm phoning Arnold Palmer," he replies.

"What?" She says.

"Yeah, I'm going to find out what's par for this hole," he replies.

Analysis:

Arnold Palmer is a famous golfer. Therefore, it is logical to assume that he knows how many times he made love with her. See the joke entitled *The Good Golf Game* for a fuller description of golf terms.

Vocabulary:

Archipelago – A collection of islands and atolls.

Atoll – A coral island which completely or nearly completely surrounds a shallow lagoon. Bikini in the Marshall Islands is the most famous atoll. It was used for early atomic testing, and gives its name to the abbreviated swimming suit.

Bellhop or Bellman – In a hotel, the man who carries your bags to your room. He is so-called because he is called by the check-in clerk's bell.

Blushes – Turns red in the cheeks on the face.

Champagne – A white bubbly wine normally used for celebrations.

Chews On – Bothers.

Hawaiian Islands – Normally, this means the island of Oahu which contains most of the population, including the city of Honolulu. The island of Hawaii is the most recent and largest island of the Hawaiian Archipelago. It is the island having all of the active volcanoes. A hot spot moves at a rate of five inches per year. Right now, this hot spot is located under the large island of Hawaii, which explains the volcanoes on this island. This island actually grows, as the hot lava meets the Pacific Ocean. Eventually, a new island will be formed when this hot spot moves far enough beyond the large island of Hawaii. Similarly, a long string of worn out islands stretches out behind the eight major islands. At one time in the distant past, these were the major islands of the Hawaiian Archipelago.

Honeymoon – A period which normally takes place immediately after a wedding, usually lasting for a week or two. This dates back to the days when a woman was thought to be a virgin before marriage, and was a period for the bride to become accustomed to having sex with her new husband.

Lagoon – A shallow body of water, usually separated from the rest of a sea or ocean by coral reefs or sandbars.

Receiver – On a telephone, the part you raise to speak and listen.

Virgin – Unused. In marriage, it means inexperienced in love making. It normally applies only the woman, but it can apply to the man as well.

The Methodist Minister

The Joke:
A Methodist Minister is speeding on the highway because he is late for a funeral at which he is supposed to be officiating. He is pulled over for speeding by a state highway patrolman. He explains his situation to the officer, and offers to give his name and address. If the officer will mail him the citation, he'll gladly pay it for he does realize that he was speeding. The officer says:

"Sorry, I can't do that. Against the rules, you know. Now, I'll need your driver's license and your registration."

The patrolman takes his time writing out the citation. No rush at all. He even reads it twice, to be sure that he hasn't missed anything. He finally hands the citation to the Minister. He then says:

"You say that you're a Methodist Minister. I happen to be a Methodist myself, and I have a little problem. Could I come see you next Sunday?"

The minister replies:

"Of course, son, and I know exactly what your problem is. Don't worry about a thing, you just bring your parents right along and I'll marry them."

Analysis:
Ethics forbids a Methodist Minister from actually calling a man a bastard, but he has found another way to get his point across.

Vocabulary:
Bastard – Used as a pejorative name for someone you dislike. Actually, of illegitimate birth. Someone born out of wedlock.

Citation – Summons to court for a misdemeanor. Issued by an officer.

Empowered – Given the power.

Ethics – What is right, and what is wrong. Motivation based on ideas of what is right and what is wrong.

Highway Patrolman – Someone who enforces the law on the open highway. They are distinguished from the police, who normally enforce the law within a city. Both are empowered to issue a citation.

Methodist – A protestant sect of Christianity.

Officiating – In this case, giving the religious service.

Registration – Short for vehicle registration.

Summons – Issued by a court. A command to appear in court.

Wedlock – Marriage.

Green Side Up

The Joke:

A lady wants to have the interior of her house painted. First, she needs an estimate. Then, she spots a crew working across the street. She calls across to the man heading the crew, and he says that he will be right over. He arrives minutes later. She explains that she wants each room to be a separate color, and asks for an estimate. He agrees, so she starts with the living room and says this room should be white. He measures the room, but first he goes over to the window, but first he goes to the window and yells across the street:

"Green side up!"

She then takes him upstairs to her bedroom, and says this room should be light blue. He again measures the room, but before that he goes to the window and yells across the street:

"Green side up!"

She goes into her bathroom, and specifies beige. Once again he takes measurements, but before he does, he goes over to a window and yells:

"Green side up!"

No matter what the room's color, the crew chief always goes over to a window and yells:

"Green side up!"

Finally she asks:

"No matter what color I specify, you always say: 'Green side up.' What is going on here?"

The crew chief replies:

"Oh, no, lady. This has nothing to do with painting your house. I have a Polish fellow laying sod across the street."

Analysis:

Sod has only two sides – one grass and the other dirt. Therefore, the crew chief is reminding the Polish guy that the grass is turned up. This is a "stupidity joke" told on the Polish guy. Please use discretion when determining whether to tell this joke.

Vocabulary:

Crew – Team.

Discretion – Good judgment is required.

Estimate – How many dollars you think it will take.

Hold the Water

The Joke:

An old lady has gone into the bar on a cruise ship. She explains that this cruise was to celebrate her birthday. Today is her birthday, and she is 84-years-old. The bartender offers to buy her a drink, since it's her birthday. She accepts his offer, and orders a scotch with a single drop of water. The man sitting to her right offers to buy her a drink also. She accepts again, and orders a drink of scotch with a single drop of water. The lady on her left offers her another drink. She accepts once again, and orders a scotch with a single drop of water. The bartender cannot hold his curiosity, and asks her why she always orders a scotch with one drop of water.

She replies:

"At 84 years of age, I've certainly learned how to hold my liquor. However, holding my water is another issue entirely."

Analysis:

The old lady has learned how to hold her liquor, but urinating is another issue.

Vocabulary:

Cruise Ship – A ship which cruises from one destination to another.

Cruises – Travels by water. Usually, a ship travels from one port to another along the coast.

Note: The above is adapted from Jim Hall and his group. To contact him, please see: murphyplus2@hotmail.com.

Harry Had a Heart Attack

The Joke:

A wife is concerned because her husband has not returned at his usual time after his Sunday round of golf. Finally, he returns home at 9 o'clock. She says:

"What happened, you're usually home by 1 o'clock?"

Her husband replies:

"Harry had a heart attack and dropped dead on the third tee. Jesus, what a game. Tee off, and drag Harry! Tee off, and drag Harry! Tee off, and drag Harry!"

Analysis:

Nothing interferes with the game of golf.

Vocabulary:

Tee off – To strike a ball from the teeing ground at the start of a hole.

Three Wishes

The Joke:

An eighty-year-old woman is sunning herself in front of her tenement in the Bronx. Suddenly, she notices something shiny under the stoop. She investigates, and finds it to be an old lamp. She is rubbing it to get some of the dirt off, when this genie appears. He offers her three wishes. She says that she wants to be young and beautiful.

POOF! In a cloud of smoke, she becomes a young, beautiful and voluptuous blond. The genie asks what she wants for her second wish. She replies that she wants to be rich.

POOF! In a second cloud of smoke, she finds herself in the middle of a great estate. She is clothed in a gorgeous gown with valuable jewelry all over her. The genie asks what she wants for her final wish. Looking around, she spies her tomcat. Change my cat to Don Juan, and make him madly in love with me.

POOF! In a third cloud of smoke, her cat is transformed into Don Juan. He sweeps her off her feet, carries her upstairs, tosses her on the bed, looks soulfully into her eyes, and asks:

"Now, aren't you sorry?"

She responds:

"Sorry about what?"

He answers:

"Sorry that you took me to the vet to be neutered when I was a little kitten."

Analysis:

The genie from a bottle or lamp, who is empowered to grant three wishes, is a common thing in literature. By rubbing the lamp, the old lady has released the genie.

Vocabulary:

Don Juan – The great Spanish lover and libertine. The subject of multiple stories in literature. It is pronounced *don jew-an* by Percy Bysshe Shelley, but as *don wan* by most other authors.

Genie – One who is confined to a bottle or lamp? Upon being released from the lamp or bottle, he or she has the power to grant three wishes.

Kitten – Young cat.

Libertine – A womanizer.

Neutered – The process of castrating a male kitten or puppy by a veterinarian. Females are spayed by a similar process, which sterilizes the subject making him or her incapable of having a new litter.

Pussycat – A female cat. See *tomcat* below.

Puppy – Young dog.

Spayed – See neutered above.

Stoop – In this case, a set of stairs leading up to a building.

Tomcat – Male cat. A female cat is called a pussycat.

Transformed – Changed.

Veterinarian – A doctor for animals. A typically used abbreviation is *vet*.

Voluptuous – Sexually desirable.

The Wooden Leg

The Joke:
A man has a car breakdown on a lonely country road. He decides to phone for a wrecker, but his cell phone won't work this far out in the country. He is hiking along this country road, when he spots a farmhouse up ahead. He goes to the farmhouse door and asks to use the farmer's telephone. While he is phoning, he notices a pig with a wooden leg out in the farmyard. When he is finished phoning, he asks the farmer if he minds if he asks him a personal question. Upon receiving a negative reply, he asks the farmer about the pig with the wooden leg. The farmer replies:

"Let me tell you about that pig. My daughter was swimming in the pond, when she suddenly got a cramp. That pig jumped into the pond and dragged her to shore. Undoubtedly, he saved her life."

The traveler says:

"But, why does he have a wooden leg?"

"Wait, that's not all. We had a fire in the house. That pig broke into the front door, woke all of us up and got us all out of the house. Undoubtedly, he saved all of our lives."

The traveler again asks:

"But, why does he have a wooden leg?"

The farmer responds:

"Well, after all that, it just didn't seem right to eat him all at once."

Analysis:
That's gratitude for you. By the way, cell phones are serviced from towers. If you are out of range from a tower, the telephone will not work.

Vocabulary:
Cramp – Doubled over in pain, due to a lack of potassium in the diet. Sometimes referred to as a muscle cramp. It consists of a muscle that is contracted and refuses to relax.
Hiking – Walking.
Wooden – Made of wood.
Wrecker – Truck which comes to help when you have a car breakdown.

The Hunting Dog

The Joke:

A man's favorite hunting dog has just died, so he is looking for a replacement. He visits a kennel. He is told by a trainer that they have plenty of dogs to choose from. But first, the trainer wants to show off a dog that he has trained. He calls Fido, and all three go in a pick-up truck to an adjacent field. The trainer says:

"OK, Fido, go count."

Fido goes into the brush, comes back and paws the ground three times. The trainer says:

"Fido says that there are three birds in the field."

"Prove it." Says the man.

Fido charges into the field, and three pheasants fly up.

"Aw, that was probably a fluke." Says the man.

"You think so. Come on Fido, get in."

They take the truck to another field. They all get out.

The trainer again says:

"OK, Fido, go count."

Again, Fido goes into the brush. He returns a few minutes later, and paws the ground seven times.

"He says that there are seven birds out there." Says the trainer.

"Prove it." Says the man.

Again, Fido charges into the field. Sure enough, seven pheasant fly up.

"Listen, I have to have that dog." Says the man.

"Oh no, Fido is not for sale." Says the trainer.

The man keeps increasing the price until the trainer finally gives in.

He finally says: "OK, he's yours. For $50,000, I suppose I could train another dog."

A few years later, the trainer runs into the man during some dog trials.

He says: "Hi, I see you're not running Fido today."

The man replies:

"Yes, that's a sad story. You see, I said: 'Go count' to Fido, and he came back with a stick, dropped it on the ground, and started humping me on the leg.

That's very embarrassing, so I said: 'No, no, Fido, go count again.' So

He went out and came back with an even bigger stick, dropped it on the ground again, and started to hump me on the leg again. So, I knew that Fido had gone crazy, so I had to shoot him."

"Boy, did you blow it!" Says the trainer.

"What do you mean, I blew it?" Asks the man.

The trainer says:

"All Fido was trying to tell you was that there more fucking birds out there than you could shake a stick at."

Analysis:

The man destroyed Fido because he thought that Fido had gone crazy, but Fido was only trying to tell him something.

Vocabulary:

Adjacent – Near. In this case, possibly joining the field where Fido made his first count and subsequent charge.

Blow – Past tense blew. Slang for making a mistake. Actually, to blow on something is to try to cool it off.

Embarrassing – Embarrassment is an emotional state experienced upon having a socially or professionally unacceptable act or condition witnessed by or revealed to others. This is known as the *present participle* form.

Fucking – Fornicating. Used in this case as a description.

Hump – Fornicate.

Hunting – In this case, seeking birds. Bird dogs track birds by air scent. Dogs can also be trained to hunt people (bloodhounds), deer, bears, etc.

Nom De Plume – Pen name. See *plumage* below.

Paw – The foot of an animal.

Paws – Scratches with a paw. In this case, the ground. An animal can also paw you to gain your attention.

Pheasant – A type of hunted bird. Any of various Old World birds of the family Phasianidae, especially the ring-necked pheasant introduced in North America, characteristically having long tails and, in the males of many species, brilliantly colored plumage.

Plumage – Feathers. Since writing used to be accomplished by dipping a feather in an ink-well, a pen name is known as a *nom de plume*. For example, Samuel Clemens was his real name, but Mark Twain was his pen name or nom de plume.

Present Participle – Anything ending in –ing.

Shake A Stick At – In this case, more than you could count.

Scent – Smell.

Subsequent – Following in time.

Trial – A test. In this case, a competition to determine qualifications.

Trainer – In this case, a dog trainer – a person who trains dogs for obedience, tricks, hunting, and work.

The Marooned Man

The Joke:

A man had been alone on an island for years. He had long since given up
hope that he would ever see civilization or another human being ever again.
He was relaxing on the beach one day when he noticed a snorkel breaking the
surf and coming towards shore. Suddenly, he sees a mask and a head which
goes with it. It's a young woman dressed in a wet suit. He rushes out to meet
her, explaining that he has been marooned on this island for years. She says:

"You mean you've been alone all these years?"

He confirms that he has indeed been alone. She offers him a cigarette, and
he accepts. She pulls a pack from a pocket in her wet suit, takes out a book of
matches from another pocket, and lights it for him. He says:

"Thank the good Lord. It's been years since I had a cigarette."

She offers him a drink, and he accepts. She reaches into a third pocket,
and draws out a flask, and hands it to him. He takes a swig, and says:

"I can't thank you enough. It's been years since I had a drink of
whiskey."

She says:

"You say you've been by yourself for years. Uh – Wouldn't you like to
play around?"

He responds:

"Oh yes, don't tell me you have a set of clubs in that wet suit too."

Analysis:

He thinks she means golf. She is thinking about foreplay as a prelude to
making love.

Vocabulary:

Civilization – An advanced state of intellectual, cultural, and material development in human society, marked by progress in the arts and sciences, the extensive use of record-keeping, including writing, and the appearance of complex political and social institutions.

Flask – A small container, such as a bottle having a narrow neck and usually a cap, especially: a flat, relatively thin container for liquor.

Foreplay – Sexual stimulation, usually as a prelude to sexual intercourse.

Isolated – Apart from everything else.

Leaven – A substance used to produce fermentation in dough or a liquid.

Marooned – Left alone. Left isolated.

Mash – A fermentable starchy mixture from which alcohol or spirits can be distilled. Usually, grain with water and yeast added.

Pocket – A small baglike attachment forming part of a garment and used to carry small articles.

Prelude – A beginning. Something that takes place before anything else.

Snorkel – A breathing device consisting of a bent tube fitting into a swimmer's mouth and extending above the surface; allows swimmer to breathe while face down in the water.

Surf – The waves of the sea as they break upon a shore or reef.

Swig – Swallow.

Wet Suit – A close-fitting, black garment made of a permeable material; worn in cold water (as by skin divers) to retain body heat.

Whiskey – Alcoholic drink. A liquor made from the fermented mash of a grain.

Yeast – A commercial leavening agent containing yeast cells; used to raise the dough in making bread and for fermenting beer or whiskey.

Give Him Two Dollars

The Joke:
A man is retiring from the U.S. Postal Service after forty years of service. The people that he delivers mail to all know that today is his last day. They are all giving him presents and money to remember him by. He stops at this one house, and the lady of the house invites him in for breakfast. At first he demurs, but she tells him that the table is already set, and a breakfast of eggs, bacon, and coffee are already prepared. Reluctantly, he agrees to eat breakfast with her. After breakfast is over, she leads him upstairs, undresses them both, and proceeds to turn him every which way but loose in bed for the next thirty minutes or so. He says:

"Thank you for an excellent breakfast and the best loving that I've had in years, but I really have to be going now."

He gets his clothes back on, and is about to leave when she hands him two dollars. He says:

"What's this for?"

She replies:

"I want you to know that breakfast was my idea, but when I told my husband about your situation and today being your last day, my husband said: 'Fuck him – give him two dollars.'"

Analysis:
The husband didn't mean for his wife to literally make love to the postman.

Vocabulary:
Demurs – Says no.
Every Which Way But Loose – A 1978 movie starring Clint Eastwood and Sandra Locke.

The Case of Priapism

The Joke:
A man walks into a pharmacy and discovers a female pharmacist behind the counter. He says:

"Excuse me, but is there a male pharmacist on duty?"

The pharmacist answers:

"No. There is only my partner and me. We own this pharmacy. But you can tell me, because I've probably heard it before."

The man explains that he has a case of Priapism.

"It is ten inches long and it won't go down. It's quite painful, and I was wondering if there's anything you can give me for it.

She says:

"I'll have to talk it over with my partner. Wait here and I'll be right back."

A few minutes later, she comes back and says:

"We can give you ten thousand dollars, and a one-third interest in the pharmacy. That's the best we can do."

Analysis:
He thinks one of the two pharmacists is going to suggest some medicine, but she and her partner make him an offer instead.

Vocabulary:
Hard On – Slang for an erection. A slang term for sexual arousal in the male is *having a hard on*. Having a hard on for someone or something can also refer to intention to harm. It can also mean the intention to get someone. For example, he had some kind of hard on for Jim, and intended to take revenge on him.

Partner – One that is united or associated with another or others in an activity or a sphere of common interest, especially: a member of a business partnership.

Pharmacist – Person who possibly runs a drug store and fills prescriptions.

Pharmacy – Drug store. Place where they fill prescriptions.

Priapism – A condition in which the penis is continually erect; usually painful and seldom with sexual arousal.

His Friend Is Blind

The Joke:

A man is taking his 12-year-old son for a walk into town. As they are walking on the sidewalk, they encounter two dogs fornicating at the curb. The boy asks:

"Gee Dad, what are they doing?"

The father says that the dog in the back is blind, so his friend is helping him to cross the street. The boy says:

"That's just like life, isn't it, Dad?"

"What do you mean, son?" asks his father.

His son says:

"Yeah, you try to help some one – and they fuck you, right in the ass."

Analysis:

That's gratitude for you.

Vocabulary:

Ass – Slang for backside or buttocks: the fleshy part of the human body that you sit on. It can also mean a donkey-like animal which is a long-eared, slow, patient, sure-footed domesticated mammal, equus asinus, related to the horse, used chiefly as a beast of burden.

Backside – The back or hind part, the rump, the buttocks. Stupidity, he couldn't find his backside with both hands.

Beast Of Burden – An animal which carries things on his back.

Chiefly – Mainly.

Chivalrous – Marked by honor, generosity, and courtesy.

Domesticated – Domestic or at home, converted or adapted to domestic use: for example, domestic animals.

Equus Asinus – African wild ass.

Equus – High-level Latin for horse. An example is equestrian, of or relating to horseback riding or horseback riders.

A low-level Latin name for horse is caballus. An example would be cavalier, a gallant or chivalrous man, especially one serving as escort to a woman of high social position; a gentleman.

Escort – Some one who accompanies some one else.

Gentleman – A man of gentle or noble birth or superior social position. A man of refinement.

Mammal – Any animal or person who suckles its young. Gives milk to the young.

Refinement – The result of refining – an improvement or elaboration.

Suckles – Feeds her young milk, from a teat. To cause or allow to take milk at the breast or udder, to nurse.

Sure-footed – Steady on the feet.

Teat – A nipple of the mammary gland.

Tit – A breast, either of two soft fleshy milk-secreting glandular organs on the chest of a woman. Now considered vulgar.

Vulgar – Crude, coarse, lacking refinement or cultivation or taste.

A Bird Is Late

The Joke:

A little bird is late flying south for the winter. On the way, he runs into a blizzard. His wings ice up, and he falls to the ground in the middle of a farmyard. A cow passes over him, and defecates on him. The manure is warm, and this revives the bird. The bird starts to sing. A cat is passing by, hears the singing, digs the bird out and eats him.

This story has three morals:

1. Not every one who shits on you is your enemy.

2. Not every one who digs you out of the shit is your friend.

3. The next time you are warm and happy, and in the middle of some really good shit, just keep your mouth shut!

Analysis:

Please pay attention to the three morals above.

Vocabulary:

Advocate – Someone who speaks for someone else. To speak, plead, or argue in favor of.

Beatification – In the Catholic Church, the first step towards canonization. Persons who have been beatified can be prayed to, and the title 'Blessed' can be put before their names.

Blizzard – Snow storm with strong winds.

Canonization – To declare (a deceased person) to be a saint and entitled to be fully honored as such. A distinction made by the Catholic Church. In the Catholic Church, the admission of one of its members to the Calendar of Saints. The evidence of the candidate's exceptional piety is contested before the Congregation for the Causes of Saints by the Promotor Fidei, popularly known as the *Devil's advocate*. Papal ratification of a favorable verdict results in beatification, and full sainthood (conferred in St Peter's Basilica, the Vatican) follows after further proof. *Capistrano* – Variant(s): or in full San Juan Capistrano. Function: Geographical name of city in SW California SE of Los Angeles, population 33826. *Deceased* – Dead.

Defecates – Has a bowel movement. Slang term is shits.

Feces / Fecal Material – Waste matter eliminated from the bowels, excrement. In this case, cow droppings.

Fertilize – Make fertile. Cause to grow things such as crops.

Migratory – Traveling. Birds that migrate go south in the winter months to avoid the cold. When it becomes warm again in the spring, they return. An example of this would be the song: 'When the Swallows Come Back to Capistrano.'

Manure – Animal feces. Fecal material, especially barnyard or stable dung, often used to fertilize soil.

Moral – The significance of a story or event. For example, 'the moral of the story is to love thy neighbor'.

Ratification – Verifying that some one or some thing is OK.

Saint – Someone canonized by the Catholic Church.

San – Spanish for saint.

Swallow – In this case, a small bird.

Broccoli

The Joke:

The Produce Manager in a grocery store is approached by a woman customer. She complains that she can't find any broccoli. The manager explains:

"I'm sorry, ma'am, but we're out of broccoli right now. However, we will get a new delivery of produce tomorrow morning, and I'm sure if you'll check back then, we'll have some broccoli." The lady thanks him, and goes away. About forty-five minutes later, however, she comes back looking for broccoli again. The manager patiently explains the situation to her again. She thanks him, and again goes back to her shopping. She comes back again in about thirty minutes with the same complaint. Again, the manager explains the situation. She thanks him again, and goes away. About forty-five minutes later, she is back with the same complaint.

The manager says:

"Spell car as in carrot."

She says: "Car."

Continuing, he says:

"Now, spell let as in lettuce."

"Let" she says.

"Now, spell fuck as in broccoli."

She answers:

"But there's no fuck in broccoli."

He says: "Lady, that's what I've been trying to tell you all this morning!"

Analysis:

There is no broccoli in the store.

Vocabulary:

Broccoli – A vegetable, used for human consumption.

Ignorant, Ignorant, Ignorant.

The Joke:

Liza and Rastus are having an argument. Liza says:

"Rastus, yo is a dumb-ass!"

"I am not." Replies Rastus.

"Yo is ign'ant, ign'ant, ign'ant!" says Liza.

"I ain't, ain't, ain't," says Rastus.

"Aw right, smarty, what do propaganda mean?" says Liza.

Rastus is silent for a moment, so Liza says:

"See, you don't know, do ya?"

"Wait just a minute, I knows dis." Replies Rastus.

"So, tell me," says Liza.

"Uh, well, it means 'If yo's the proper goose, I's the proper gander,'" responds Rastus.

Analysis:

The author does not mean to say anything derogatory or demeaning towards African-Americans. The above joke is included only because it is typical of a certain type of joke once common in the southern United States.

Before the days of political correctness, this type of Liza and Rastus or colored joke was heard commonly in the southern United States.

Nowadays, it is seldom heard at all.

Vocabulary:

Argument – A quarrel; a dispute.

Dumb-ass – A stupid person: stupid thing or stupid action.

Gander – Male goose.

Geese – Plural of goose (More than one).

Goose – Female goose.

Propaganda – Information, ideas, or rumors deliberately spread widely to help or harm a person, group, movement, institution, nation, etc.

Proper – Right. Marked by suitability or rightness or appropriateness.

Southern United States – A section of the southeastern United States, normally considered to be comprised of the old Confederacy (The eleven states on the side of the South during the American Civil War – Missouri was a 12th state, but did not actually secede from the union upon joining the Confederacy later in the War).

I Have To Have Some Right Now

The Joke:
Liza and Rastus are riding along in their car. Rastus suddenly says:
"Liza. Honey, I's got to have some right now!"
Liza replies:
"Rastus, you crazy? We's right in the middle of a whole bunch of houses."
Rastus mulls this over for a few minutes. Finally, he says:
"Liza, I'll tell ya what I'm gonna do. I is going to pull the car over to the curb, then spread a blanket and some tools under the car. We'll get under the car, and if any body asks any questions, I'll tell 'em I is fixing the car."
Liza thinks this over for a few minutes, and finally consents. They do as Rastus has suggested, and fifteen minutes later thing are going along nicely. After a few more minutes, Rastus hears this voice above him say:
"Hey fellow, what you doing down there?"
"Oh, uh, I is fixing the brakes." Replies Rastus.
"Well, fellow, you aren't doing such a hot job. The car just rolled down the hill five minutes ago," responds the voice.

Analysis:
Rastus thought he was doing something really intelligent. Unfortunately, the car rolled down the hill, exposing him and Liza.
See previous joke for disclaimers concerning this type of joke.

Vocabulary:
Curb – The raised wall at the edge of a city street. A concrete border or row of joined stones forming part of a gutter along the edge of a street. It also means to put constraints on – An example would be to curb your temper.
Disclaimer – Disavowal. Denial or renunciation, as of a claim, title, etc. A refusal to accept responsibility.
Exposing – Indecent. Appearing naked. Laying open (to danger, attack, ridicule, etc.); leaving unprotected; making accessible or subject to ridicule.
Pull Over – In this case, to put a car at the side of a street or road.

The Grand Dame of the Confederacy

The Joke:

An older woman living in Charleston, SC has decided to do a good deed for Christmas. She phones Fort Jackson, and asks to speak to one of their company commanders. She introduces herself, and gives her address. She explains that she knows that some of their enlisted men do not go home for Christmas. She asks the company commander to send ten of his enlisted men to have Christmas luncheon with her. Then she says:

"Just one thing, don't send any Jewish kids, because this is a restricted neighborhood."

Christmas day arrives, and the doorbell rings. The butler answers the door. A couple of seconds later, he returns and asks the lady of the house to come to the front door. She does, and finds ten of the biggest and blackest men imaginable. She exclaims:

"There must be some mistake!"

The HNIC says:

"No, ma'am, dat dere Captain Goldberg – he don't make no mistakes."

Analysis:

Little does the lady suspect that the company commander that she is speaking to is Jewish.

Vocabulary:

Butler – A household employee who is charged with serving dishes during a meal. He may also be charged with responsibility for answering the door.

Company Commander – The commander of a company in the U.S. military.

Confederacy – The eleven states in the southeastern U.S. which seceded from the Union. This started the American Civil War.

Fort Jackson – A military installation in the vicinity of Charleston, SC.

Good Deed – A usually praiseworthy act. A feat or exploit. Humor: No good deed goes unpunished.

Grand Dame – A woman, especially an older one, of great dignity or prestige. The origin is French and literally means great lady.

HNIC – Head Nigger In Charge. A slang expression.

Jewish – A member of the Jewish faith.

Neighborhood – A district or area with distinctive characteristics. For example, a neighborhood of fine homes; an ethnic neighborhood.

Restricted – No Jews allowed. Excluding or unavailable to certain groups. Such restrictions are now against the law.

Two Drinks, Please

The Joke:

It is just after the historic, landmark decision of the Earl Warren Supreme Court banning segregation in 1954. Two black men walk into a bar in Atlanta, Georgia. They order a drink apiece. The bartender excuses himself, and goes running to see his boss. Breathlessly, he says:

"Boss, I have a couple of niggers out here trying to buy a drink. What should I do?"

"Charge them $25 a drink," replies the boss.

The bartender thinks that is a great idea, and turns to leave. But, when he reaches the door of his boss' office, he turns and asks:

"Boss, what'll I do if they pay it?"

"Well don't just stand there; throw the rest of the white trash out!" Responds his boss.

Analysis:

Money talks, and bullshit walks. If the two black men are willing to pay $25 for a drink, then the boss is not only willing to accept them, but orders the bartender to throw all the whites out of the bar.

Vocabulary:

Afrikaans – An official language of the Republic of South Africa; closely related to Dutch and Flemish. It is usually considered a lower dialect of the Dutch language. If history interests you, investigate the Boer Wars. Of particular interest is the 1980 Australian movie entitled 'Breaker Morant' about the second Boer War.

Apartheid – Separation of the races, particularly Africans from Coloreds from Whites in the nation of South Africa on the southern tip of Africa.

Banning – To prohibit, especially by official decree. To forbid.

Boer Wars – Either of two wars: the first when the Boers fought England in order to regain the independence they had given up to obtain British help against the Zulus (1880-1881); the second when the Orange Free State and Transvaal declared war on Britain (1899-1902).

Breaker Morant – Harry 'Breaker' Harbord Morant (9 December 1864 – 27 February 1902) was an Australian drover, horseman, poet, soldier and convicted war criminal whose skill with horses earned him the nickname "The Breaker".

Breathlessly – Without breath at a normal rate. Tired from running. Breathing with difficulty. Gasping for breath.

Bullshit – Otherwise known as BS. This literally means manure from a bull. It is vulgar slang for foolish, deceitful, or boastful language.

Caucasian – White: a member of the Caucasoid race.

Earl Warren – (March 19, 1891 – July 9, 1974) was the 14th Chief Justice of the United States and the only person elected Governor of California three times. He was Chief Justice from October 2, 1953 until June 23, 1869.

Historic – Will be remembered throughout history. Having importance in or influence on history.

Landmark – In this instance, an event marking an important stage of development or a turning point in history.

Nigger – Derogatory name for African-Americans. It is a corruption of the word Negro (meaning black in Portuguese). An insult. Not used in polite society. Do not use this term unless you're ready to fight.

Segregation – Separation of the races, particularly African-Americans from Whites in the southeastern U.S. It was similar to Apartheid in South Africa. The primary difference was that all coloreds were considered Negroes in America. Indeed, anyone with any black blood was considered to be a Negro.

Supreme Court – The highest court in the U.S. It is considered to be the head of one of the three branches of the U.S. Government.

Trash – A person of low morality. An uneducated and illiterate person. Also, rubbish or worthless material.

White – Usually, a member of the Caucasian race.

In a Grocery Store

The Joke:
The manager of a grocery store notices that a woman buys three cans of dog food every week. He meanders on over, and asks:
"Hi, what kind of dog do you have?"
"Oh, I don't have a dog."
He responds:
"Oh, if you don't mind my asking, what do you do with the dog food?"
"I feed it to my husband." She answers.
"Oh, Ma'am, please don't do that. It is not pasteurized or sanitized. It really is not for human consumption." He says.
"Nonsense, he loves it. Sometimes, he won't accept anything else. Don't worry about it." She says.
About six weeks later, the same woman comes in. She is dressed entirely in black, and doesn't purchase any dog food.
Again he walks over and says:
"Howdy, Ma'am. I'm glad to see you didn't buy any dog food today."
"Yes, my husband passed away last week," she sniffles.
He responds:
"I'm very sorry, but I did try to warn you about that dog food."
"Oh, no. It wasn't the dog food."
"Well, excuse me, but how did he pass away exactly?" he asks.
"Well, a truck ran over him while he was sitting in the middle of the street licking his balls," she says.

Analysis:
Is her husband a dog, or isn't he?

Vocabulary:
Balls – Slang name for testicles.
Meanders – To follow a winding and turning course. In this case, to walk slowly over to.
Sniffles – To weep or whimper lightly with spasmodic congestion of the nose.

The Kid Learned Everything

The Joke:

A company has a policy whereby the children are allowed to accompany their father or mother for one day to see what their parent does for a living. At the end of the day, each child is presented with a scale model of the warehouse, complete with loading docks, trucks and even a perimeter fence.

The next day, the son's mother is appalled to hear him say:

"All right, fella, back that rig up just a cunt hair."

She goes flying into the living room, and says:

"You! You go up to your room this instant without your supper. And boy is your father going to hear about this when he gets home!"

The kid gets about half way up the stairs, and his mother suddenly says:

"Wait a minute! What about all this stuff on the rug?"

The kid looks down at the mess on the rug, and then says:

"Fuck it! Leave it for the night shift."

Analysis:

As evidenced by his last statement, the kid learned everything he needed to know after only one day in the warehouse.

Vocabulary:

Appalled – Filled with consternation or dismay.

Cunt Hair – Slang for a very small amount, about the distance represented by the thickness of a female pubic hair.

Cunt – Offensive. Used as a disparaging term for a woman.

Fella – Short for fellow.

Night Shift – A group of men which relieves the day shift usually about 4 pm in the warehouse.

Rig – In this case, a truck.

The Flirting Lady

The Joke:
A middle-aged woman is checking out in the grocery store. She notices that the boy bagging her groceries is young and quite handsome. In short, he is a real hunk. She attempts to flirt with him, but he doesn't seem to respond. On her way to the parking lot, she finally says:

"You know, I have an itchy pussy."

He answers:

"Well, you'll have to point it out, Ma'am. All of these Japanese cars look the same to me".

Analysis:
The kid who has bagged her groceries, and is carrying them to her car thinks that an itchy pussy is a type of Japanese car. She is trying to tell him that she is horny. In other words, she is trying to seduce him.

Vocabulary:
Flirt – To make sexual advances.

Horny – Slang for ready to have sex.

Hunk – Slang for a sexually attractive man with a well-developed physique.

Itchy Pussy – Slang phrase for being sexually aroused. Used by women to indicate that they are ready to have sex.

Make/Made – Slang for seduce/seduced.

Score – A sexual conquest.

Seduce – Induce to have sex. Examples are: "Harry finally seduced Sally"; "Harry scored with Sally last night."; "Harry made Sally"

The Ventriloquist

The Joke:

A ventriloquist has just spent the night with a farmer in his farmhouse. The following morning, wanting to have some fun and realizing that the farmer doesn't know that he is a skilled ventriloquist, he requests a tour of the farmyard. The unsuspecting farmer complies, and starts the tour immediately. The first animal they come across is a cow. The ventriloquist asks:

"Good morning and how are you this fine morning?"

Seeming to respond, the cow answers:

"Fine, but you know the farmer milks me every morning and his hands are very cold. It would be nice if his hands were warmer."

Continuing in this fashion, the ventriloquist interviews each farm animal. Then, he notices that the farmer is becoming increasingly nervous as he continues the interviews. He asks the farmer:

"Is there anything wrong?"

The farmer replies:

"You see that ewe over there. Well, she's a big liar. You can't believe anything that she says."

Analysis:

The farmer is engaged in having sexual relations with this female sheep. He is afraid that she will tell on him.

Vocabulary:

Bestiality – Sexual relations between a human being and an animal. At Common Law, bestiality was considered a crime against nature and was punishable by death.

Ewe – Female sheep. It is pronounced to rhyme with you. The male sheep is called a ram and a baby sheep is called a lamb.

Liar – Someone who doesn't tell the truth.

Sexual Relations – Between a man and a female sheep is accomplished by placing the hind legs of the sheep in the man's boots.

Shepherd – Some one who takes care of sheep.

Ventriloquism – The art of projecting one's voice so that it seems to come from another source, as from a wooden figure.

Ventriloquist – One who practices the art of ventriloquism.

The Head Is Larger Than the Shaft

The Joke:

Everyone knows that the head of the penis is larger than its shaft, but no one knows why. The University of Manchester in England is determined to find the answer. After months of arduous research, they conclude that it is because it gives more pleasure to the man during sexual intercourse.

However, they need confirmation of their research, so they send off to the University of Milan in Milan, Italy. After a few months, the University concludes that it is because it gives more pleasure to the woman during sexual intercourse.

Now they have a conflict, so they send off to the University of Warsaw in Warsaw, Poland to resolve the issue. After a couple of months, the University of Manchester still hadn't received a reply. So they decide to call the University of Warsaw. Finally, upon reaching the University's Department of Sexuality, they receive their answer: To keep the hand from slipping off, of course.

Analysis:

The University of Warsaw is referring to masturbation.

Vocabulary:

Arduous – Characterized by effort to the point of exhaustion.

Conclude – Decide by reasoning; draw or come to a conclusion.

Confirmation – Additional proof that something that was believed (some fact or hypothesis or theory) is correct.

Head – The top of something.

Issue – An important question that is in dispute and must be settled.

Shaft – The long slender part of something.

The Column of Smoke

The Joke:

A U.S. Cavalry Indian Scout is proceeding ahead of the rest of his troop. He is on the lookout for hostile Indians. Suddenly, he spots a column of smoke on the distant horizon. Riding to investigate, he encounters a scene of total carnage which would do justice to Dante's Inferno. Although the settlers have drawn their wagons into a circle, it appears to have had little effect on the hostile Indians who attacked them. There are burning wagons everywhere in the circle, and arrows protruding from the dead bodies of the pioneers. Almost all the dead bodies had been scalped. Buzzards are circling lower and lower. Suddenly, he hears the sound of a low moan. Going to check it out, he finds a young woman spread-eagled, face-up, and nude in the sand. He asks what happened, and is told by the young woman:

"The Indians attacked, and killed and scalped everyone. Then, they raped me and left me to die in the sand. Oh, thank God you're here."

The scout dismounts, undoes his belt buckle, and says:

"Well, ma'am, I guess today just isn't your day."

Analysis:

The young lady thinks that the scout is going to rescue her. Instead, he intends to rape her again.

Vocabulary:

Buzzards – Birds which eat dead bodies. Scavengers. New World vultures that are common in South America and Central America and the southern United States.

Carnage – Slaughter: the savage and excessive killing of many people.

Carnivorous – Flesh-eating or predatory.

Cavalry – Soldiers mounted on horseback.

Column – Anything that approximates the shape of a column or tower.

Dante's Inferno – A reference to the Italian poet Dante Alighieri and a part of his most famous poem *The Divine Comedy*.

Drawing The Wagons Into A Circle – A standard defensive maneuver for wagon trains.

Enmity – The bitter attitude or feelings of an enemy or of mutual enemies; hostility; antagonism.

Horizon – The line at which the sky and Earth appear to meet.

Hostile – Characterized by enmity or ill will.

Indians – The Indians referred to here are not residents of India, but are the original Americans encountered by Columbus. He thought he had reached India, and so he named the natives Indians. Although the natives he met were largely peaceful, they had a reputation for being hostile savages who scalped their dead victims. They are sometimes referred to as red Indians or American Indians to distinguish them from residents (or descendants of residents) of India.

Necrophagy – Necrophilia: feeding on corpses or carrion.

Pioneers – People who venture into unknown or unclaimed territory to settle.

Predatory – Living by preying on other organisms.

Scalped – Removal of the skin covering the top of the human head.
A portion of this skin with its attached hair, cut from a body especially as a battle trophy or as proof in claiming a bounty.

Scavengers – Scavenging, or Necrophagy, is a carnivorous feeding behavior in which a predator consumes corpses or carrion that were not killed to be eaten by the predator or others of its species. Scavengers play an important role in the ecosystem by contributing to the decomposition of dead animal remains.

Scout – Somebody, especially a soldier, who is sent to gather information about an enemy's position or movements. In this case, the enemies are American Indians.

Settler – One who settles in a new region. In this case, one who moves west to settle new land.

Spread-Eagled – Positioned with the arms and legs stretched out.

Expands Twelve Times

The Joke:

A sixth-grade teacher stands in front of her students, and asks:

"Class, what part of the human anatomy expands to twelve times its normal size when it is stimulated?"

Seated in the front row, little Mary starts to giggle uncontrollably. She tries to cover her mouth with her hand, so the rest of the class won't know.

In the back, little Johnnie raises his hand and is recognized by the teacher.

He stands and says:

"The iris of the human eye expands twelve times when stimulated by light."

The teacher says:

"That is the correct answer, Johnnie. And, Mary, you have a very dirty mind, and when you grow up, you're going to be extremely disappointed."

Analysis:

Little Mary was thinking of a man's penis, and she is going to be very disappointed to find that it doesn't grow to twelve times its size even when it fills with blood.

Vocabulary:

Iris of the human eye – The round, pigmented membrane surrounding the pupil of the eye, having muscles that adjust the size of the pupil to regulate the amount of light entering the eye. The larger it gets, the smaller the pupil gets.

Uncontrollably – Impossible to control or govern.

The Case of Tennis Elbow

The Joke:

A man goes to his doctor for his annual physical examination. After a little while, the doctor says:

"According to this printout from the computer, you have tennis elbow."

He answers:

"Doctor, that's ridiculous. I don't play tennis, or any other game which is close such as hardball or squash."

The doctor responds:

"The computer's not infallible, but it usually doesn't make a mistake. I'll tell you what, take another sterilized bottle home. I'll run the urine sample again free of charge."

The man agrees, and leaves the doctor's office for home. He is annoyed at the computer for diagnosing an ailment which he doesn't have. So, he decides to play a little game on the computer. When he stops the car at home, he raises the hood and uses the oil dipstick to put a little oil in the container. Next, he urinates in the bottle and tells his wife and his daughter to urinate in it. As a final step, he goes into the bathroom and masturbates into the bottle. He mixes it all up in the bottle.

The next morning, he goes to the doctor's office and he hands the bottle to the technician, who runs the test. About an hour later, the doctor calls him into his office, and says:

"This is the darnedest printout I've ever seen."

Feigning innocence, the man says:

"What does the printout say?"

The doctor says:

"According to this printout, your car needs to have the oil changed, your daughter is pregnant, your wife has a urinary tract infection, and if you don't stop jerking off, you'll never get rid of tennis elbow."

Analysis:

This is one heck of a smart computer. Not only does it know that the patient has tennis elbow, but it also knows that the car needs an oil change, the daughter is pregnant, and his wife has a urinary infection. Unfortunately, the computer doesn't exist in the real world.

133

Vocabulary:

Darnedest – A euphemistic word for damnedest. most amazing or extraordinary.

Dipstick – A graduated rod for measuring the depth or amount of liquid in a container, as of oil in a crankcase.

Euphemistic – Substituting a mild term for a harsher or distasteful one.

Feigning – Faking. To give a false appearance of. To represent falsely. Pretend to. To imitate so as to deceive.

Innocence – The state or quality of being not chargeable for, or guilty of, a particular crime or offense.

Handball – A game similar in scoring to volleyball that is played by two or more players who hit a ball against a wall with their hands usually.

Inelastic – Lacking elasticity; unyielding or inadaptable.

Infallible – Incapable of failure or error. Doesn't make any mistakes.

Inflammation – In this case, a response of body tissues to injury or irritation; characterized by pain and swelling and redness and heat.

Also, excitement: the state of being emotionally aroused and worked up. As examples: 'His face was flushed with excitement and his hands trembled.' and 'He tried to calm those who were in a state of extreme inflammation.'

Jerking Off – A slang term for masturbation.

Masturbates – Sexual stimulation, especially of one's own genitals (self masturbation), often to the point of orgasm.

Microorganism – Any organism of microscopic size.

Orgasm – A frenzy; great excitement; esp., the climax of sexual excitement, as in intercourse, normally accompanied in the male by ejaculation.

Squash – In this case, a game played in an enclosed court by two or four players who strike the ball with long-handled rackets.

Also, the edible fruit of a squash plant; eaten as a vegetable.

Also, to compress with violence, out of natural shape or condition. Example would be: 'crush an aluminum can' or 'squeeze a lemon.'

Sterlize – To make free from live bacteria or other microorganisms.

Technician – Someone whose occupation involves training in a specific technical process. In this case, a computer technician, who is trained to do urine analysis through the computer.

Tendon – A cord or band of inelastic tissue connecting a muscle with its bony attachment.

Tennis Elbow – A painful inflammation of the tendon at the outer border of the elbow resulting from overuse of lower arm muscles (as in twisting of the hand).

Urinary Tract Infection – Infection of the kidney, ureter, bladder, or urethra. This is commonplace in women.

Send Me Some Water

The Joke:
A man is struggling in the Sahara desert. He has been without water for the past three days. Buzzards are circling lower and lower just above him. Finally, he decides that he cannot go any further. He struggles to the crest of a sand dune, drops to one knee, and says:

"Please, Lord, if you can hear me – send me some water."

About this time, one of the buzzards defecates, and it lands on this fellow's face. He reaches up and wipes it off his forehead. He looks closely at it, and says:

"Please. Lord, don't hand me any shit – I'm serious!"

Analysis:
The man thinks that God has sent him some feces.

Vocabulary:
Buzzards – Any diurnal bird of prey of the genus *Buteo*, typically having broad wings and tail and a soaring flight.

Crest – The top line of a hill, mountain, or wave.

Defecates – Slang would be: shits. Stool: have a bowel movement.

Diurnal – Of, or belonging to, or active during the day. An example would be: 'Diurnal animals are active during the day.'

Sahara Desert – The world's largest desert (3,500,000 square miles) in northern Africa.

Sand Dune – A ridge of sand created by the wind.

Soaring – To rise, fly, or glide high and with little apparent effort.

The Mohel

The Joke:

A mohel has retired after forty years of service to his synagogue.

Throughout this period, he has diligently saved and preserved the foreskins after they have been removed. There are literally hundreds of thousands of these foreskins in his collection. His friend, Abraham, is famous for his fine leatherwork, so he goes to him, explains his situation, and requests that Abraham make him something out of all these foreskins. Abraham agrees, and says that he will contact the retired mohel in about three weeks. Three weeks later, Abraham is finished, and asks the retired mohel to come see what he has made for him. The retired mohel accedes, and goes to see what his friend has made for him. When he arrives, Abraham proudly shows him a wallet in a small box. Says the mohel:

"You mean that a small wallet is all I get after forty years of service?"

"Not so fast, if you rub it, it will turn into a complete set of luggage," replies Abraham.

Analysis:

When excited and filled with blood, the penis swells. The foreskin will obviously do the same.

Vocabulary:

Accede – To give one's consent, often at the insistence of another; concede.

Assiduity – Persistent application or diligence; unflagging effort.

Constant personal attention and often obsequious solicitude.

Brit Milah – The rite or ceremony of male circumcision, usually performed on the eighth day of life.

Circumcision – Surgery that removes the foreskin (the loose tissue) covering the glans of the penis. Circumcision may be performed for religious or cultural reasons, or health reasons. Newborn circumcision diminishes the risk for cancer of the penis and lowers the risk for cancer of the cervix in sexual partners. It also decreases the risk of urinary tract infections and lowers the risk of sexually transmitted diseases, including especially HIV. The Latin "circum-" means around (or about). Circumcision is, literally, a cutting around. Circumcision dates back to prehistoric times. It is one of the oldest surgical operations known to have been performed by people.

Diligently – Earnest and persistent application to an undertaking; steady effort; assiduity.

Foreskin – The fold of skin which covers the head (the glans) of the penis. Also called the prepuce.

Literally – In a literal manner; word for word.

Mohel – The plural is mohelim, pronunciation: moy'el, mo'hel) is a Jewish man trained in the practice of Brit Milah (circumcision).

Obsequious – Bootlicking: attempting to win favor from influential people by flattery.

Prepuce – See foreskin above.

Preserve – Continue: keep or maintain in unaltered condition; cause to remain or last.

Solicitude – The state of being solicitous; care or concern, as for the well-being of another.

Synagogue – The place of worship for a Jewish congregation.

Wales

The Joke:

In England, a young man is summoned to the General Manager's office. The young man is praised for the excellent job that he's been doing. The General Manager then says:

"You've been selected to attend a training course in Cardiff."

The young man protests, saying:

"Sir, there's nothing from Wales except football players and prostitutes."

The GM indignantly replies:

"My wife is from Wales."

Thinking fast, the young man responds:

"On yeah, what position does she play?"

Analysis:

Thinking fast, the young man doesn't want to imply that his boss's wife is a prostitute.

Vocabulary:

Cardiff – The largest city and capitol of Wales.

Football – In Europe and the United Kingdom, the game of soccer is referred to as football. Sometimes, the phrase American football is used to distinguish this sport from soccer or football as it is known throughout the rest of the world.

Wales – One of the four countries that make up the United Kingdom of Great Britain and Northern Ireland; during Roman times, the region was known as Cambria.

The British Lady on the Train

The Joke:

As each passenger boards a train in England, he or she is subjected to loud barking and ferocious behavior on the part of the lapdog of a lady already seated on the train. The conductor approaches, and says politely:

"Excuse me, ma'am, but your pet is creating quite a disturbance. If you don't mind, I'd like to take her and put her back in the baggage car. I can assure you that it is quite warm and comfortable back there, and no harm will come to her."

The old lady responds indignantly:

"Young man, you most certainly will not put my precious Fifi back in your filthy baggage car. I'll have you know that she is my constant traveling companion, and I never go anywhere without her. Furthermore, I'll have you know that I'm a very close personal friend of the President of this railroad, and if you give me any more trouble, I can assure you that you'll regret it."

The conductor shrugs his shoulders and walks away.

A few minutes later, he hears the sounds of a tremendous commotion coming from this car, and goes rushing back.

He arrives to find this English lady beating an American tourist over the head with her parasol. He breaks them apart, and says:

'Here, here, what's going on here?"

The old lady answers:

"This … this American savage just threw my Fifi off the train!"

The conductor whips around on the American, saying:

"You Americans can't seem to do anything right – You drive on the wrong side of the road, you can't spell simple little words like honour and colour correctly, and now you've just thrown the wrong bitch off the train."

Analysis:

This joke depends on the two meanings of the term bitch. It can mean a female dog. It can also mean a woman of bad character; a woman of foul disposition such as the old lady in the story.

Vocabulary:

Bitch – The female of the dog or some other carnivorous mammal. A lewd or immoral woman: a malicious, spiteful, or overbearing woman —sometimes used as a generalized term of abuse.

Commotion – Disturbance: a disorderly outburst or tumult.

Ferocious – Fierce; savage; violently cruel.

Indignantly – Feeling or expressing anger or scorn, especially at unjust, mean, or ungrateful action or treatment.

Lapdog – A dog small and tame enough to be held in the lap.

Magnum Opus – A great work, especially a literary or artistic masterpiece. The greatest single work of an artist, writer, or composer.

Parasol – A light, usually small umbrella carried as protection from the sun.

Spelling – Sometimes, the same word is spelled differently between America and England. Most of the specifically American spelling rules come from Noah Webster, the Connecticut-born educator and lexicographer whose magnum opus was his 1828 *American Dictionary of the English Language*.

Umbrella – A screen or shade, usually of cloth stretched over a folding radial frame, carried for protection against the rain or sun.

A Half Head of Lettuce

The Joke:
In England, this obnoxious bloke wants to buy just a half head of lettuce. He is told that it is not sold that way. Flying into a rage, he breaks a head of lettuce into two parts, and proceeds to the cashier. The cashier asks him to wait while he checks with his boss to see if it's all right to sell him a half a head of lettuce. He goes to the grocery store manager, and says:

"Some big obnoxious ass-hole wants to buy a half of a head of lettuce."

Suddenly, he susses out that the man has followed him to his manager's office and twigged to every word that he has said. Thinking quickly and turning to the man, he says:

"And this gentleman has agreed to buy the other half."

Analysis:
Knowing that you may find yourself in England some day, the author has set the scene in England and used British terminology. See appendix II for some common English terms.

Vocabulary:
Bloke – British and Australian: an informal word for man.

Lettuce – Any of various plants of the genus *Lactuca*, especially *L. sativa*, cultivated for their edible leaves.

Obnoxious – Objectionable: causing disapproval or protest; 'a vulgar and objectionable person.'

Susses Out – Chiefly British: to inspect or investigate so as to gain more knowledge —usually used with **out**.

Twigged – Looked at; observed, saw, understood.

The German Shepherd and the Pekinese

The Joke:

A large German Shepherd and a small Pekinese find themselves together at a vet's. The German Shepherd says:

"Hi, what are you in for?"

The Pekinese answers:

"You know how it is when you're lying around bored all day. I started on my mistress' slippers, then I moved to the drapes, and finally I wound up destroying part of the furniture. So, she has me in here to be put down. What are you in for?"

The Shepherd says:

"Well, my mistress came out of the shower, and dropped something on the rug. There she was – nude and groping around on the rug. Well, what can I say? I'm a man, you know."

The Pekinese says:

"Oh, then you're in to be put down too."

The German Shepherd says:

"Actually, I just came in to have my nails done."

Analysis:

The German Shepherd's mistress really enjoyed the sex she had with him. She enjoyed it so much that she even has the dog in the vet's for a pedicure.

Vocabulary:

Euthanasia – An easy or painless death. Mercy killing.

German Shepherd – Any of a breed of large dog somewhat resembling a wolf, with a bushy tail and erect ears, developed in Germany to herd sheep, now often used as a guard dog,

Pedicure – A cosmetic treatment of the feet and toenails.

Pekinese – A Chinese breed of small short-legged dogs with a long silky coat and broad flat muzzle.

Put Down – In this case, to subject (an animal) to euthanasia. To kill him or her.

Vet – Short for veterinarian.

Veterinarian – The study of the diseases of animals including their diagnosis, prevention and treatment. One who practices veterinary medicine.

Three Convicts

The Joke:

One night three convicted felons escape from a maximum security prison. They are of three different ethnic backgrounds. There are one Frenchman, one Italian, and one Pole. Running through the woods, they can hear the bloodhounds closing on their trail. Fearful that capture is imminent, the Italian says to the others:

"Quick! Up in the trees!"

Each escaped convict scurries up into a separate tree. As the police are passing underneath, the Italian makes a mistake and rustles some leaves. As the police are looking up in the tree, they hear a sound: "Who, who." "Come on, they're getting away, it's just an owl" says one of the policemen.

As they are passing under his tree, the Frenchman makes a mistake, and snaps a twig. As the police are looking up in the tree, they hear a sound: "Caw, caw." "Come on, they're getting away, it's just a crow" says one of the policemen.

As they are passing under his tree, the Pole makes a mistake, and snaps a branch. As the police are looking up in the tree, they hear a sound: "M-o-o, m-o-o."

Analysis:

It takes a dumb Polack, indeed, to imitate a cow in a tree. It takes an even dumber Polack to think the police will buy it.

Vocabulary:

Bloodhound – One of a breed of hounds with a smooth coat, drooping ears, sagging jowls, and a keen sense of smell.

Ethnic – Cultural: denoting or deriving from or distinctive of the ways of living built up by a group of people.

Felon – Person convicted of a serious crime, such as murder or armed robbery. A less serious crime, such as speeding is called a misdemeanor.

Imminent – Close in time; about to occur.

Maximum Security – Having more restrictions than others of its kind.

Misdemeanor – A misdeed. In law, a criminal offense that is less serious than a felony and generally punishable by a fine.

Rustles – To move with soft fluttering or crackling sounds.

Scurries – Runs hastily; scampers.

Twig – A small, slender branch or shoot of a tree or shrub.

The Little Green Rat

The Joke:

Washington is suddenly infested with rats. This is a major problem for the city. The government officials try everything, but nothing seems to work. Finally, in desperation, they place an ad in every newspaper requesting anyone who knows of any way to rid the city of this horrible nuisance to please contact the white house.

One day shortly thereafter, a little man dressed in a green suit shows up at one of the gates, and asks to see the President. He is about to be turned away when he mentions that he is there in response to the advertisement in the papers. He is immediately admitted to see President Bush. He offers to rid the city of its rats for only $500. He is immediately taken up on the offer by the President himself.

He places the sack he has been carrying on the floor, takes out a small bright green rat, and walks out the door. The green rat follows him. As the man walks through the city, every rat falls in behind him and the little green rat.

They proceed to the Potomac River. When they reach it, the little green rat jumps in. All the other rats jump in and drown themselves, thus ridding Washington of the problem.

Returning to the White House, the man accepts his five hundred dollars and is about to leave, when he is stopped by President Bush, who sidles up to him and whispers:

"By any chance, do you have any little green Democrats in that bag?"

Analysis:

Now that Washington is rid of its rats, President Bush would like to be rid of all the Democrats, too.

Vocabulary:

Nuisance – One that is inconvenient, annoying, or vexatious; a bother.

Infested – Invaded in great numbers; an example would be "the roaches infested our kitchen"

Sidles – Advances in an unobtrusive, furtive, or coy way.

The Simultaneous Arrivals

The Joke:

Three men arrive before St. Peter at exactly the same exact time. St. Peter says:

"It's highly unusual for any one to appear up here simultaneously from the same location on Earth."

Turning to the first man, he asks:

"What's your story?"

The man replies:

"I was just coming out the front door of my apartment building when this refrigerator fell on me, killing me instantly."

The man standing behind him says:

"St. Peter, I think I can explain that. You see, I came home early and found my wife dressed in a filmy negligee. There was someone else in my apartment, but I couldn't find him. I searched and searched, but to no avail. Finally, I became so enraged that I picked up the refrigerator and threw it out the window. As a result, I had a heart attack, and here I am."

St. Peter turns to the third man, and says:

"What's your story?"

The third man responds:

"Well, St. Peter, I was just sitting in this refrigerator minding my own business, when suddenly ... ."

Analysis:

The man sitting in the refrigerator was playing around with the second man's wife. When he was interrupted by her husband coming home early, he hid in the refrigerator.

Vocabulary:

Filmy – Of, resembling, or consisting of film; gauzy. An example would be: *filmy* lingerie.

Negligee – A woman's loose dressing gown, often of soft, delicate fabric.

Refrigerator – An appliance, cabinet, or room for storing food or other substances at a low temperature.

To No Avail – It was not a success; it was useless.

Constipation

A woman goes to her doctor, and complains that she hasn't had a bowel movement in about a week. The doctor prescribes some suppositories for her, and asks her to return the following week. When she returns the following week, she complains that the suppositories have not worked: she still is unable to defecate. The doctor prescribes more suppositories, and asks her to come back the following week. When she again complains that she is unable to have a bowel movement, it suddenly dawns on the doctor that she may not have been taking the suppositories rectally. He says:

"Wait a minute. You haven't been eating those suppositories, have you?"

She answers sarcastically:

"Of course I've been eating them. What do you think I've been doing with them – jamming them up my ass?'

Analysis:

The doctor should know better. His patient has been eating her suppositories.

Vocabulary:

Alimentary – Concerned with food, nutrition, or digestion.

Anus – The opening at the lower end of the alimentary canal through which solid waste is eliminated from the body. Known colloquially as the ass-hole.

Ass – Buttocks: the fleshy part of the human body that you sit on.

Bowel – Intestines: the part of the alimentary canal between the stomach and the anus.

Bowel Movement – A euphemism for defecation. The discharge of waste matter from the large intestine; defecation.

Constipation – Irregular and infrequent or difficult evacuation of the bowels; can be a symptom of intestinal obstruction or diverticulitis.

Defecation – The elimination of fecal waste through the anus.

Diverticulum – A small bulging sac pushing outward from the colon wall is a diverticulum.

Diverticulitis – Inflammation of a diverticulum in the digestive tract (especially the colon); characterized by painful abdominal cramping and fever and constipation,

Euphemism – An inoffensive or indirect expression that is substituted for one that is considered offensive or too harsh.

Rectum – The last 6 to 8 inches of the large intestine. The rectum stores solid waste until it leaves the body through the anus.

Rectally – Of, relating to, or situated near the rectum.

Sarcastically – Of, having the nature of, or characterized by sarcasm; sneering, caustic, cutting, etc. Using or fond of using, sarcasm.

Suppository – A small plug of medication designed to melt at body temperature within a body cavity other than the mouth, especially the rectum or vagina. It is also called a *bougie*.

The Religious Parrot

The Joke:

The owner of a pet shop indicates that a parrot called Sam is for sale. The parrot knows the Jewish services in Hebrew. A prospective buyer called Abraham asks for and receives proof that the parrot can actually say the services in Hebrew. He buys the parrot, takes it home, and prepares to go to the synagogue because it's the beginning of Rosh Hashanah.

Since it's the beginning of a new Jewish year, the line outside the synagogue is quite long. Abraham proceeds to place bets with everyone in line that he has a parrot who can say the services in Hebrew. When he gives out of money, he finally stops.

Then he turns to Sam, and says:

"OK, Sam, do your thing."

But, Sam is silent. Abraham implores him:

"Sam, say something."

But, Sam continues his silence.

So, Abraham is forced to pay off all those he has wagered with. He seethes throughout the service. Finally, when the service is over he rushes home. He goes straight to the kitchen, and seizes a meat cleaver. He is about to finish him off, when Sam says:

"Oi veh! Wait for Yom Kippur – we'll clean up. We'll get 10-to-1 odds."

Analysis:

Sam has sucked everyone in the line into believing that he can't speak Hebrew or say the services. He wants to wait until Yom Kippur and place the bets again.

149

Vocabulary:

Canaan – An ancient region made up of Palestine or the part of it between the Jordan River and the Mediterranean Sea. In the Bible it is the Promised Land of the Israelites.

Canaanitic – A group of ancient languages belonging to the Semitic subfamily of the Afro-Asiatic family.

Entreat – Bid: ask for or request earnestly.

Hebrew – The ancient Canaanitic language of the Hebrews that has been revived as the official language of Israel. Also, a member or descendant of a Semitic people claiming descent from Abraham, Isaac, and Jacob; an Israelite; a Jew.

Implores – To beg for urgently; entreat.

Meat Cleaver – A butcher's knife having a large square blade.

Oi Veh – Is an exclamation of dismay or exasperation in Yiddish meaning "oh woe."

Rosh Hashanah – This is sometimes referred to as the Jewish New Year. The start of the civil year in the Hebrew calendar. It is the New Year for people, animals, and legal contracts. Jews believe Rosh Hashanah represents either analogically or literally the creation of the World, or Universe. The middle class are allowed a respite of ten days, until Yom Kippur, to repent and become righteous; the wicked are "blotted out of the book of the living."[1]

Seethes – To be in a state of turmoil or ferment. Angry.

Semitic – Of or relating to the Semites or their languages or cultures.

Also, of, relating to, or constituting a subgroup of the Afro-Asiatic language group that includes Arabic, Hebrew, Amharic, and Aramaic.

Synagogue – The place of worship for a Jewish congregation.

Wagered – An agreement under which each bettor pledges a certain amount to the other depending on the outcome of an unsettled matter.

Yiddish – A dialect of High German including some Hebrew and other words; spoken in Europe as a vernacular by many Jews.

Yom Kippur – It is also known as the *Day of Atonement*, and is the holiest day of the year for religious Jews. Its central themes are atonement and repentance. Jews traditionally observe this holy day with a 25-hour period of fasting and intensive prayer, often spending most of the day in synagogue services. Yom Kippur completes the annual period known in Judaism as the High Holy Days.

Jump!

The Joke:

Two guys are watching the evening news on TV in a bar. One guy is Jewish and the other is Polish. They are watching a young woman threatening to jump from a ledge, and kill herself. The Jew says:

"Tell you what, I bet that she'll jump. If she does, you pay me twenty dollars. If she doesn't jump, I'll pay you twenty dollars. Okay?"

They bet, and a few minutes later, she jumps. The Polish guy gets up and pays the Jewish guy his twenty dollars. About ten minutes later, the Jewish man turns to the Pole and says:

"Friend, I just can't take the twenty dollars. This was a repeat of the afternoon news. I knew she was going to jump."

And the Jew tries to give the Pole back his twenty dollars. But the Pole refuses the money, saying that he knew it was a repeat since he also saw the news earlier in the day. The Jew says:

"If you knew it was a repeat, how come you took the bet?"

The Pole responds:

"Well, I didn't think she would be stupid enough to jump again."

Analysis:

This is a stupidity joke. The polack really doesn't realize that he is watching a replay.

Vocabulary:

Ledge – A horizontal projection forming a narrow shelf on the wall of a building.

Congratulations

The Joke:

A man flies to Japan to compete in a golf tournament the following day. He hires a prostitute who doesn't speak English for the evening. During the evening, she keeps repeating in Japanese:

"Um-pe-tao. Um-pe-tao. Um-pe-tao."

The following day, he is paired with another American. But the remainder of his foursome is Japanese. On the fourth tee, one of the Japanese golfers hits a hole-in-one.

He turns to his American partner, and says:

"I would like to congratulate that guy, but I don't know any Japanese. Wait a minute, maybe I do know some Japanese after all."

He walks up to the Japanese golfer, and says:

"Um-pe-tao, um-pe-tao."

The Japanese turns to him and says:

"What do you mean – I got it in the wrong hole?"

Analysis:

The American thinks that he knows some Japanese – but he doesn't understand what he's saying.

Vocabulary:

Hole-in-one – In golf, this refers to getting the ball in the hole in one stroke.

The Helper

The Joke:

A man is getting married, and he is still a virgin. He goes to his friend, and explains the situation. His friend is nonplussed because there just isn't time to teach him everything he might like to know. However, he offers to take the room next door during the honeymoon. If the groom gets into any trouble, he is to come to the door and whisper his problem. The friend will answer all of his questions through the door.

Everything goes well for the wedding. The bride and groom check in to the hotel for their honeymoon. The new groom goes into the bathroom to take his shower. His new bride suddenly has to defecate, but doesn't want to go into the bathroom while he is taking a shower. She searches around, finds a shoebox in the closet, and proceeds to take her dump in the box. He opens the door, and says:

"OK, dear, I'm through with my shower."

Startled, she leaps into the bed.

He comes across the floor, and steps in this box full of excrement. He exclaims:

"Jesus, there's shit in this box!"

A voice comes from the room next door:

"Roll her over. Roll her over."

Analysis:

The groom has stepped in the box on the floor. But his friend in the next room thinks that the groom has his penis stuck in the rear of his bride. The friend gives advice based on this assumption.

Vocabulary:

Bride – A woman who is about to be married or has recently been married.

Defecate – To stool: have a bowel movement.

Excrement – Body waste: waste matter (as urine or sweat but especially feces) discharged from the body.

Groom – Short for a bridegroom. A man who is about to be married or has recently been married.

Honeymoon – A holiday or trip taken by a newly married couple. An early harmonious period in a relationship.

Non-plussed – At a loss. Filled with bewilderment.

Take A Dump – Euphemism for defecating. Also known as shitting or pooping. Also can be seen as **taking** a crap, **taking** a shit, dropping a load, etc.

Startled – Excited by sudden surprise or alarm and making a quick involuntary movement.

Virgin – A person who has not experienced sexual intercourse. Also a chaste or unmarried woman; a maiden.

The Ex-Schoolteacher

The Joke:

A madam in a brothel notices that among her three new recruits, the ex-schoolteacher is getting most of the repeat business. She doesn't know why, so she decides to eavesdrop outside their doors.

The first recruit is an ex-housekeeper. The madam listens and hears her say that the shoes go under the chair, the shirt goes across the back of the chair, and the trousers go on the chair after the contents are emptied on the dresser. She understands why the ex-housekeeper isn't getting much repeat business.

The second recruit used to be a hairdresser. The madam listens, and hears her say to be very careful of her hair. Don't muss it up during sex. That's not very hard to figure out either.

The madam decides to listen outside the door of the ex-schoolteacher. For a long time, there are only the usual sounds. Then, the madam hears the ex-schoolteacher say:

"You come right back here and do it again. We're going to keep right on doing it until we get it right."

Analysis:

The ex-schoolteacher knows how to please her customers. She's going to make them repeat until they get it right.

Vocabulary:

Brothel – Whorehouse: a building where prostitutes are available.

Eavesdrop – To listen in: to listen without the speaker's knowledge.

Hairdresser – One who cuts or arranges hair.

Household – A domestic unit consisting of the members of a family who live together along with nonrelatives such as servants.

Housekeeper – One who is employed to perform or direct the domestic tasks in a household. Also, a housewife.

Madam – In this case, a woman in charge of a brothel. Also, used without a name as a form of respectful or polite address to a woman.

Prostitute – One who sells one's body; exchanges sex for money.

Repeat Business – Business from satisfied customers: further patronage that a business receives from customers who were happy with their previous service from the business.

Whore – Prostitute; any woman who engages in promiscuous sexual intercourse.

Whorehouse – A place where prostitutes are for hire; a brothel.

The Baseball Game

The Joke:

It is Liza's birthday. She has never seen a baseball game, so Rastus decides to take her to the stadium. Everything is going fine, and he even buys her a hot dog with mustard and a drink. In the third inning, the batter receives four balls. He throws his bat towards his dugout, and starts to walk to first base. Liza yells:

"Run, man, run!"

Rastus explains that the man has got four balls, and is entitled to walk to first base.

Liza turns, and yells:

"Strut, man, strut!"

Analysis:

Liza believes that the batter has four testicles. He shouldn't walk – he should strut!

Vocabulary:

Batter – In this case, the player at bat.

Birthday – An anniversary of the day on which a person was born (or the celebration of it). In the U.S., we wish someone a Happy Birthday. The same is true in Germany. But in many others (including countries using a Romance language), they wish the subject a Happy Anniversary.

Diamond – In this case, the square formed by the four bases.

Dugout – Either of two low shelters on either side of a baseball diamond where the players and coaches sit during the game.

Hot Dog – A frankfurter, especially one served hot in a long soft roll.

Liza And Rastus Jokes – A type of joke told in the U.S. South. Rastus and Liza were names given to Negro men and women. Many of these jokes are derogatory, but this one is funny because it displays ignorance. That is, this joke is humorous rather than malicious.

Mustard – A pungent powder or paste prepared from the seed of the mustard plant, used as a food seasoning or condiment, and medicinally in plasters, poultices, etc.

Romance Language – Languages derived from Latin (the Roman language).

Strut – A proud stiff pompous gait.

Stadium – A large structure for open-air sports or entertainments.

Testicles – The testicles produce and store sperm, and they are also the body's main source of male hormones (testosterone). A slang term is balls.

His Friend Is Dead

The Joke:
   Two hunters are out in the woods when one of them collapses. He doesn't seem to be breathing and his eyes are glazed. The other guy whips out his cell phone and calls the emergency service. He gasps:
   "My friend is dead! What can I do?"
   The operator says:
   "Calm down. I can help. First, let's make sure he's dead."
   There is a silence, and then a shot is heard.
   Back on the phone, the guy says:
   "OK, now what?"

Analysis:
   The friend is now dead.

Vocabulary:
   Calm Down – Become quiet or calm, especially after a state of agitation.
   Collapses – Falls down or inward suddenly; caves in.
   Gasps – Pants: breathes noisily, as when one is exhausted.
   Glazed – Glassy: (used of eyes) lacking liveliness.

What Do You See?

The Joke:

Sherlock Holmes and Dr. Watson go on a camping trip, and after finishing their dinner they retire for the night, and go to sleep. Some hours later, Holmes wakes up and nudges his faithful friend.

"Watson, look up at the sky and tell me what you see."

"I see millions and millions of stars, Holmes" exclaims Watson.

"And what do you deduce from that?"

Watson ponders for a minute.

"Well, astronomically, it tells me that there are millions of galaxies and potentially billions of planets. Astrologically, I observe that Saturn is in Leo. Horologically, I deduce that the time is approximately a quarter past three. Meteorologically, I suspect that we will have a beautiful day tomorrow. Theologically, I can see that God is all powerful, and that we are a small and insignificant part of the universe." He asks:

"What does it tell you, Holmes?"

"Watson, you idiot!" Holmes exclaims, "Somebody's stolen our tent!"

Analysis:

Holmes is calling his friend an idiot because he doesn't seem to realize that the tent they fell asleep under has been stolen while they slept.

Vocabulary:

Astronomically – Of or relating to astronomy. Also, of enormous magnitude; immense.

Astronomy – The scientific study of matter in outer space, especially the positions, dimensions, distribution, motion, composition, energy, and evolution of celestial bodies and phenomena.

Celestial – Of or relating to the sky or the heavens.

Horologically – Having to do with the measurement of time.

Meteorologically – Having to do with the weather.

Nudges – Pushes against gently, especially in order to gain attention or give a signal.

Theologically – Having to do with the study of religion and God.

The Ugly Baby

The Joke:

A woman gets on a bus with her baby. The bus driver says:

"That's the ugliest baby that I've ever seen. Ugh!"

The woman goes to the rear of the bus and sits down, fuming. She says to a man next to her:

"The driver just insulted me!"

The man says:

"You go right up there and tell him off – go ahead, I'll hold your monkey for you."

Analysis:

The man has mistaken the woman's baby for a monkey.

Vocabulary:

Fuming – In this case, a state of resentment or vexation.

Vexation – Annoyance: anger produced by some annoying irritation.

Looking Good

The Joke:

A man walks into a bar and orders one shot of whiskey. Then he looks into his shirt pocket and orders another shot. After he finishes, he looks into his shirt pocket again and orders another shot. The bartender is curious and asks: "Every time you order a shot, you look in your shirt pocket. Why?"

The man replies:

"I have a picture of my lawyer in my pocket and when he starts to look good to me, I go home."

Analysis:

When the lawyer looks good, it's time to go home.

Vocabulary:

None.

Help Me Decide

The Joke:

Three men are stranded on a desert island: an Englishman, a Frenchman, and a Pole. They have been on the island for a year when they come across a lamp lying in the sand. They rub it and, of course, a genie appears.

The genie says to them:

"Well, gentlemen, traditionally I give the person who finds the lamp three wishes. But, in this case, since there are three of you, I will give you each one wish."

The Englishman speaks right up: "I know what I want. I wish to be back in Piccadilly Circus in my favorite club having a pint with all of my mates."

Poof! He disappears.

Next the Frenchman says: "I wish to be back in Paris in a nice little restaurant with a bottle of good wine and a beautiful woman by my side."

Poof! He disappears.

The Polish guy is sitting there thinking and thinking.

"And what would you like, my friend?" asked the genie.

"Gee, I don't know," says the Polish guy. "It's so hard to make up my mind. Boy, I sure wish those other guys were here to help me decide."

Analysis:

Guess which two guys are back on the island.

Vocabulary:

Mates – British informal: a chum; buddy; pal: often used as a familiar form of address.

I Want a Whore with Syphilis

The Joke:

A young kid appears at the door of a brothel. The Madam is amused, and asks him what he wants. He says:

"I want a whore with syphilis."

The Madam asks:

"Why do you want a whore with syphilis?"

He responds:

"If I get it, I give it to my sister. She gives it to my father. My father gives it to my mother. My mother gives it to the milkman. And that son of a bitch ran over my bicycle."

Analysis:

The milkman ran over the boy's bicycle. The boy wants his revenge.

Vocabulary:

None.

The Not So Intelligent Dog

The Joke:

A man goes to visit his friend. He spots a big Saint Bernard sitting at a table holding a poker hand in his paw. He asks:

"Is that dog really playing poker?"

His friend answers in the affirmative, so the man says:

"Boy that must be a really intelligent dog."

"Not really," replies his friend.

"Why do you say that?"

"Because every time he has a good hand, he wags his tail," answers his friend.

Analysis:

A cardinal rule of playing poker is to maintain a straight face no matter whether the cards you have been dealt are good or bad. Indeed, a slang term for not showing any emotion is to remain pokerfaced.

Vocabulary:

Affirmative – Asserting that something is true or correct, as with the answer "yes": an affirmative reply. The opposite is negative, meaning "No".

Cardinal – Of foremost importance; paramount: a cardinal rule; cardinal sins.

Dealt – Distributed (playing cards) to players in a game.

Negative – Expressing, containing, or consisting of a negation, refusal, or denial: gave a negative answer to our request. Saying: "No". See affirmative above.

Paw – The foot of an animal, especially a quadruped, which has claws or nails.

Pokerfaced – A face lacking any interpretable expression, as that of an expert poker player.

Quadruped – An animal, especially a mammal, having four limbs specialized for walking.

Saint Bernard – The St. Bernard Dog is a very large breed of dog, a working dog from the Swiss Alps, originally bred for rescue.

Wags His Tail – Tails wag to the right when dogs are happy and see something they want to approach and to the left when they are frightened and confronted with something they want to run away from, claim the researchers.

The Collateral

The Joke:

A very well-dressed gentleman walks into a midtown branch of the Chase Bank and asks for a loan of $10,000 for two weeks.

The loan officer asks for some identification and credit references.

The applicant declines and the officer refuses to grant the loan. The applicant then asks to speak to the boss of the officer. He talks to the branch manager, who also tells him that the loan would be impossible. The man then demands to see someone higher up. This goes on and on, and the problem keeps getting kicked upstairs, until finally the man is ushered in to see David Rockefeller.

"Yes, sir," says Mr. Rockefeller, "what can I do for you?"

"I need a loan of $10,000 for two weeks," Says the man.

Mr. Rockefeller asks for identification and credit references, and again, the man declines.

"However, I am willing to put up my Rolls-Royce as collateral. It is parked right out front." So saying, he takes the keys to his car out and drops them on the desk.

"Well," says Mr. Rockefeller, "a $150,000 car as collateral for a two-week $10,000 loan is good enough for me." The two men shake hands. The applicant is issued the check.

Two weeks later, he returns. He goes up to the officer he first spoke with, and says, "I would now like to repay my loan." The loan officer, upon seeing the man, snaps to attention. He says: "Sir, I have strict instructions that when you come in, I should send you in immediately to see Mr. Rockefeller."

The man is once again ushered in to see David Rockefeller. He sits down and pays back the loan with $200 interest. Once they have concluded their business, Mr. Rockefeller says: "Sir from the license plates on your car, I was able to run a check on you. You are one of the wealthiest men in the world! Why would you want to leave your car here, in exchange for a $10,000 loan?"

"Where else could I find such a great parking place so cheap?" says the man.

Analysis:

The parking place for two weeks was worth the $ 200.00. Only in Manhattan.

Vocabulary:

Applicant – A person who requests or seeks something such as assistance or employment or admission or, in this case, a loan.

Concluded – Ended: completed: having come or been brought to a conclusion.

Midtown – A central portion of a city, between uptown and downtown.

Rolls-Royce – A large, expensive, and comfortable car of very high quality made by a company in the UK (Vickers). It is sometimes simply called a Rolls.

Vickers – In 1999, Vickers sold Rolls-Royce to Volkswagen.

The Grandmother

The Joke:

Little Red Riding Hood's grandmother is lying in bed when the wolf bursts in through her door.

"Give me all your money," he demands, snarling and showing his teeth.

"Oh, no, you don't," says the grandmother pulling a revolver out from under the pillow and training it on the wolf.

She says:

"You're going to eat me, like it says in the book!"

Analysis:

The grandmother wants the wolf to perform cunnilingus on her.

Vocabulary:

Canids – Any of various widely distributed carnivorous mammals of the family Canidae, which includes the foxes, wolves, dogs, jackals, and coyotes.

Clitoris – A female sexual organ homologous to the penis.

Cunnilingus – Oral stimulation of the vulva or clitoris.

Homologous – Corresponding or similar in position, value, structure, or function.

Little Red Riding Hood – A girl in a fairy tale who meets a wolf while going to visit her grandmother. The reference to the book is a reference to this story.

Oral – Of or relating to the mouth.

Penis – The urethra emerges at the glans, the rounded tip of the penis. The penis is the counterpart of the clitoris in the female. The male organ of copulation in higher vertebrates.

Pillow – A cloth case, stuffed with something soft, such as down, feathers, or foam rubber, used to cushion the head, especially during sleep.

Revolver – A pistol with a revolving cylinder (usually having six chambers for bullets).

Urethra – The transport tube leading from the bladder to discharge urine outside the body.

Vulva – The external genital organs of the female, including the labia majora, labia minora, clitoris, and vestibule of the vagina.

Wolf – Any of several large predatory canids (genus Canis) that live and hunt in packs and resemble the related dogs.

First Blow Job

The Joke:

   A man goes into a bar and orders twelve shots of whiskey. The bartender lines up a dozen shot glasses on the bar, and then fills them with whiskey. Quickly the man downs one after the other until he has finished all twelve. The bartender asks what he is celebrating.

   "My first blow job," says the man.

   "Oh, in that case, let me buy you one more!" says the bartender.

   "No, if twelve won't get the taste out of my mouth, nothing will," says the man.

Analysis:

   Instead of receiving a blow-job, the man was giving it.

Vocabulary:

   None.

The Horse and Buggy

The Joke:

It is a hundred and fifty years ago. A couple has just married, and are on their way home in the buggy. A rabbit darts across the road. The horse, startled, rears up in the traces. Looking straight at the horse, the man says: "That's **one**."

As they continue, some leaves brush the ear of the horse, and he rears up again. Looking straight at the horse, the man says:

"That's **two**."

When they get home, the man starts to tie the horse to the hitching post.

As he is doing this, the horse reaches over and bites him on the shoulder.

The man says:

"That's **three**."

He goes running into the house. He comes out a few seconds later with a big 44-caliber pistol.

Blam! He kills the horse.

His new bride starts yelling at the man:

"What have you just done, you idiot! That was our only transportation. Now, how are we going to get around? You're such a hothead!"

The man turns to her, and says:

"That's **one**."

Analysis:

You only get three chances. His wife has just used one.

Vocabulary:

Caliber – The diameter of the bore of a firearm, usually shown in hundredths or thousandths of an inch and expressed in writing or print in terms of a decimal fraction: *.45 caliber.*

Darts – Moves with sudden speed.

Hitching Post – A fixed post with a ring to which a horse can be tied to prevent it from straying.

Hothead – A quick-tempered or impetuous person.

Traces – In this case, two side straps or chains connecting a harnessed draft animal to a vehicle or whiffletree.

Transportation – A facility consisting of the means and equipment necessary for the movement of passengers or goods.

Whiffletree – In the Northeastern U.S., the pivoted horizontal crossbar to which the harness traces of a draft animal are attached and which is in turn attached to a vehicle or an implement. Also called *singletree, swingletree*; also called regionally *whippletree.*

The Jar Full Of $20 Bills

The Joke:
A man is having a drink in a bar when he notices a huge jar full of $20 bills behind the bar. He calls the bartender over and asks him what the jar is for. The bartender says:

"We have this little game we play here. We have a donkey tethered out back. You put $20 in the jar. If you can make the donkey laugh, you can have the whole jar."

"That doesn't sound very difficult," says the man. He hands the bartender $20, and goes out back. About 10 minutes later, the donkey can be heard laughing: "Hee, haw – hee, haw!"

The man comes back, collects all the money, and leaves.

Three years go by.

The man comes back for another drink, and notices another huge jar of $20 bills behind the bar. He calls the bartender over and asks him what the new jar is for.

The bartender says:

"Since you won the first time, we've changed the name of the game. Now you put $20 in the jar and if you can make the donkey cry, you can have the whole thing."

"That doesn't sound very difficult," says the man. He hands the bartender $20, and goes out back. About 10 minutes later, the donkey can be heard crying. The donkey is very upset – boy, is he upset!

The man comes back, and indicates that he will take all the money in the jar.

The bartender says:

"We'll give you the money. You won it fair and square, but you have to tell us how you did it."

"Sure," says the man. "The first time, I told him that mine was longer than his – the second time, I proved it to him."

Analysis:
I can certainly understand how the donkey would be upset the second time. The fact that the man is better hung than the donkey is certainly something to think about.

Vocabulary:

Domesticated – Converted or adapted to domestic use; "domestic animals".

Donkey – The domesticated ass (Equus asinus).

Hung – Vulgar Slang: Having large genitals. Used of males.

Tethered – Confined or restricted with or as if with a rope or chain.

Upset – To make someone feel sad, worried, or angry.

There Is No Sound and No Smell

The Joke:
A lady goes to her doctor in the UK. She says:

"Doctor, I have this sensation all day long as though I'm breaking wind, but there is no sound, and there is no smell."

The doctor says:

"I want you to take this prescription down to the chemist and have it filled. Then I want you to take one of those pills after each meal and come see me next week at the same time.

The next week, the lady returns, and the doctor asks:

"Well, how is it?"

The lady responds: "Oh, doctor, it's much worse!"

"Worse, how's that?" He asks.

"Well, I still have a sensation all day long as though I'm breaking wind, but now each time accompanying it, there is a terrible loud noise."

"Oh, great!" replies the doctor. "We've got your ears sorted out. Now we can start on your nose."

Analysis:
The farts have both a smell and a noise associated with them. The doctor is trying to cure both.

Vocabulary:
Breaking Wind – A polite term for fart: a reflex that expels intestinal gas through the anus.

Chemist – British: pharmacist

Sensation – A perception associated with stimulation of a sense organ or with a specific body condition: the **sensation** of heat; a visual **sensation**.

Sorted Out – Cured.

It Has To Come Off

The Joke:

A soldier in Vietnam contracts a venereal disease. He goes to see the Army doctor who tells him that his penis will have to be amputated. He goes to see the Navy doctor, who confirms that his penis will have to be cut off. He then goes to the Air Force doctor, who also says that his penis will have to be amputated. He decides to see the Vietnamese doctor downtown, to get a second opinion. He examines the soldier. The man says:

"How about it, Doc? Are you going to have to amputate?"

The doctor responds:

"Oh, no, I'm not going to amputate."

The soldier breathes a sigh of relief and says:

"I saw three American doctors at the base, and they all said they would have to amputate."

The Vietnamese doctor responds:

"Amelican doctors knife crazy – cut, cut, cut – it not necessary to amputate, it fall off by itself."

Analysis:

If the soldier will just wait, his penis will fall off by itself.

Vocabulary:

Amputate – To cut off (a projecting body part), especially by surgery.

Venereal Disease – A communicable infection transmitted by sexual intercourse or genital contact.

Same Old, Same Old

The Joke:

A man is seeing his psychiatrist and complaining about his sex life. The psychiatrist asks:

"How many times a week do you have sex?"

"Once. On each Saturday morning," replies the man.

"And you never have sex except on a Saturday morning? That's the problem. Your sex life is too predictable, too boring. Here's what I want you to do. Get off work early one day. Drive home and park in the driveway, go in the front door. Find your wife and throw her on the couch. Rip off all of her clothes, and make love to her right on the couch."

The man demurs, but the psychiatrist insists. The man goes home, and returns the following week. The psychiatrist asks:

"Well, how was it?"

The man says:

"It was the same old, same old – but I have to admit that her bridge club did seem to get a large charge out of it."

Analysis:

Her bridge club watched while her husband made love to her.

Vocabulary:

Demurs – Voices opposition; objects.

Large charge – Enjoyment.

The Breakfast Together

The Joke:
A young couple is having marital problems. They go to a marriage counselor, and he says:

"First, we should start by discussing your sex life. For instance, how often do you make love?"

The young man says:

"Well, doctor, we make love every Monday, Wednesday and Friday at 10 o'clock."

"You mean," says the doctor, "that you make love on schedule?"

The man says:

"Of course, doesn't everyone?"

"No, no, no," replies the doctor. "Love is a very beautiful, spontaneous thing. When the feeling comes on you, you've got to act on it. Be a little impulsive now and then. Now go out this week and try to follow your feelings. Then come back next week and we'll discuss it."

The following week, when the couple comes in, they are holding hands and the doctor can see that there is a certain glow about them. They are even smiling at each other, and they are acting a little shy. So the doctor says:

"I see that it's been a special week for you. Would you like to tell me about it?"

"Well, Doctor," says the man, smiling and looking at his wife, "the day after we saw you we were having breakfast, and I looked across at her and she looked back at me, and before we knew it, we were making love right there on the table. It was very exciting!"

The doctor is very pleased for them. He says:

"That is wonderful!"

"Yes," says the man "but we can't eat in the Howard Johnson's any more."

Analysis:
The man and his wife were having breakfast in the Howard Johnson's restaurant. Love making on top of the table is frowned upon at your local Hojos.

Vocabulary:

Counselor – Someone who gives advice about problems.

Frowned Upon – Regarded something with disapproval or distaste.

Impulsive – Proceeding from natural feeling or impulse without external stimulus.

Marital – Of or relating to the state of marriage.

Schedule – A plan for an activity or event.

Spontaneous – Happening or arising without apparent external cause; self-generated.

There Are No Fish Here

The Joke:

Two Poles have just finished cutting a hole in the ice. Suddenly, they hear a voice above them say:

"There are no fish here."

They move on, and cut another hole in the ice. Again, they hear the voice above them say:

"There are no fish here."

Again, they move and cut another hole in the ice. Again, the voice above them says:

"There are no fish here. The rink is closed."

Analysis:

The two Poles are in the middle of a skating rink, which is closed.

Vocabulary:

Curling – A game originating in Scotland in which two four-person teams slide heavy oblate stones toward the center of a circle at either end of a length of ice.

Hockey – A game played on ice in which two opposing teams of skaters, using curved sticks, try to drive a puck into the opponent's goal.

Rink – An area surfaced with smooth ice for skating, hockey, or curling.

Skating – The sport of gliding on skates.

Doggy Fashion

The Joke:

A man is seeing his psychiatrist and complaining about his sex life. The psychiatrist asks:

"How many different positions have you tried?"

"Positions?" says the man.

"You know. You're on the top and she is on the bottom. She is on the top and you are on the bottom. Doggy fashion," says the doctor.

"Oh, no, doctor, you don't understand. My wife is very religious. She wouldn't go for something different," says the man.

"Does she drink?" asks the doctor.

"Yes, she does with dinner," answers the man.

"Here's what I want you to do. Mix up a big pitcher of martinis and serve it with dinner the next time you eat together. Loosen her up a little bit, and she'll go for it. Try it doggy fashion. She'll love it!" says the doctor.

"Doc, I don't know," says the man.

"I refuse to take no for an answer. Try it, she'll love it! Come to see me this same time next week."

When the man arrives next week, the doctor asks:

"Well, how was it?"

"It was okay, I guess," says the man.

"What do you mean, you guess?" says the doctor.

"Well, it did take me twenty-two martinis," says the man.

"Twenty-two martinis!" exclaims the doctor.

"Yes, it took me sixteen to get her out in the front yard," says the man.

Analysis:

By doggy fashion, the doctor didn't mean in public.

Vocabulary:

Doggy Fashion – An act of sex in the manner of dogs.

In Public – Publicly: in a manner accessible to or observable by the public; openly.

Martini – A cocktail made of gin (or vodka) with dry vermouth.

Positions – Sexual positions. Positions for sexual intercourse.

Savoir Faire

The Joke:

Two men are having dinner together one evening, when one asks the other:

"How would you define savoir faire?"

"That is very difficult," replies the other.

But perhaps I could give you an example.

"Savoir faire is when you come home unexpectedly, and find your wife in bed with another man. You say: "Don't mind me, carry on.""

The second man says:

"That is a good example, but perhaps a better example would be if you came home unexpectedly and found your wife in bed with another woman, and you said: 'Don't mind me, carry on.'"

The waiter, who has been listening to all this and is French, says:

"Excusez moi, Messieurs, but savoir faire is when you came home early, find your wife in bed with another man, and say: 'Don't mind me, carry on.'

And he can, that is savoir faire."

Analysis:

Most men would develop a not-so-slight performance problem if we were caught in the middle of an act of sexual intercourse.

Vocabulary:

Excusez moi – Means 'excuse me' in English.

Orgasm – The moment of most intense pleasure in sexual intercourse.

Performance Problem – There is a discrepancy between the sought-after results and the actual results. During sex, good performance is causing your partner to have an orgasm.

Savoir Faire – The ability to say or do the right or graceful thing. Taken from the French, it literally means: 'To know how to do.'

The Greatest Man Who Ever Lived

The Joke:

A schoolteacher tells her class that she will give a dollar to anyone who can name the greatest man who ever lived.

Immediately, an Italian boy raises his hand. She says:

"Yes, Tony."

The boy says:

"Christopher Columbus."

"No, Tony. Christopher Columbus was a great man and a great Italian explorer, but that is not the name I am looking for."

Right away a little English girl raises her hand. The teacher says:

"Yes, Martha."

The girl says:

"Winston Churchill."

"No, Martha. Winston Churchill was a great man and a great statesman, but that is not the name I am looking for."

From the back of the room, Irving Goldstein raises his hand. The teacher says:

"Yes, Irving."

"Jesus Christ."

"That is correct, Irving. Please come up and get your dollar."

When Irving comes up, the teacher asks him:

"How is it that a Jewish kid like you knows the correct answer to that question?"

"Well," replies Irving. "Of course, I knew it was Moses – but business is business."

Analysis:

The Jewish kid wants the dollar worse than he wants everyone to know that the greatest man on Earth was Moses.

Vocabulary:

Christopher Columbus – The Italian navigator who discovered the New World in 1492 in the service of Spain while looking for a route to China (1451-1506).

Jesus Christ – A teacher and prophet born in Bethlehem and active in Nazareth; his life and sermons form the basis for Christianity (circa 4 BC – AD 29)

Moses – The Hebrew prophet who led the Israelites from Egypt across the Red sea on a journey known as the Exodus; Moses received the Ten Commandments from God on Mount Sinai.

Winston Churchill – British statesman and leader during World War II; he received the Nobel Prize for Literature in 1953 (1874-1965).

The Polish Salesman

The Joke:

A Polish guy walks into a hardware store to apply for a job. The Jewish owner is more interested in his ability to sell than in his clerical ability.

The owner sees a customer coming in the door and says:

"Okay, just to make sure you know what I'm talking about, watch me!"

The customer walks up and asks where the grass seed is. The owner tells him that it is in the third aisle on the fourth shelf down. When the Man comes back to the cash register with the grass seed, the owner says:

"Do you need a lawnmower? We have a special sale on lawnmowers at the moment."

"What do I need a lawnmower for? I don't even have any grass yet," says the customer.

"Maybe not now, but eventually you will. And then you'll need a lawnmower and you won't be able to get one any cheaper than what we're selling them for right now," says the owner.

"Hmmm, I guess you're right. Okay, I'll take the lawnmower too," says the customer.

After the customer leaves, the owner says to the Polish guy:

"So, do you think you can do that?"

"Sure," responds the Polish guy.

"Okay, I have to make a deposit at the bank. I'll only be gone for a few minutes, but while I'm away, watch over the store for me. And remember, if anyone comes in, *sell, sell, sell!*" says the owner.

A few minutes later, a woman comes in. She goes up to the Polish man at the cash register and asks where the Kotex is. She is told that it's in the fifth aisle on the second shelf down. When she returns to the register to pay for it, he asks:

"Do you want to buy a lawnmower?"

She responds:

"What would I want a lawnmower for?"

He says:

"Well, you can't be having any fun riding the rag this weekend, so you might as well be out mowing the grass."

Analysis:

The Polish guy assumes the woman needs the Kotex for this weekend.

Vocabulary:

Kotex – A sanitary napkin: a disposable absorbent pad (trade name Kotex); worn to absorb menstrual flow.

Riding The Rag – Vulgar slang for having a menstrual period.

The Genitals Have Been Blown Away

The Joke:

A soldier in Vietnam has his genitals blown off. The doctor doesn't know what else to do, so he grafts on a baby elephant's trunk.

The soldier is discharged, and returns to the U.S.

A few months later, he is on a date with a new young lady. As they are seated at a table in a restaurant, the trunk comes up over the edge of the table, grabs a dinner roll, and ducks back under the table.

The girl is fascinated, and says:

"Say, could you do that again?"

The ex-soldier replies:

"Yes, but I'm not sure my asshole could take another roll."

Analysis:

The roll was jammed up the man's anal orifice.

Vocabulary:

None.

Name Calling

The Joke:

A young lady goes to confession. She confesses that her boyfriend has called her "A rotten bitch." The priest is very sympathetic, and asks what happened.

The girl replies that she doesn't know, so the priest inquires further.

"Did he kiss you on the mouth like this?"

"Yes."

"And did he kiss you on the neck like this?"

"Yes."

"And did he unbutton your blouse like this?"

"Yes."

"And did he make love to you like this?"

"Yes."

"And then what?" says the priest.

"I told him that I had Syphilis," replies the girl.

"Oh, you rotten bitch!" exclaims the priest.

Analysis:

The priest is also taken aback when he learns that the girl he is making love to has Syphilis.

Vocabulary:

None.

He Snores

The Joke:

A man is driving across the country, when he starts to get very sleepy. Not wanting to fall asleep at the wheel, he decides to check into a motel. When he reaches the next town, he goes from one motel to the other, but they are all booked.

When he reaches the far edge of town, he walks into the lobby of the last motel. He goes up to the manager and says:

"Please, do you have a room? Even just a bed, anything at all?"

The manager says:

"I'm sorry, Sir, we're all booked up. But there is one thing I can think of. There is a double room with only one occupant, and he might be happy to split the cost with you."

"Great!" says the man, "I'll take it!"

"Hold on," says the manager. "There is a problem I have to tell you about. This guy snores."

"That's not a problem at all," says the man. "Right now I could sleep through anything."

The manager replies:

"No, you don't understand. This guy snores so loudly that the people in the adjoining rooms have been complaining for the past two nights. I'm not sure if this is going to be worth it for you."

"Believe me, it will be fine," says the man.

The next morning, the man comes bouncing into the lobby, looking cheerful and well-rested.

Manager spots him, and says:

"Sure looks like you slept pretty well!"

"Never better," replies the man.

"So you didn't have any problem with that guy's snoring?" The manager asks.

"No," says the man. "I shut him up real quick."

The incredulous manager asks:

"How in the world did you do that?"

"Well," says the man, "he was sound asleep and snoring when I first entered the room. I must admit that his snoring was pretty loud. But I just went over, gave him a kiss on the cheek, and said: 'Goodnight, cutie!' He sat bolt upright all night long, watching me like a hawk."

Analysis:

The man shut his roommate up by kissing him on the cheek.

Vocabulary:

Snore – To breathe during sleep with harsh, snorting noises caused by vibration of the soft palate.

No Sex Tonight

The Joke:

A guy goes into a tavern and sits down. He sees a beautiful young woman at the other end of the bar, and after a few minutes of watching her sit there alone, he musters up his courage and goes over. He asks her very politely:

"Excuse me, is this seat taken?"

He is shocked and dismayed when she turns around, and says very loudly:

"HELL NO! I WON'T SLEEP WITH YOU TONGHT! NOW, GET AWAY FROM ME!"

Completely humiliated, he slinks back to his seat and sits down.

A few minutes later, she comes over to the seat and joins him. She says:

"I'm sorry. You see, I'm a graduate student in psychology, and I am doing a research project to see how people respond to embarrassing situations.

I hope that I wasn't too rough on you."

The man reflects on this for a few seconds. Then he shouts:

"THREE HUNDRED DOLLARS!"

Analysis:

The man believes that turnabout is fair play. If she can do it, then he can do it. Or: What's sauce for the goose is sauce for the gander.

Vocabulary:

Aghast – Struck with fear, dread, or consternation.

Consternation – A state of paralyzing dismay.

Dismayed – Aghast: struck with fear, dread, or consternation.

Gander – Male goose. See goose below.

Goose – Any of various wild or domesticated water birds of the family Anatidae, and especially of the genera *Anser* and *Branta*, characteristically having a shorter neck than that of a swan and a shorter, more pointed bill than that of a duck. The female of such a bird.

Humiliated – Broken: subdued or brought low in condition or status.

Musters – Causes to come together; gathers.

Sleep With – Slang for sleep together: have sexual intercourse with.

Slinks – Moves in a quiet furtive manner; sneaks: slinks away ashamed.

Psychology – The science of mind and behavior.

Sauce – A liquid or soft mixture served with food to add flavor or enhance its general appeal.

Tavern – An establishment licensed to sell alcoholic beverages to be consumed on the premises.

Turnabout – A change or reversal of opinion, attitude, etc.

The Lion Tamer

The Joke:

A circus was touring a series of small towns in Florida. Suddenly, the lion tamer had a heart attack, and was seriously incapacitated in a local hospital.

The ringmaster decided to place an ad in the local newspaper. Only two applicants show up: One is a tall, willowy blonde dressed in a trench coat. The other is a nondescript gentleman.

The skeptical ringmaster says:

"Okay, there is a gun, a whip, and a chair just inside the cage door. There is only Leo in the cage. Now, who wants to be first?"

The man, imitating Sir Galahad, says:

"Ladies first."

The young woman bypasses the gun, whip, and chair. She proceeds directly to the center of the cage.

Leo looks: no whip, no gun, and no chair. He lets out a huge roar, but the young lady doesn't move. He lets a second roar, but the young lady still doesn't move. He leaps off his pedestal, spitting and snarling. The young lady opens her trench coat, and she is not wearing anything underneath. Leo drops to the ground. He lies down, rolls over and over, and starts licking her feet. The ringmaster exclaims:

"Well, I'll be damned."

He turns to the second applicant, and asks:

"Well, can you top that?"

The second applicant responds:

"Sure, just get that stupid lion out of there."

Analysis:

When the ringmaster asks the second applicant if he can top that, he means in lion taming.

Vocabulary:

Gracile – Slender and graceful.

Incapacitated – Deprived of strength or ability; disabled.

Lion Taming – The practice of taming lions, either for protection, whereby the practice was probably created, or, more commonly, entertainment, particularly in the circus. Every circus had a lion act, whereby trained lions were required to perform tricks in front of an audience.

Nondescript – Lacking distinctive qualities; having no individual character or form.

Pedestal – A support or foundation.

Ringmaster – The person in charge of performances in a circus ring.

Series – Similar things placed in order or happening one after another.

Sir Galahad – Galahad was the natural son of Lancelot. His name may be of Welsh origin or come from the place name Gilead in Palestine. His name is associated with gallant behavior.

Skeptical – Marked by or given to doubt; questioning.

Top That – In this case, top the highest position or rank.

Trench Coat – A military style raincoat; belted with deep pockets.

Willowy – Gracile: slender and graceful.

Gay Spiders

The Joke:

A father is on his back porch in Houston watching his young daughter playing in the backyard. He is admiring how cute she is, so young and innocent. Then he notices that she suddenly stops playing, crouches down, and starts staring at the ground underneath a bush. He walks over to see what she is looking at. Underneath the bush, he sees two spiders mating.

His daughter asks:

"What are they doing, Daddy?"

Her father answers:

"They're mating."

The little girl then asks:

"What do you call the spider on the top?"

"That's a Daddy Longlegs." says the father.

"Oh," says the girl, "So is the other one a Mommy Longlegs?"

"Actually, no," replies the father. "Both of them are Daddy Longlegs."

The little girl stands up immediately, stamps her foot down on the two spiders, and says:

"That might be okay in California or Massachusetts, but we're not having any of that shit in Texas!"

Analysis:

Homosexuality is frowned upon in Texas.

Vocabulary:

Daddy Longlegs – Spiders – Any of various arachnids of the order Phalangida, with a small rounded body and long slender legs.

Mating – Coupling: the act of pairing a male and female for reproductive purposes.

Straight Down the Fairway

The Joke:

A woman is out on the golf course for her very first time, and she is having great difficulty. Every shot either slices or hooks, and she can't seem to get any shots that come close to landing on the fairway. A golf pro happens to walk by and sees her struggling. As she gets more and more frustrated, he walks up to her and says:

"Excuse me, ma'am, but I think I can help you with that."

"You can?" says the woman, tears beginning to well up in her eyes.

"Sure I can. Don't you worry about a thing," comforts the golf pro.

"Here, I'll show you." With that, he reaches his arms around her and grabs the club, his hands on top of hers. He says:

"You hold the club like this. Now, it might make it a little easier for you if you think of holding it just like you hold your boyfriend's, uh, male member."

"O-o-h-h-h," replies the woman, the light bulb going off inside her head. She looks the golf pro straight in the eye, smiles, grips the club, and WHACK! She hits the ball 350 yards down the fairway.

"Wow!" shouts the golf pro, "That was fantastic! Tiger Woods couldn't even hit it like that! That was incredible! Now try it again," he says, "but this time, take the club out of your mouth."

Analysis:

If she can hit straight down the fairway with the club in her mouth, think what she could do without it in her mouth.

Vocabulary:

Fairway – In golf, the area between the tee and putting green where the grass is cut short.

Frustrated – Defeated: disappointingly unsuccessful.

Hooks – In golf, the course of a ball that curves in a direction away from the dominant hand of the player propelling it, as to the left of a right-handed player.

Slices – In golf, the course of a ball that curves in the direction of the dominant hand of the player propelling it, as to the right of a right-handed player.

Tiger Woods – Eldrick Tont "Tiger" Woods (born December 30, 1975) is an American professional golfer whose achievements to date rank him among the most successful golfers of all time. Currently the World No. 1 golfer.

Graphic Art

The Joke:

Two school administrators are talking about the drug problem in their respective public schools. One of the administrators says:

"You know, we reduced the drug problem in our school just with the use of graphic art."

The second administrator says:

"Really, what did you do?"

The first administrator says:

"Well, we made posters and got a hundred of them printed up. On the left-hand side of the poster, we had a big circle. Underneath it, we wrote: 'This is your brain.'

On the right-hand side of the poster, we had a little tiny circle. Underneath it we wrote: 'This is your brain on drugs.'

It's simple, it's direct, and it was very effective. By putting up those posters all over our school, we were able to reduce the drug problem by 40%!"

The second administrator replies:

"That's very interesting, because we did a similar thing in our school. But in our school, we were able to reduce the drug problem by 95%."

The first administrator says:

"That's even more amazing. What did you do?"

The second administrator explains:

"Well, we also had posters made up. They were quite similar to yours, but on our poster, we had a little tiny circle on the left-hand side. Underneath it, we put: 'This is your ass-hole.' On the right-hand side of the poster, we had a very large circle. Underneath it, we put: 'This is your ass-hole in prison.'"

Analysis:

Due to the pederasty in prison, the anal orifice is enlarged. The victim is called a punk or the girlfriend of his assailant. View the 1979 Clint Eastwood film *Escape from Alcatraz* for a full discussion of this problem. The film also stars Patrick McGoohan as the warden. Pay particular attention to Eastwood's altercations with other inmate Wolf. This film is based on the real life story of convict Frank Morris.

Vocabulary:

Alcatraz – A rocky island of western California in San Francisco Bay. It was a federal military prison from 1859 to 1933 and a federal prison until 1963. It is now a tourist attraction. The island has long been known as "the Rock." Since closing, it has become a major tourist attraction in San Francisco.

Alimentary – Concerned with food, nutrition, or digestion; eating.

Altercation – An angry or heated discussion or quarrel; argument.

Anal – Of or related to the anus.

Anus – The opening at the lower end of the alimentary canal through which solid waste is eliminated from the body.

Ass-hole – Slang term for the anal orifice.

Convict – A person serving a sentence in a jail or prison. A person who has been convicted of committing a crime.

Drug Problem – Drug abuse is an increasing problem in our affluent societies and carries great social and economic costs through its impacts on crime and health.

Girlfriend – In this context, slang for a man who is the sexual partner of another man.

Inmate- One of several residents of a dwelling (especially someone confined to a prison or hospital).

Orifice – An aperture or hole that opens into a bodily cavity.

Pederasty – A man who has sexual relations, especially anal intercourse, with a boy or other man.

Prison – A place for the confinement of persons in lawful detention, especially persons convicted of crimes.

Punk – In this context, slang for a young man who is the sexual partner of an older man.

Warden – The chief official in charge of a prison.

The Virgin

The Joke:
A millionaire decides that he wants to get married, but he wants to marry a virgin. This is not an easy thing to find in this day and age, but he starts scouring the countryside. After a few months of looking, the millionaire is out on a date one night and thinks he may have finally found his ideal.

The young lady seems extremely innocent, so after dinner, as they are riding in the back of his limousine, the man unzips his fly and whips out his cock. He asks:

"Do you know what this is?"

The young woman replies:

"Yes, that's a wee-wee."

Impressed by her innocence, the man determines to marry her. He informs her of his intentions. A month later, they get married. On their wedding night in the hotel room, the husband sits down on the bed next to his wife. He pulls out his penis and says:

"Now that we're married, you should know the proper name for things. This is my cock."

"No, it's not!" replies his wife. "Cocks are 12-inches long and black! That's definitely a wee-wee."

Analysis:
His wife is not as innocent as the millionaire thought.

Vocabulary:
Innocent – Free from evil or guilt.

Millionaire – A person whose material wealth is valued at more than a million dollars.

Penis – The male organ of copulation in higher vertebrates, homologous with the clitoris.

Scouring – Moving over territory to search for something.

Virgin – A person who has never had sex.

Aids or Alzheimer's Disease

The Joke:

A woman's urine analysis comes back from the lab. The doctor calls her husband in. He says:

"According to this report, your wife has either Aids or Alzheimer's Disease.

The husband asks:

"Doctor, what would you suggest?"

The doctor replies:

"Well, you know that shopping center close to your house?"

The husband confirms that he does.

Then, the doctor says:

"Well, drop her off in the middle of that shopping center. If she can find her way back home, don't fuck her."

Analysis:

If the wife can find her way back from the mall, she obviously does not have Alzheimer's disease. The only alternative is that she must have Aids. Therefore, she shouldn't have sexual intercourse with anyone.

Vocabulary:

None.

What Do You Think I Am

The Joke:

George Bernard Shaw is at a party. He has been having an argument about an hour about ethics. He has been arguing situation ethics – a starving man will steal food, a man will do things to protect his family that he wouldn't do to protect himself, etc. His opponent is arguing absolute ethics – a man learns about ethics at six-years-of-age and doesn't deviate from that for the rest of his life. Shaw tires of the argument, and says:

"Okay, just stay behind me and listen. I'll go prove my point."

He approaches this young, debutante type and says:

"Excuse me, young lady. Do you know who I am?"

"Why, yes," she replies, "You're George Bernard Shaw, the famous playwright."

He says:

"That is correct, young lady. Listen carefully; I have a proposition for you."

She is surprised, for Shaw was about eighty at the time.

"I'll give you 100,000 pounds to spend the night with me."

She thinks about it for a moment, and then says:

"All right."

"On second thought, that's too much. I'll give you 30 pounds."

"Really," she says indignantly, "What do you think I am?"

"We've already determined that," says Shaw, "We are now haggling over price."

Analysis:

Shaw proved his point. Situation ethics won.

Vocabulary:

Debutante – A young woman making a formal debut into society.

Dramatist – Someone who writes plays.

Ethics – Motivation based on ideas of right and wrong.

Haggling – To bargain, as over the price of something; dicker.

Indignantly – Feeling or expressing anger or scorn, esp. at unjust, mean, or ungrateful action or treatment.

Playwright – A dramatist: someone who writes plays.

Proposition – In this case, an offer of a private bargain, especially a request for sexual relations.

Situation Ethics – The view that ethical judgment applies to whole situations, rather as aesthetic judgment is formed in response to total works of art.

The Green Circles

The Joke:
   A woman at the doctor's office complains that she has green circles on the inside of her thighs. He examines her and asks:
   "Are you a lesbian?"
   She answers testily:
   "Yes, I am. Why do you ask?"
   The doctor straightens up and says:
   "I'm afraid that you're going to have to go home and break the news to your girlfriend that her earrings aren't real gold."

Analysis:
   The green circles are left by her sexual partner.

Vocabulary:
   Lesbian – A woman whose sexual orientation is to women.
   Thighs – The portion of the human legs between the hips and the knees.

The Bollocks of the Bull

The Joke:

An American tourist is sitting in a café in Madrid, Spain. He is trying to decide what he wants to order, when a waiter walks by. On the plate he is carrying are two big round hunks of meat, about the size of grapefruits.

The man calls the waiter over, points to the plate, and says:

"That's what I want!"

"I'm sorry, sir, but that is the special, and there is only one order of the special available each day," says the waiter.

"What kind of a special is that?" asks the man.

"You see, Sir," says the waiter, "those are the testicles of the bull killed today in the bullfight. It is our most popular item, and you have to reserve it many days in advance."

"When is the next free day?" asks the man.

The waiter checks his book, and says:

"Tuesday."

"All right, then," says the man, "put me down for Tuesday."

Finally, Tuesday arrives and the man excitedly goes to the café and sits at his regular table. "I'd like the special, please." He orders.

When the waiter arrives, though, on the plate there are just two small pieces of meat about the size of grapes.

"Hey, what is this?" He says.

"Ah, Senor, what can I say? Sometimes, the bull wins."

Analysis:

The testicles on the plate came from the matador.

Vocabulary:

Bollocks – Testicles.

Matador – The principal bullfighter who is appointed to make the final passes and kill the bull.

My Dad Has Two of Those

The Joke:
   A grandfather in England decides to give his children a break. He takes his small grandson out to the zoo. While there, he has to go to the bathroom to urinate. Since he doesn't know what else to do, he takes his grandson along to the urinal. The boy says:
   "My father has two of those."
   The old man is somewhat surprised, and asks the young boy to explain.
   The young boy says:
   "He has a small one that he uses to pee with like that, and a much larger one that he uses to clean the teeth of the au pair girl with."

Analysis:
   The father has been having oral sex with the au pair girl.

Vocabulary:
   Au Pair – A domestic assistant working for, and living as part of, a host family. Typically, au pairs take on a share of the family's responsibility for childcare as well as some housework, and receive a small monetary allowance for personal use. They are often foreign-nationals of the country in which they are working. The title comes from the French term *au pair*, meaning "on a par" or "equal to", indicating that the relationship is intended to be one of equals: the au pair is intended to become a member of the family, albeit a temporary one, rather than a domestic servant.

That's for Pearl Harbor

The Joke:

A Chinese man is enjoying a drink at a bar. Suddenly, without any warning, he is knocked to the ground by this other bar patron. He asks:

"Jesus, what's that for?"

The other patron answers:

"That's for Pearl Harbor."

"But I'm Chinese, not Japanese," protests the Chinese man.

"Oh, Chinese or Japanese, it's all the same to me," says the other patron, and he stalks off.

The Chinese asks the bartender:

"What was all that about?"

"Oh," replies the bartender, "that was just old Sol Goldberg blowing off some steam. Don't pay him any attention."

A few minutes later, the Chinese man walks over to the Jewish patron, and knocks him to the ground. The Jewish man asks:

"What's that for?"

"That's for the Titanic," responds the Chinese.

"What?" says the Jewish guy.

"Yes, iceberg, Goldberg, it's all the same to me," says the Chinese.

Analysis:

The Chinese is annoyed to be attacked in the bar, particularly when his attacker makes no distinction between Chinese and Japanese.

Vocabulary:

Pearl Harbor – A harbor on Oahu to the west of Honolulu; location of the United States naval base that was attacked by the Japanese on 7 Dec 1941. This attack started WWII for the U.S.

Titanic – On 12 April 1912 the White Star Line's royal mail steamer Titanic, a ship many considered unsinkable, set sail on its maiden voyage from Southampton in England. Four days into the crossing, at 23:40 on 14 April 1912, she struck an iceberg and sank at 2:20 the following morning, resulting in the deaths of 1,517 people in one of the deadliest peacetime maritime disasters in history.

Baseball in Heaven

The Joke:

Two ninety-year-old Jewish men have been friends all their lives. Sam is about to pass away, so Moe comes for a last visit. Moe says:

"Sam, you know that we have both loved baseball, so I want you to do me one final favor. Somehow, you have to tell me whether there is baseball in heaven."

Sam answers:

"Moe, you've been my dearest friend for many years. This last favor, I'll do for you." And with that, Sam passes on.

Moe is sound asleep around midnight, when he hears this distant voice: "Moe, it's me, Sam."

Moe sits up suddenly, and says:

"Is that you, Sam?"

Sam assures Moe that it is he, and he's calling straight from heaven. Sam says: "I have some good news and some bad news for you."

Moe says: "Give me the good news first."

Sam says: "The good news is that there is baseball here in heaven,"

Moe responds: "Really, that's wonderful. But, what's the bad news?"

Sam says: "The bad news is that you're pitching this coming Tuesday."

Analysis:

Moe will be dead by this coming Tuesday.

Vocabulary:

None.

The Gorilla Hunter

The Joke:

A great white hunter in Africa has achieved a world-wide reputation as a gorilla hunter. Whenever a zoo needs a new gorilla, they rely on this man to go out and hunt down the gorilla they need. Finally, his fame reaches such proportions that he is interviewed by a leading weekly magazine from the U.S. He describes what he does to capture a gorilla:

"We go out and form a huge circle around a clearing with a tall tree in its middle. Then, we continue to tighten the circle while beating drums. The frightened gorilla finally reaches the tree and shinnies up into it. Then I go up in the tree, and shake it until the gorilla loses his balance and falls to the ground. At this point, my trusty dog rushes in and bites the gorilla in the testicles. While the gorilla is rolling over and over in pain, my bearers throw a net over the gorilla and toss him into a cage."

The reporter asks for permission to go along on the next hunt. This is granted, and the reporter shows up for the next hunt. He notices that a gun-bearer comes along, and asks the hunter for an explanation. He is told not to worry about the gun-bearer, since he is only for back-up and is never used.

Things go quite well on the hunt, and the party has succeeded in capturing two gorillas. On the third day, the party tracks a third gorilla. He is isolated and the circle closes. The frightened gorilla shinnies up the tree. The great white hunter climbs the tree, and shakes it as usual. The gorilla shinnies back down the tree, grabs the great white hunter, and throws the hunter out of the tree. As he is falling, the hunter yells:

"Shoot the dog! Shoot the dog! Shoot the dog!"

Analysis:

Now, the reporter knows what back-up means.

Vocabulary:

Gun-bearer – Some one who carries a rifle.

Shinny – Clamber: climb awkwardly, as if by scrambling.

Custer's Last Stand

The Joke:

A bar is being completely renovated in Manhattan in New York City. As part of the grand re-opening, the owner has commissioned a painting to be hung over the bar in his new establishment. His instructions to the artist have been very specific:

"I do not want a traditional rendering of Custer's Last Stand. Rather, I want a painting of your impression of what Custer must have been thinking at the beginning of the Battle of Little Bighorn. I do not want to see this painting in advance. I want it delivered under drapes, to be unveiled as a surprise as part of the ceremony celebrating the re-opening of my new establishment."

So saying, he sends the artist off to achieve the painting. On opening night, as part of the grand re-opening ceremony, he personally pulls the drapes covering the picture. The audience is aghast. The painting is of American Indians in every conceivable position of sexual intercourse. In the center of the painting is a large cow with a halo over its head. The owner turns to the artist, and asks:

"What is this?"

The artist replies that it represents what Custer must have been thinking as he rode over the hill at the beginning of the Battle of Little Bighorn.

"Holy cow, look at all those fucking Indians!"

Analysis:

The owner got what he paid for (but he doesn't like it).

Vocabulary:

Aghast – Struck with fear, dread, or consternation.

Battle Of Little Bighorn – Sited on a river in the West Central US, rising in Northern Wyoming and flowing north to the Bighorn River. Its banks were the scene of the defeat (1876) and killing of General George A. Custer and his entire cavalry command by Sioux Indians.

Commissioned – The act of granting certain powers or the authority to carry out a particular task or duty. That is, the painting.

Drapes – To cover, dress, or hang with or as if with cloth in loose folds.

Halo – An aura: an indication of radiant light drawn around the head of a saint or holy object.

Impression – An effect, feeling, or image retained as a consequence of experience.

Rendering – A depiction or interpretation, as in painting or music.

Renovated – The process of improving a structure. Two prominent types of renovations are commercial and residential.

Traditional – Consisting of or derived from tradition; "traditional history"; "traditional morality".

Unveiled – Removed a veil or covering from.

The Gunfighter

The Joke:

A young gunfighter rides his horse into Dodge City. He trots up to the largest saloon he sees and dismounts. As soon as he walks through the swinging doors, he is met with the lively music of a tinkling piano and sees some beautiful women dancing on the stage. He is absolutely awestruck, though, to see the famous Doc Holliday playing poker at one of the tables.

The gunfighter strolls right over to the legendary man, who is at that moment looking at his cards. He says:

"Excuse me, but are you Doc Holliday, friend to gunfighter and lawman alike?"

Doc Holliday slowly puts down his cards and says:

"Why, yes, I am. Are you going to start some trouble?"

"No, no!" says the gunfighter, holding up his hands. "I was just wondering if you could critique my shooting style."

Doc Holliday relaxes, smiles, and replies:

"Sure, son, I'd be happy to."

In a split second, the Colt .45 comes out of the young man's holster, and he fires a shot. The bullet knocks the cufflink off the piano player's right sleeve. The piano player doesn't even miss a beat. He just keeps on playing, the dancing girls keep dancing, and the people just keep on drinking and playing cards.

The gunfighter twirls the gun, and then smoothly slips it back into its holster. A split second goes by, and out comes the gun again. He blasts off a second shot, and this one blows the cufflink off the piano player's left sleeve. The cufflink makes an arc through the air, and then clatters to the floor at the feet of Doc Holliday. Again, the piano player doesn't miss a beat, and just keeps playing away. The girls are still doing the can-can, people are still drinking, and the gambling wheels still keep spinning.

Doc Holliday says:

"That's some mighty fancy shooting there, young man."

Replies the kid:

"Thank you, sir."

"However, I do have two suggestions for you," says Doc Holliday.

"Yes, please tell me," says the gunfighter.

"Well," says the Doc, rolling himself a cigarette, "I noticed on your first shot that there was a slight hesitation on your equipment, and I think there might be a little burr on the hammer of your gun. Go down the street here, to Al's gunsmith shop, and ask Al to file that off for you."

The kid says:

"Great! Thanks! What is the second suggestion?"

"When you get finished in Al's," answers Doc Holliday as he lights up his cigarette, "go across the street to the general store. Ask Fred in the general store to dip your entire gun in bear grease."

"Bear grease!" The kid exclaims. "Why?"

"Because," replies Doc, letting out a puff of smoke, "when Wyatt finishes playing that tune on that piano, he's going to shove that gun up your ass."

Analysis:

Wyatt Earp is playing the piano in this saloon. He seems imperturbable and absolutely unflappable. However, when he finishes playing the piano, he is going to shove the gunfighter's gun up his ass. It seems the least he can do to the gunfighter, since he ruined two of his best cufflinks.

Vocabulary:

Arc – In this case, a curved path.

Bear Grease – Soft or melted bear fat, especially after rendering.

Burr – A rough edge or ridge left on metal or other material by cutting or drilling.

Clatters – Moves with a rattling sound.

Critique – Review: an essay or article that gives a critical evaluation (as of a book or play).

Colt .45 – A six-shot revolver invented by Samuel Colt and used throughout the West. The gunfighter's pistol in this story.

Cufflinks – Decorative fasteners worn by men or women to fasten the two sides of the cuff on a dress shirt or blouse.

Dismounts – Gets off or down, as from a horse.

Doc Holliday – John Henry "Doc" Holliday (August 14, 1851 – November 8, 1887) was an American dentist, gambler and gunfighter of the American Old West, who is usually remembered for his friendship with Wyatt Earp and his involvement in the Gunfight at the O.K. Corral.

Dodge City – A town of southwestern Kansas on the Arkansas River; formerly a rowdy cow town.

Gunfighter – Gunfighter, also gunslinger, is a 20th century name, used in cinema or literature, referring to men in the American Old West who had gained a reputation as being dangerous with a gun.

Hammer – The part of a gunlock that strikes the percussion cap when the trigger is pulled.

Holster – A case of leather or similar material into which a pistol fits snugly and which attaches to a belt, strap, or saddle so that it may be carried or transported.

Imperturbable – Not easily perturbed or excited or upset; marked by extreme calm and composure. See unflappable below.

Legendary – So celebrated as to have taken on the nature of a legend.

Percussion Cap – A thin metal cap containing an explosive substance, such as fulminate of mercury, that explodes on being struck.

Poker – Any of various card games played by two or more players who bet on the value of their hands.

Rolling – Rotating on an axis or moving along a surface by rotation; turning over and over as if on an axis or a pivot. Rolling your own cigarettes was the custom before machine rolling of cigarettes.

Sleeve – The part of a garment that is attached at the armhole and that provides a cloth covering for the arm.

Twirls – Turns in a twisting or spinning motion.

Unflappable – Imperturbable: not easily perturbed or excited or upset; marked by extreme calm and composure. See imperturbable above.

Wyatt Earp – Wyatt Berry Stapp Earp (March 19, 1848 – January 13, 1929) was an American officer of the law in various Western frontier towns, farmer, teamster, buffalo hunter, gambler, saloon-keeper, miner and boxing referee.

The Golfing Couple

The Joke:

A man and his wife were so enamored of the game that they had their house constructed so that the picture window of their master bedroom looked out over the eighteenth green of their favorite golf course. One evening over dinner, the wife asked:

"Dear, if I were to pass away would you still play on the same golf course?"

He thinks for a minute before responding:

"Well, I hadn't thought about it, but since they don't know me anywhere else in this town, I suppose so."

Getting a little upset, his wife then asks:

"And would you use the same house?"

Again he reflects before answering:

"Well, with the cost of mortgage money being what it is, I suppose so."

Getting angrier, she asks:

"And would you use the same master bedroom?"

He answers:

"Well, honey, the house only has one master bedroom."

Blowing her stack, she asks:

"And would you let her use my golf clubs?"

He replies:

"Oh, no, she's left-handed."

Analysis:

Well, at least she won't be using the same golf clubs. For those unfamiliar with the game, left-handed golfers use an entirely different set of clubs.

Vocabulary:

Blowing His/Her Stack – Informal: To lose one's temper.

Enamored – Marked by foolish or unreasoning fondness.

Picture Window – A large, usually single-paned window that provides a broad outside view.

The New Minister

The Joke:

A young Methodist Minister is assigned to a small town in the rural South. He is worried that what he has learned in Union Seminary in New York City will not relate to his new parishioners in this rural setting. There are only three churches in town. There is his Methodist Church, a Southern Baptist Church and the local Catholic Church. Then, he spots a large sign in front of the Baptist Church announcing a Revival Meeting on Wednesday night. Since the sign says: "Come and Bring Your Friends", he decides to attend to see how it is done.

Up on the rostrum is an eighty-year-old Baptist Minister giving one of his usual fiery sermons: "All have sinned, and come short of the Glory of God. You're all going to Hell. Repent now and be saved."

The young Methodist Minister is very impressed. He asks the old Baptist Minister how he manages to get such enthusiasm and fire into his sermons.

The old Baptist replies:

"Well, Sonny, you see the pitcher on the podium?"

"Sure, but every speaker has water on the podium with him." replies the young Methodist.

"Sonny, that wasn't water – that was White Lightning in that pitcher." says the old Baptist.

"White Lightning?" says the new Minister.

"Sonny, where are you from?" says the old Baptist.

Upon learning that his fellow minister is from New York City, he informs him that White Lightening is alcohol – bootleg whiskey. Fascinated, the young Methodist asks if the old Baptist can get him a bottle. He promises to use this White Lightning in his first sermon, and invites the old Baptist to hear his first sermon next Sunday.

The young Methodist Minister gives his first sermon on the following Sunday. After the sermon, the old Baptist Minister comes up and congratulates him.

He says:

"However, you did make a few mistakes."

Completely stoned, the Methodist Minister asks:

"Mistakes, wha's that?"

"Well," replies the old Baptist, "there were ten commandments – not twelve, there were twelve apostles – not ten, and the way I interpret the Bible, David killed Goliath with a slingshot – he didn't throw him down and tromp the shit out of him. And then when you got to the announcements, well, let's just put it this way, there's going to be a Taffy Pull at Saint Peter's next Thursday, and not vice versa."

Analysis:

Thank God for mistakes! Otherwise, we'd be in for a lot of boring sermons.

Vocabulary:

Bootleg – To make, sell, or transport (alcoholic liquor) for sale illegally.

Moonshine – Illegally distilled whiskey. Also called regionally white lightning. To distill and sell liquor illegally.

Podium – A stand for holding the notes of a public speaker; a lectern.

Repent – To feel remorse, contrition, or self-reproach for what one has done or failed to do; be contrite.

Revival – Bringing again into activity and prominence.

Rostrum – A dais, pulpit, or other elevated platform for public speaking.

Rural – Of, relating to, or characteristic of the country. The opposite of urban.

Stoned – Slang: Drunk or intoxicated.

Tromp – To tread heavily, especially to crush underfoot; to utterly defeat an opponent.

Union Theological Seminary – An independent college of theology, located in Manhattan, in New York City.

Urban – Relating to or concerned with a city or densely populated area. The opposite of rural.

Vice Versa – With the order or meaning reversed; conversely.

White Lightening – Slang for homemade whiskey, especially strong corn whiskey, typically colorless and usually not aged. Chiefly Southern U.S. See also *Moonshine* above.

The Mexican Bordello

The Joke:

Two American tourists visit a Mexican bordello. They enjoy themselves thoroughly. As they are about to leave, one has to use the men's bathroom. Finding it occupied, the visitor asks his buddy to stand guard while he uses the lady's rest room. A few minutes later, his buddy hears a loud scream. A few minutes later, his buddy appears through the door, doubled over in pain. He asks:

"Good Lord, what happened?"

His friend replies that he decided to try the three buttons on the stall. He says:

"When I pressed the first button, cologne sprayed my buttocks. Then, a towel dried my entire ass.

When I pressed the second button, a powder puff dusted my entire bottom with talcum powder.

Then I decided to try the third button. Before I could stop it, a rubber dildo hit me in the balls at least ten or twelve times."

Analysis:

Next time, learn to read *Spanish*. Serves you right.

Vocabulary:

Ass – Buttocks: the fleshy part of the human body that you sit on. Also, any of several hoofed mammals of the genus Equus, resembling and closely related to the horses but having a smaller build.

Balls – Slang for testicles.

Bordello – A whorehouse: a building where prostitutes are available.

Cologne – A perfumed toilet water made of alcohol and aromatic oils.

Dildo – A vibrating device that substitutes for an erect penis to provide vaginal stimulation.

Doubled Over – Bent over or curled up, usually with laughter or pain.

Serves You Right – As one deserves, especially to punish justly: It will serve you right if she never speaks to you again.

Stand Guard – Watch over so as to protect. To prevent anyone else from entering.

Talcum Powder – A fine, often perfumed powder made from purified talc for use on the skin.

A Hundred and Eleven

The Joke:
A man is traveling on a dirt road when his car breaks down. Walking down this dirt road, he finally spots a farmhouse. He knocks, and an older gentleman answers the door. He explains his situation, and asks to phone for a wrecker to come look at his car. The old farmer says that it's getting late in the afternoon, and it wouldn't be possible to find a garage still open which would come out this time of night.

However, for $ 25.00, he offers to give the young man room and board for the night. Tomorrow morning, he agrees to take the young man to town to find a garage. Tired, the young man readily agrees.

During supper, the young man can hardly avoid looking at the farmer's daughter. She is very good-looking and extremely nubile. After dinner, the old farmer and the young man retire to the parlor to have some brandy and smoke cigars. The old farmer says:

"During dinner, I noticed you were eying my daughter."

The young man starts to protest, but the old farmer cuts him off with:

"Sonny, you got any sporting blood in you?"

The young man nods affirmatively.

The old farmer then says:

"I'll make a bet with you. If you can get it off my daughter more times than I can get it off my wife, I'll let you spend the night for nothing. However, if I can get it from my wife more times than you get it off my daughter, you have to pay me double, or $ 50.00 for the night."

The young man accepts the wager.

That evening, the young man sleeps with the farmer's daughter. She is hell in bed, and turns him every way but loose. Two or three hours later, he does it again. Around five in the morning, he worries because the farmer might get it up twice. He decides to add a third time for insurance. Exhausted afterwards, he can only put three hash marks over the head of the bed.

The next morning, the old farmer comes bounding into the young man's bedroom and asks:

"Well, sonny, how'd you do?"

Too exhausted to do anything else, the young man points to the three hash marks over the bed.

The old farmer exclaims:

"A hundred and eleven. Damn, you beat me by one."

Analysis:

Actually, a hundred and ten times isn't bad – for an old man.

Vocabulary:

Bounding – To leap forward or upward; spring.

Brandy – An alcoholic liquor distilled from wine or fermented fruit juice.

Catalyst – A substance that initiates or accelerates a chemical reaction without itself being affected.

Fermented – The process of fermentation in wine is the catalyst function that turns grape juice into an alcoholic beverage. To speed fermentation, normally, some yeast or other catalyst is added.

Nubile – Sexually mature and attractive. Ready for marriage – used about young women.

Parlor – A room in a private home set apart for the entertainment of visitors.

Room and Board – Sleeping accommodations and meals.

Wager – Bet: stake on the outcome of an issue.

I Want To Buy a Skoda

The Joke:
A man walks into a car sales agency in England, and says:
"I want to buy a new Skoda."
The salesman says:
"Great! We have plenty of them in stock. But first we have to make sure that you are compatible with the car. You'll have to take a medical test. Don't worry; the agency will pay for it."
The man agrees to take a medical exam. After taking the test, he says:
"OK, now I'll take my Skoda."
The salesman says:
"Not so fast, we don't have the results back yet. Come back tomorrow morning."
The following morning, the man returns to the agency. He says:
"OK, now I'll take the Skoda.'
The salesman replies:
"Sorry, I can't sell it to you."
"Why?" asks the man.
"It says right here in the medical report that you've been circumcised, and it takes a perfect dork to buy a Skoda," retorts the salesman.

A second punch-line:
"It says right here in the medical report that you have hemorrhoids, and it takes a perfect asshole to buy a Skoda," retorts the salesman.

Analysis:
The use of the words *dork* and *asshole* are prime examples of double entendres.

Vocabulary:

Asshole – Vulgar slang for the anus. Also, a thoroughly contemptible, detestable person. It can mean either.

Circumcised – Male circumcision is the removal of some or the entire foreskin (prepuce) from the penis.

Dork – In slang, a stupid, inept, or foolish person. Also vulgar slang for the penis. It can mean either.

Euphemism – An inoffensive or indirect expression that is substituted for one that is considered offensive or too harsh. An example would be calling a janitor a sanitary engineer.

Foreskin – The fold of skin that covers the glans of the penis; prepuce: in circumcision it is completely or partly removed. See prepuce below.

Hemorrhoids – Swelling and inflammation of veins in the rectum and anus. It is characterized by puffy skin just outside the anus.

Penis – The male organ of copulation ('member' is a euphemism).

Prepuce – A loose fold of skin covering the glans clitoridis. It can pertain to either male or female anatomy. See foreskin above.

Retorts – To reply, especially to answer in a quick, caustic, or witty manner.

Skoda – A car famous for its unreliability and mechanical faults. The roots of this famous Czech automobile lay in the bicycle manufacturing business established by Vaclav. It is made in the Skoda Works in Czechoslovakia. It is named after Emil von Skoda (1839-1900), a Czech engineer and industrialist.

Ten Years from Now

The Joke:

A man in the former Soviet Union wants to buy a new car. He goes to the Soviet bureau of transportation to order it. He is informed that he will have to put his money down now, but there is a ten-year wait before he will receive the car. Nevertheless, he fills out the multiple forms and has them processed through the various agencies. He signs in countless places. Finally, he gets to the last agency where they put the stamp on all his papers. He pays them his money. They say:

"Come back in ten years and get your car."

He asks:

"Morning or afternoon?"

They say:

"We're talking about ten years from now. What difference does it make?"

He replies:

"The plumber is coming in the morning."

Analysis:

This joke is a lampoon against the Soviet economy. Whether it concerns a new car or just plumbing, it takes ten years.

Vocabulary:

Lampoon – To satirize: ridicule with satire.

Plumbing – The pipes, fixtures, and other apparatus of a water, gas, or sewage system in a building.

Soviet Union – A former federal republic in East Europe and central and North Asia: the revolution of 1917 achieved the overthrow of the Russian monarchy and the USSR was established in 1922 as a Communist state.

Ode to Obama, Reid and Pelosi

I do not like this Uncle Sam,

I do not like his health care scam,

I do not like these dirty crooks,

Or how they lie and cook the books,

I do not like when Congress steals.

I do not like their secret deals,

I do not like this speaker Nan,

I do not like this 'YES, WE CAN'.

I do not like this spending spree—

I'm smart; I know that nothing's free.

I do not like your smug replies,

When I complain about your lies.

I do not like this kind of hope.
I do not like it. Nope, nope, nope!

Go green – recycle Congress in 2010!

Note: The above copied from Jim Hall and his group. See murphyplus2@
hotmail.com.

Dirty Ditties

There once was a man from Kent,
Who had a dork so long it was bent.
It really was no trouble,
He just stuck it in double,
And instead of coming, he went.

There once was a man from Boston,
Who drove a little red Austin.
There was room for his ass,
And a gallon of gas,
But his balls hung out, and he lost 'em.

There once was a girl named Myrtle,
Who had an affair with a turtle.
Her swelling abdominal
Was really phenomenal,
Which proved that the turtle was fertile.

There once was a girl named Alice,
Who used a dynamite stick for a phallus.
They found her vagina
Over North Carolina,
And the rest of her ass over Dallas.

There once was a man from Nantucket,
Who had a dick so long that he could suck it.
As he said with a grin,
As he wiped off his chin,
If my ear were a cunt, I could fuck it.

There once was a man from Racine,
Who invented a masturbating machine.
On the eighty-ninth stroke,
The Goddamned thing broke,
And pounded his balls into cream.

There once was a man from Racine,
Who invented a screwing machine.
Both concave and convex,
It would fit either sex –
And could jerk itself off in between.

There once was a man named McFarr,
Who went to bed with a Hollywood star.
When he first saw her gashie,
He asked for his mashie –
And believed he could make it in par.

There once was a man named Dave,
Who kept a dead whore in his cave.
A bit of a shit,
You'll have to admit –
But think of the money he saved.

There once was a man named MacGruder,
Who wooed a girl from Bermuda.
The girl thought it crude,
To be wooed in the nude -
But MacGruder was cruder, he screwed her.

There once was a man named Cass,
Whose balls were made out of brass.
When he rubbed them together,
They played *Stormy Weather* –
And lightning shot out of his ass.

There once was a man named McNair,
Who was screwing his girl on the stair.
When the banister broke,
He re-doubled his stroke –
And finished her off in mid-air.

There once was a queer named Broom,
Who took a lesbian up to his room.
They argued all night,
As to who had the right –
To do what, and with which, and to whom.

There once was a senator from Mass,
Who was searching around for a lass.
He lucked out, and found her,
But he fucked up and drowned her –
And that was the end of his ass.

Old Mother Hubbard,
Went to the cupboard
To get her poor dog a bone
But when she bent over,
She caught it from Rover –
The dog had a bone of his own.

All men are one of a kind,
They fuck just for fun, but you find
Women are not just about,
To consider it without –
Some other motive in mind.

Short Takes

While she is shopping in a department store, a woman notices that the man next to her is shying away from her dog. She says: "Don't worry, he won't bite."

He says: "I know that, Lady, but I'm afraid from the way that he keeps raising his hind leg that he's going to kick me to death."

Why is it awful to be an egg?
1. You only get laid once.
2. You only get eaten once.
3. The only one who ever sits on your face is your own mother.
4. It takes 4 minutes to get hard. Only 2 minutes to get soft.
5. You come in a box with eleven others.

A Polish guy is out hunting in the woods. Suddenly he comes upon a clearing, and there before his eyes is a beautiful, totally naked woman.

She looks at him seductively, and says:

"I'm game!"

So he shoots her.

Two Polish men rent a rowboat and go fishing on a lake. They catch quite a few fish, and have almost two dozen by the end of the afternoon. One man says to the other:

"Why don't we come back to the very same place tomorrow?"

"Great idea," his friend answers.

So the first man takes a piece of chalk, and draws an "X" on the bottom of the boat.

"Don't be stupid!" The friend says. "How do you know that we'll get the same boat tomorrow?"

A Polish guy comes home early from work, and finds his wife in bed with another man. He runs over to the dresser and pulls out a gun. He then puts it up to his own head.

When his wife starts laughing, the husband says:

"Don't laugh, you're next."

Two men are playing golf at a country club. One of the men is just about to sink an important putt, when he looks up and sees a funeral procession going by. He stops, straightens up, takes off his golf cap, and holds it over his heart until the procession has gone by.

As he puts his hat back on his head, his friend says:

"That was a really nice thoughtful gesture."

As the man returns to his putt, he says:

"After twenty years of marriage, it's the least I could do."

A woman calls her butler into her bedroom. She says:

"Charles, take off my dress."

"Yes, Madam," he replies, and removes the dress.

"Charles, take off my bra." She says.

"Yes, Madam," he replies, and removes the bra.

"Charles, take off my shoes and stockings." She says.

"Yes, Madam," he replies, and removes the shoes and stockings.

"Now, take off my panties," she says.

"Yes, Madam," he replies, and removes the panties.

She then says:

"I'm warning you, Charles. If I ever catch you wearing my clothes again, you're fired!"

An Anglican minister arrives at JFK Airport. He gets a devout Irish Catholic cabdriver for his trip into the city. The Anglican minister says:

"Take me to the Christ Church in Manhattan, please."

The cabbie drives from the airport into Manhattan, goes straight up Fifth Avenue, and stops in front of St. Patrick's Cathedral. The minister is incensed. He says:

"Sir, I asked you to take me to the Christ Church!"

The cabbie replies:

"Pastor, I know this town well. If He's home at all, He'll be in Saint Patrick's!"

A troop ship docks during the Korean War. After awhile, an argument breaks out between a soldier and his wife standing on the dock. She keeps shouting: "EF." And he keeps shouting back: "FF." This argument has been going on for quite some time, when a soldier turns and asks his sergeant what is going on.

"Oh," He responds: "she wants to eat first."

229

What bird is traditionally associated with warlike tendencies and aggression?
The Hawk.
What bird is associated with peace and love?
The Dove.
What bird is traditionally associated with childbirth and the delivery of children?
The Stork.
What bird is associated with birth control?
The Swallow.

A boy surprises his parents making love. He asks:
"What are you doing?"
His father answers:
"Son, we're making a baby brother or sister for you."
The Son replies:
"Well, could you turn mommy over, Dad?
I think I'd rather have a puppy."

A madam is giving her girls instructions on their coming move to Las Vegas. She says:
"Josie, you were $25 here in New York, but you're going to be $50 in Las Vegas. Madeline, you were $50 here in New York, and you're going to be $100 in Las Vegas. And Mary, you're $10 here and you're going to be $10 there – until you learn that the customer comes first."

Yes, I've been married seventeen years. If I'd strangled her on the first night, I'd be out by now.

I miss my ex-, but my aim is improving.

I'd like to help you out – which way did you come in?

Get in, sit down, buckle up, and shut up.

Everybody pays to ride in this car – gas, grass, or ass?

Save a tree, eat a beaver.

How's my driving – call 1-800-EAT-SHIT!

Gun control means using both hands.

Guns don't kill people, drivers with cell phones do.

My other auto is a 9mm.

A man once said to me: "Remember, if it's got either tits or tires, it's going to cost you a lot of money and cause you a lot of heartache!"

A little boy and little girl are taking a bath. Suddenly, the little girl breaks out into tears and says:
"Mommy, I don't have one of those."
Her mother says:
"Don't worry, if you have one of these (pulling up her dress), you can get all of those you want."

A Scottish drunk is passed out at the curb. Three ladies pass by on their way to church. Curious, one of the ladies goes over to see what the drunk has under his kilt. Horrified, she jumps back. Then she removes a blue ribbon from her hair, and ties it around his private part. Then she goes back across the street, and she and her friends proceed to church. A few hours later, the drunkard wakes up and goes to the woods to urinate. He lifts his kilt – Then he says:
"I don't know where you've been Laddie, but you won first prize!"

A husband and wife are getting ready for bed. After they get in bed, the man gets up again, and goes into the bathroom. He comes back with a glass of water and two aspirin. He gets back in bed, and holds out the water and aspirin to his wife. She says:
"What are those for?"
"They're for you." He replies.
The wife says:
"Why? I don't have a headache."
The husband smiles, and says:
"Right, gotcha!"

New Zealand – That's where the men are men, and the sheep are afraid.

Please engage brain before opening mouth.

A young bull is talking to an older colleague and looking at a herd of young heifers:

"Let's run down, leap over the fence, and get us one of those cows."

The older bull responds:

"Let's walk down, roll under the fence, and get all of those cows."

A man talking to his boss: If only the good die young, you've got to be immortal.

Two lawyers are standing at a bar having a drink together. Suddenly a young, beautiful woman walks into the room. One of the lawyers leans over to the other one and whispers:

"Man, I sure would love to screw her."

The other lawyer whispers back:

"Out of what?"

A man walks up to a lady on the street and asks:

"Can I paint you in the nude?"

She replies:

"But, I'm not a model."

"That's okay; I'm not really an artist either," says the man.

A blonde is driving down a road. Suddenly, she sees another blonde sitting in a rowboat in the middle of a field. She pulls the car over to the side of the road. She gets out, and says:

"It's blondes like you that give the rest of us a bad name. And if I could just swim, I'd swim out there and kick your ass."

Sign on the wall of an automotive repair shop:

Tune-up $15, $25 if you watch, $35 if you help

A man chases every woman in the neighborhood. The other wives decide that it's time to clue his wife in. They find her in the kitchen, and inform her of the situation. She does not seem perturbed. She says:

"Oh, I know all about that."

One of the women asks:

"You know all about this? And it doesn't disturb you?"

The wife answers affirmatively.

The head of the delegation asks:

"Why?"

"Well," responds the wife, "You see that dog under the table? He chases every car that comes down the street, but if he ever caught one, he wouldn't know how to operate it."

There are three types of orgasm:
1. The religious orgasm – Oh God, Oh God, Oh God!
2. The positive orgasm – Oh Yes, Oh Yes, Oh Yes!
3. The fake orgasm – Oh Jim, Oh Jim, Oh Jim!

There are four kinds of foreplay:
1. Australian foreplay – Brace yourself, Sheila.
2. American foreplay – Ready or not, here I come.
3. Black foreplay – Wake up, bitch.
4. Jewish foreplay – Half an hour of begging.

It is just after the fall, and Adam has just finished making love to Eve. God happens by, and asks:

"Hi, Adam, where's Eve?"

Adam replies:

"We just finished making love, so Eve is down in the creek washing up."

"Oh, no!" exclaims God, "Now, all of the fish will smell like that."

God says to Adam: "I have some good news, and some bad news.

First the good news: I gave you a large brain and a large penis.

Now the bad news: I only gave you enough blood to operate one at a time."

Scientists have discovered a food that instantly diminishes a woman's sex drive by 90%. It's called Wedding Cake.

The government announced that its new emblem is going to be a condom.

It more clearly represents what the government does. A condom stands up to inflation, halts production, destroys the next generation, protects a bunch of pricks, and gives you a sense of security while its screwing you.

On a crowded airliner, a five-year-old boy is throwing a wild temper tantrum. No matter what his frustrated, embarrassed mother does to try to calm him down, the boy continues to scream furiously and kick the seats around him.

Suddenly, from the rear of the plane, an elderly minister slowly walks forward up the aisle. Stopping the flustered mother with an upraised hand, the minister leans down and whispers something into the boy's ear. Instantly, the boy calms down, gently takes his mother's hand and quietly fastens his own seatbelt.

As the minister slowly makes his way back to his seat, one of the stewardesses takes him by the sleeve and asks:

"Excuse me, Reverend, but what magic words did you use on that little boy?"

The old man smiles, and gently says:

"I told him that if he didn't cut that shit out, I'd kick his fucking ass to the moon."

Sweden was the only European country to switch from driving on the right (like the English) to driving on the left (like the French). The Polish sent over an observation team. The Swedish set a time of 3 am in the morning of a certain day when all the bells were rung all over the country. All the vehicles pulled over to the side of the road. Ten minutes later, the bells were rung all over the country again and all the vehicles pulled over to the other side of the road and proceeded to drive on.

The Polish Observation Team recommended the same approach. At 3 am, bells all over Poland would be rung. All cars would pull over to the side of the road. Ten minutes later, bells would ring all over Poland and all the cars would pull across the road and keep going. If that worked, one week later they would switch over all the trucks.

A jockey develops a reputation for bringing home horses that are long-shots as winners. He is besieged by reporters, and finally consents to an interview. He is asked by the reporters:

"Do you have any secret to bringing home as winners these long-shot horses?"

He confirms that he does indeed have a secret, namely that he recites poetry to the animals during the races. Asked for a sample by the reporters, he recites:

"Roses are red,
Violets are blue,
Horses that lose,
Are made into glue."

A man down on his luck goes on to his wife and tells her:

"Look, dear, we're low on money now, and we're going to have to cut down on some luxuries."

He then adds scornfully:

"If you would learn how to cook, we could fire the chef."

Retorts his wife:

"In that case, if you would learn how to make love, we could fire the chauffeur."

A metal worker receives an order from a chemical manufacturer for a number of very large cages. When the man delivers the cages to the factory, he is ordered to set them up in the laboratory. He asks the scientist what he will be keeping in the cages.

"Oh," says the scientist, "we're going to be using some lawyers for some very dangerous experiments."

"But," replies the man, "don't you usually use rats for these experiments?"

"Yes," says the scientist, "but you know, you get so attached to the rats."

A schoolteacher is attempting to find out what her pupil's parents do for a living. She is getting the usual responses – lawyer, doctor, chief of the fire department, etc. When she reaches little Joseph, he responds that his father plays the piano in a whorehouse. Shocked and embarrassed, the schoolteacher switches the subject to history.

After school, the teacher visits Joseph's house and knocks on the door. Joseph's father answers it and says:

"Yes? Can I help you?"

She says:

"Your son Joseph is in my third-grade class. What is this I hear about you playing a piano in a whorehouse for living?"

Responds the father:

"Actually, I'm a lawyer, but you can't tell *that* to an eight-year-old kid."

One day the Pope gets a message from God. God says to him:

"Since you have been such a good Pope, I wanted you to be the first to he know."

"The first to know what?" says the Pope.

God says:

"I have some good news and some bad news. The good news is that I have decided that from now on, the world will have only one religion."

"That's wonderful!" says the Pope. "Now everyone will be peaceful and get along with one another. That's great! But what's the bad news?"

God says:

"In a few days, you will be receiving a phone call from Salt Lake City."

A student asks whether light bulbs are good to eat. The teacher:

"No, of course not – why do you ask?"

The student:

"I was passing by the master bedroom, and I heard Dad say: 'Turn out the light, and I'll eat it.'"

A man and a woman are attending the same cocktail party. She says:

"You know, you look just like my third husband."

"Oh, really?" he says. "How many times have you been married?"

"Twice." she replies.

Two gay men are watching a dog licking his balls. One says to the other:

"I wish I could do that."

The other replies:

"I think you'd better pet him on the head first."

Then, there was the case of the dyslexic atheist. He wrote:

"There is no Dog!"

The newlywed man goes into the master bedroom. He grabs a pillow, a blanket, and some sheets. He goes back to the living room, and starts to make his bed on the couch. His wife comes out a few minutes later, and asks:

"What are you doing out here?"

"Honey, it's Lent." He replies.

"Oh, no!" she exclaims, "To whom, and for how long?"

A little girl accompanies her father to the barber shop.

The little girl starts to consume a Twinkie. Then she decides to go close to her father. The barber notices her and says:

"Sweetheart, you're going to get hair on your Twinkie."

She smiles sweetly and replies:

"I know. I'm going to get boobies on my chest, too."

A woman goes into a card shop. She walks around and around, looking at all the different displays. She finally goes over to the manager. He says:

"May I help you, miss?"

She replies:

"I'm not sure; do you have any 'Sorry I Laughed at Your Dick' cards?"

A young boy is in the bathtub, studying his penis. He says to his mother:
"Mommy, is this my brain?"
His mother looks down, and says:
"No, son. Not yet."

The musician Prince is final conclusive proof that Jimi Hendrix actually did screw Liberace.

The cowboy is final conclusive proof that the American Indian did screw the buffalo.

A client asks a prostitute, after having unprotected sex with her:
"How was I?"
The prostitute responds:
"I have some bad news and some good news for you."
The client says:
"What's that?"
The prostitute says:
"You're better than Magic Johnson."

A man catches his wife in bed with his best friend. He is thoroughly irate, tells his wife off in no uncertain terms, and orders her to leave his house and never return. Then, he turns to his best friend and says:
"As for you – Bad dog! Bad dog! Bad dog!"

A nun gets on a bus in midtown Manhattan. She walks right past the fare box, and doesn't put anything in. The bus driver says:

"Will the lady who forgot to pay her fare come up and put it in now?"

Receiving no response, he cranks up the bus and proceeds to the next stop.

When he reaches it, he says:

"Will the lady dressed all in black who forgot to pay her fare two stops ago please come up and put it in now?"

Again receiving no response, he cranks up the bus and proceeds to the next stop. By this time, the nun has taken out her Bible, and is reading it.

Upon reaching the next stop, the driver says:

"Will the lady dressed all in black, wearing a rosary, who is reading her Bible, who forgot to pay her fare three stops ago please come up and put it in now." The man sitting next to her says:

"Excuse me, Sister, but I think he is referring to you."

Without turning her head, the nun says:

"I know, fuck him!"

A man is thinking of entering this contest at the local bar to see who has the longest dick. He tells his wife, and she says:

"Dear, I don't want you exposing that thing in public."

He says:

"But honey, first prize is $100."

She answers:

"I don't care. I still don't want you to display that whole thing in public."

He goes and wins the contest, anyway. When he comes home that night, he confesses to his wife. She says:

"You didn't take out that entire thing, did you?"

He replies:

"Shucks no, honey, just enough to win!"

A man and his wife go to their honeymoon hotel for their 25th anniversary.

She says: "Twenty-five years ago, what were you thinking on that first night?"

He replies: "I was thinking that I was going to fuck your brains out."

She asks: "And what are you thinking now?"

He replies: "Well, I guess it must have worked."

There are four kinds of sex:

HOUSE SEX – When you are newly married and have sex all over the house in every room.

BEDROOM SEX – After you have been married for a while, you only have sex in the bedroom.

HALL SEX – After you've been married for many, many years you just pass each other in the hall and say "FUCK YOU".

COURTROOM SEX – When your wife and her lawyer fuck you in the divorce court in front of many people for every penny you've got.

A man and a woman started to have sex in the middle of a dark forest. After about 15 minutes of it, the man finally gets up and says: "Damn, I wish I had a flashlight!" The woman says: "Me too, you've been eating grass for the past ten minutes!"

One day Mr. Johnson, the president, called his vice-president, Jim, into his office and says: "We have to make some cutbacks, so either Jack or Evelyn will have to be laid off." Jim looks at Mr. Johnson and says: "Evelyn is one of my best workers, but Jack has a wife and two kids. I'm really in a quandary. I don't know who I want to fire." The next morning Jim waits for his employees to arrive. Evelyn arrives first, so Jim says: "Evelyn, I've got a problem. You see, I've got to lay you or Jack off and I don't know what to do." Evelyn replies: "You'd better jack off, then. Because you're not touching me!"

For two years, a young attorney had been taking his vacations at this country inn. The last time he'd finally had an affair with the innkeeper's daughter. Looking forward to an exciting few days, he dragged his suitcase up the stairs of the inn. Then he stopped short.

There sat his lover with an infant on her lap! "Helen, why didn't you write when you learned you were pregnant?" he cried. "I would have rushed up here, we could have gotten married, and the baby would have my name!"

"Well," she said, "when my folks found out about my condition, we sat up all night talking and talking and decided it would be better to have a bastard in the family than a lawyer."

A lawyer is standing in a long line at the box office. Suddenly, he feels a pair of hands kneading his shoulders, back, and neck. The lawyer turns around. "What the hell do you think you're doing?" "I'm a chiropractor, and I'm just keeping in practice while I'm waiting in line." "Well, I'm a lawyer, but you don't see me screwing the guy in front of me, do you?"

Richard Nixon, Jimmy Carter, and Bill Clinton are on the titanic. When it starts to sink Carter yells, "Quick, save the women and children!" Nixon: "Screw the women and children" Clinton: "Do we have time?"

Monica Lewinsky wants to have a dress cleaned. She takes the dress to the dry cleaner's, and says:
"I'd like this dress cleaned."
The guy behind the counter is about ninety years old, and somewhat deaf.
Cupping his hand behind one ear, he says:
"Come again."
Monica replies:
"No, mustard this time."

Signs posted on Churches:
God so loved the world that He did not send a committee.
It is unlikely there'll be a reduction in the wages of sin.
No God — No Peace. Know God — Know Peace.
Fight truth decay — study the Bible daily.
Free Trip to heaven. Details Inside!
If you're headed in the wrong direction, God allows U-turns.
How will you spend eternity — Smoking or Non-smoking?
Have trouble sleeping? We have sermons — come hear one!

The town fathers were looking for a way to increase attendance and participation at their regular meetings. One member suggested bringing in a hypnotist. The officials agreed, a famous hypnotist was hired, publicity distributed, and everyone was pleased.

A few weeks later the meeting hall was packed, and the town's people sat fascinated as the hypnotist withdrew a pocket watch. The hypnotist began chanting… "Watch the watch, watch the watch, watch the watch…"

The crowd became mesmerized as the watch swayed back and forth, light gleaming off its polished surface. Hundreds of pairs of eyes followed the swaying watch, until suddenly the hypnotist's fingers slipped and the watch fell to the floor…

"Oh, shit!" said the hypnotist.

It took three weeks to clean up the town hall.

A man is seated in a movie theater next to a gorgeous blonde. He tries putting his hand on her knee, but she brushes him away. Curious, he looks to see who she is with. It turns out that she is with Al Capone, but old Scarface is thoroughly absorbed in the movie. He decides to try again. Once again, he places his hand on the knee of the gorgeous blonde. Once again, she pushes his hand away, but this time she scribbles him a note on a matchbook and sneaks it to him. He opens the book of matches, and it reads:

"When you get to the balls, act natural! Elliott Ness."

One day a man was waking along the beach when he tripped over a lamp. He turned around and kicked the lamp again out of anger. A few seconds later, a genie popped out of the lamp, but the genie was angry that the man had kicked his lamp.

Reluctantly, the genie said, "Even though you kicked me, I still have to give you three wishes. However because of what you did, I will also give double what you wish for to the person you hate the most: your boss."

So the man agreed and made his first wish. "I want lots of money", he said. Instantly 22 million dollars appear in the man's bank account and 44 million appeared in his boss' account.

For his second wish, the man wished for a couple of sports cars. Instantly a Lamborghini, Ferrari and a Porsche appeared, but at the same time outside his boss' house appeared two of each car.

Finally the genie said, "This is your last wish, you should choose carefully", and so the man replied… "I've always wanted to donate a kidney…"

Three black dudes are urinating off a bridge. The first dude exclaims:
"Man, dat dere water cold!"
The second dude:
"Yeah, deep, too."
The third dude:
"Yeah, muddy, too."

A young lady received a red-wood cedar splinter in her derriere while she was playing around on her back porch. She decided to visit a doctor to have it removed. The doctor prescribed some pills, and told her to come back next week. She asked why the doctor didn't just pull out the splinter. The doctor replied that it was too much government paperwork, explaining:
"Before you can remove a redwood from a recreation area in the State of California, you have to file an Environmental Impact Statement."

Here's to the girl in the little red shoes.
She hasn't got her cherry, but that's no sin,
She still has the box that it came in.

Diapers and politicians should be changed frequently – and for the same reason.

"Behind every successful man stands a surprised mother-in-law."
Voltaire

A teacher instructs her middle-school class to come up to the blackboard and write something that causes excitement. When it comes little Johnnie's turn, he comes up to the blackboard and makes a single dot. When asked by the teacher what's so exciting about that, Johnnie explains that it's not a dot, but a period. When the teacher says that she still doesn't see what is exciting about a period, Johnnie replies:

"I don't know either, but I heard my older sister say to my father that she had missed two periods in a row. You should see what kind of excitement that caused around our house!"

A father was fed up with cursing around the house, so he told his two sons that the first one who used another curse word the next morning would receive a beating. The next morning, he asked the oldest son what he wanted for breakfast. He replied that he wanted some damned cereal. The father was outraged, beat him, and told him to go to school without any breakfast. Then the father turned to the second son and asked what he wanted for breakfast. The second son replied:

"Whatever it is, you bet your sweet ass that I don't want any of that damned cereal that got my brother a beating."

The best thing about a Yugo is its rear window heater. It makes it possible to keep your hands warm while you're pushing the car.

A man ran his hand over the bald head of an employee, and said:
"Hmmm, it feels just like my wife's keister."
Unperturbed, the employee ran his hand over his bald pate, and said;
"So it does, so it does."

Rastus is climbing a mountain when he loses his footing. Falling, he reaches out and grabs a branch protruding from a cliff. He cries:
"Lord, Lord, save me!"
A voice above him answers:
"Rastus, do you believe?"
Rastus answers:
"Oh, yes, Lord – I believes!"
The voice queries:
"Rastus, do you believe I delivered Daniel from the Lion's den?"
Rastus answers:
"Oh, yes, Lord – I believes!"
The voice continues:
"And Jonah from the mouth of the whale?"
Rastus answers:
"Oh, yes, Lord – I believes!"
The voice says:
"Rastus, let go that branch!"
Rastus responds:
"Is there anyone else up there?"

The following story is based on the theory that women are contentious by nature:

If you marry one woman, she will nag you to death.

If you marry two women, they will fight over you constantly, and you won't have any peace.

If you marry three women, two of them will gang up on the third, and you won't have any peace either.

But if you marry four women, they will pair off and make friends with each other. There will be peace and harmony in the harem, and they will leave you alone.

Though humorous, the above story is false. Actually, the Islamic population had been depleted by wars. Thus, there were many more available women than there were available men. This situation was resolved by allowing each man to have four wives. In other words, this was done to counterbalance a

Shortage of males in the Islamic population.

Queen Victoria decided that it was time to pick a quarrel with Siam (presently called Thailand), and take the country over for England. Accordingly, she sent a new ambassador to Thailand with very specific instructions. After presenting his credentials to the King (Rama IV or King Mongkut), the new English ambassador proposed an exchange of gifts – England could request anything from Thailand, and in return Thailand could request anything from England. The King said that since it was England's proposal, England should choose first. The English ambassador chose the Emerald Buddha. Since the Emerald Buddha was considered the symbol of the country, several courtiers placed their hands upon the hilts of their swords. They looked to the King for permission to dispatch this arrogant foreigner. After the King had been successful in dissuading his courtiers from violence and re-establishing calm in his court, he gave permission for England to have the Emerald Buddha. Taken aback, the English ambassador asked what Thailand would like in return. The King replied that Thailand would like the Emerald Buddha back. Supposedly, Queen Victoria was so impressed by this story that she decided to leave Thailand as a buffer state between Burma and French Indo-China. In other words, she decided to leave the Thais alone.

Supposedly, the above story is true. Unfortunately, most of the Thai people themselves are ignorant of this tale.

Actually, the word *Siam* means *South* in Chinese. Since Thailand is unique in Asia in maintaining its freedom from foreign domination, the word *Thai* in the Thai language means *free*. This resulted in the renaming of the country in 1939 to Thailand or "land of the free."

Among its many distinctions is the voluntary abolition of slavery. Every slave born before a certain date would remain a slave. Every child born to a slave family after a certain date would be free.

A farmer and a lawyer suffered a head-on collision. They both staggered out of their wrecked cars. The farmer returned to his car, took out a package containing some whiskey, and came back. He said:

"Here, you look pretty badly shaken up. I think you ought to have a sip of this. It'll steady your nerves."

So the lawyer did. At the farmer's urging, he had several more drinks. Finally, he was feeling no pain. He noticed that the farmer wasn't drinking, so he asked if he didn't want a little nip too.

The farmer replied:

"No thanks, I'm waiting for the highway patrolman."

Two campers were hiking when they spotted a grizzly bear in the distance. One camper immediately dropped his knapsack, took out a pair of tennis shoes and started to put them on. The other camper asked:

"What are you doing? You can't possibly outrun a grizzly bear."

His friend replied:

"I don't have to outrun the grizzly bear. I just have to outrun you."

There is only room for one more in Heaven, but there are three applicants – a surgeon, an engineer, and an economist. Saint Peter decides to give the opening to the oldest profession.

The surgeon stepped forward, and said:

"I'm your man. Right after God created Adam, he operated. He created Eve from Adam's rib. So surgery has to be the oldest profession."

The engineer protested:

"No. You see, before God created Adam and Eve, he took the chaos that prevailed and built the earth in six days. So engineering had to precede surgery."

Finally, the economist spoke up and said:

"Wait a minute. Who do you think created all that chaos?"

Mirabeau, a French revolutionary, once said that Talleyrand "would sell his soul for money, and he would be right, for he would be exchanging dung for gold."

"The income tax has made more liars out of the American people than golf has." Will Rogers

"We declared war on poverty and poverty won." Ronald Reagan

"History shows that over a long period of time government will spend whatever the tax system raises plus as much more as it can get away with."
Milton Friedman

Gaffe: One of those infrequent occasions when politicians tell the truth.

Historically, women are responsible for civilizing men. Were it not for women, men would still be living in caves and running around in skin tights carrying clubs.

An elderly man was trying to help the victim of an accident lying on the sidewalk. Suddenly, he was shoved aside by someone pushing his way to forefront. The intruder said:
"Let me at him. I was just trained in first aid."
The elderly fellow obliged, and the newcomer began carrying out the steps he had learned in first aid class. At one point the old guy tapped the newcomer on the shoulder and said:
"When you get to the part about calling a doctor, I'm right here."

Niccolo Machiavelli was dying. They called a priest to give Machiavelli the Last Rites. Upon arriving, the priest urged Machiavelli to repent of his sins and renounce Satan. Eyes closed, Machiavelli said nothing. Again the priest said more loudly:
"Will you repent of your sins and renounce Satan?"
Opening one eye, Machiavelli whispered:
"Father, at a time like this, one tries not to make new enemies."

"I'm an excellent housekeeper. Every time I get a divorce, I keep the house." Zsa Zsa Gabor

Paraprosdokian Sentences

A **Paraprosdokian** is a figure of speech in which the latter part of a sentence or phrase is surprising or unexpected in a way that causes the reader or listener to reframe or reinterpret the first part. It is frequently used for humorous or dramatic effect, sometimes producing an anticlimax.

I asked God for a bike, but I know God doesn't work that way. So I stole a bike and asked for forgiveness.

Do not argue with an idiot. He will drag you down to his level and beat you with experience.

I want to die peacefully in my sleep, like my grandfather. Not screaming and yelling like the passengers in his car.

Going to church doesn't make you a Christian any more than standing in a garage makes you a car.

The last thing I want to do is hurt you. But it's still on the list.

Light travels faster than sound. This is why some people appear bright until you hear them speak.

If I agreed with you we'd both be wrong.

We never really grow up; we only learn how to act in public.

War does not determine who is right – only who is left.

Knowledge knows a tomato is a fruit; Wisdom is not putting it in a fruit salad.

The early bird might get the worm, but the second mouse gets the cheese.

Evening news is where they begin with 'Good evening', and then proceed to tell you why it isn't.

To steal ideas from one person is plagiarism. To steal from many is research.

A bus station is where a bus stops. A train station is where a train stops. On my desk, I have a work station.

How is it that one careless match can start a forest fire, but it takes a whole box to start a campfire?

Some people are like Slinkies ... not really good for anything, but you can't help smiling when you see one tumble down the stairs.

Dolphins are so smart that within a few weeks of captivity, they can train people to stand on the very edge of the pool and throw them fish.

I thought I wanted a career; turns out I just wanted pay checks.
A bank is a place that will lend you money, if you can prove that you don't need it.

Whenever I fill out an application, in the part that says "If an emergency, notify:" I put "DOCTOR".

I didn't say it was your fault, I said I was blaming you.

I saw a woman wearing a sweat shirt with "Guess" on it...so I said "Implants?"

Why does someone believe you when you say there are four billion stars, but check when you say the paint is wet?

Women will never be equal to men until they can walk down the street with a bald head and a beer gut, and still think they are sexy.

Why do Americans choose from just two people to run for president and 50 for Miss America?

Behind every successful man is his woman. Behind the fall of a successful man is usually another woman.

A clear conscience is usually the sign of a bad memory.

You do not need a parachute to skydive. You only need a parachute to skydive twice.

The voices in my head may not be real, but they have some good ideas!

Always borrow money from a pessimist. He won't expect it back.

A diplomat is someone who can tell you to go to hell in such a way that you will look forward to the trip.

Hospitality: making your guests feel like they're at home, even if you wish they were.

Money can't buy happiness, but it sure makes misery easier to live with.

I discovered I scream the same way whether I'm about to be devoured by a great white shark or if a piece of seaweed touches my foot.

Some cause happiness wherever they go. Others whenever they go.

There's a fine line between cuddling and holding someone down so they can't get away.
I used to be indecisive. Now I'm not sure.

I always take life with a grain of salt, plus a slice of lime, & a shot of tequila.

When tempted to fight fire with fire, remember that the Fire Department usually uses water.

You're never too old to learn something stupid.

To be sure of hitting the target, shoot first, call whatever you hit the target.

Nostalgia isn't what it used to be.

Some people hear voices. Some see invisible people. Others have no imagination whatsoever.

A bus is a vehicle that runs twice as fast when you are after it as when you are in it.

Change is inevitable, except from a vending machine.
If you are supposed to learn from your mistakes, why do some people have more than one child?

Dinner Invocation

This senior lady (Mary Maxwell), a resident of a retirement community (Home Instead), was asked to give the invocation at a dinner/convention of retirement community managers. She does so, but then decides to add a few words of her own as a part of her invocation. Enjoy!

After giving a standard invocation, the lady proceeded to add the following remarks.

As long as I have the microphone, there are a few things that I forgot to mention. First of all, just to introduce myself a little, over the years I've noticed that the two things most people want to know about you are the two things that they're far too polite to ask. So let's get that out of the way. I'm 72 years old. And I weigh 145 lbs.

As you know, we seniors are not very likeable – let alone lovable. So Lord, could you please continue to keep people at home patient and aware of the way we are? And Lord, please remind them that the thing about old age is that you don't get a chance to practice.

This is the first time I've ever been old. And it just sort of crept up on me. There were signs. Random hair growth – that's special. Particularly that first time you go to brush a hair off your lapel and discover it's attached to your chin. You turn your left turn signal on in the morning and leave it on all day. Non life-threatening skin growths large enough to name after deceased pets and relatives begin to appear. And neck tissue seems to develop a life of its own.

Last November, I was afraid to leave the house Thanksgiving week. Aren't you quick? You do strange things as you age, like driving up to a curbside mailbox and ordering a cheeseburger and fries. And Lord, I know you're aware that one Sunday at church I put my Dillard's bill in the collection basket by mistake.

And last Easter after services at St. Cecilia's Cathedral here in Omaha, my husband stopped to speak to a friend and I went on out to the car to go home. The gentleman sitting behind the wheel said: "Oh, are you going home with me?" And I said: "Oh, Archbishop, I'm so sorry!"

I won't even mention driving into the wrong end of the carwash. People get so excited when you do that. I don't know why the lady in the other car was screaming like that. I was just as surprised to see her as she was to see me. I also won't mention discovering that you're wearing mismatched earrings, and going home to change them – and ending up wearing the other mismatched pair.

254

And you know, Lord that it's hard for old people to exercise. I did try to jog once, but it make's the wine just jump right out of your glass. Well, Lord, you understand seniors and their care. And so does Home Instead.

And I have here a poem I found in a local retirement home newsletter that I have always thought spoke volumes about Home Instead:

Blessed are they, who understand my faltering step and shaking hand,
Blessed are they, who know my ears today must strain the things they say,
Blessed are they, who seem to know that my eyes are dim and my wits are slow,
Blessed are they, who looked away when I spilled coffee at table today,
Blessed are they, with cheery smiles, who take the time to chat for awhile,
Blessed are they, who know the ways to bring back memories of yesterdays,
Blessed are they, who make it known I'm loved, respected and not alone.

Just like you. To us, it's Christmas. That's Home Instead, Lord. Bless them all. And at the end of the evening, please help me find my car in the parking lot.
Amen.

The below was written by Regina Brett, 90 years old, of the Plain Dealer, Cleveland, Ohio.

"To celebrate growing older, I once wrote the 45 lessons life taught me. It is the most requested column I've ever written.
My odometer rolled over to 90 in August, so here is the column once more:
1. Life isn't fair, but it's still good.
2. When in doubt, just take the next small step.
3. Life is too short to waste time hating anyone.
4. Your job won't take care of you when you are sick. Your friends and parents will. Stay in touch.
5. Pay off your credit cards every month.
6. You don't have to win every argument. Agree to disagree.
7. Cry with someone. It's more healing than crying alone.
8. It's OK to get angry with God. He can take it.
9. Save for retirement starting with your first paycheck.
10. When it comes to chocolate, resistance is futile.
11. Make peace with your past so it won't screw up the present.
12. It's OK to let your children see you cry.
13. Don't compare your life to others. You have no idea what their journey is all about.
14. If a relationship has to be a secret, you shouldn't be in it.
15. Everything can change in the blink of an eye. But don't worry; God never blinks.
16. Take a deep breath. It calms the mind.
17. Get rid of anything that isn't useful, beautiful or joyful.
18. Whatever doesn't kill you really does make you stronger.
19. It's never too late to have a happy childhood. But the second one is up to you and no one else.
20. When it comes to going after what you love in life, don't take no for an answer.
21. Burn the candles, use the nice sheets, and wear the fancy lingerie. Don't save it for a special occasion. Today is special.
22. Over prepare, and then go with the flow.
23. Be eccentric now. Don't wait for old age to wear purple.
24. The most important sex organ is the brain.
25. No one is in charge of your happiness but you.
26. Frame every so-called disaster with these words 'In five years, will this matter?'
27. Always choose life.

28. Forgive everyone everything.
29. What other people think of you is none of your business.
30. Time heals almost everything. Give time time.
31. However good or bad a situation is, it will change.
32. Don't take yourself so seriously. No one else does.
33. Believe in miracles.
34. God loves you because of who God is, not because of anything you did or didn't do.
35. Don't audit life. Show up and make the most of it now.
36. Growing old beats the alternative — dying young.
37. Your children get only one childhood.
38. All that truly matters in the end is that you loved.
39. Get outside every day. Miracles are waiting everywhere.
40. If we all threw our problems in a pile and saw everyone else's, we'd grab ours back.
41. Envy is a waste of time. You already have all you need.
42. The best is yet to come…
43. No matter how you feel, get up, dress up and show up.
44. Yield.
45. Life isn't tied with a bow, but it's still a gift."

Note: we are indebted for the last eight pages to David R. Gibson of DRG Associates. He can be reached at: davegibson@msn.com

A SPANISH Teacher was explaining to her class that in Spanish, unlike English, nouns are designated as either masculine or feminine. 'House' for instance, is feminine: 'la casa.' 'Pencil,' however, is masculine: 'el lapiz.'

A student asked, 'What gender is 'computer'?' Instead of giving the answer, the teacher split the class into two groups, male and female, and asked them to decide for themselves whether computer' should be a masculine or a feminine noun. Each group was asked to give four reasons for its recommendation.

The men's group decided that 'computer' should definitely be of the feminine gender ('la computadora'), because:
1. No one but their creator understands their internal logic.
2. The native language they use to communicate with other computers is incomprehensible to everyone else.
3. Even the smallest mistakes are stored in long term memory for possible later retrieval.
4. As soon as you make a commitment to one, you find yourself spending half your paycheck on accessories for it.

(THIS GETS BETTER!)

The women's group, however, concluded that computers should be Masculine ('el computador'), because:
1. In order to do anything with them, you have to turn them on.
2. They have a lot of data but still can't think for themselves.
3. They are supposed to help you solve problems, but half the time they ARE the problem.
4. As soon as you commit to one, you realize that if you had waited a little longer, you could have gotten a better model.

The women won.

An elderly man is stopped by the police around 1 a. m. and is asked where he is going at this time of night.

The man replies, "I am going to a lecture about alcohol abuse and the effects it has on the human body".

The officer then asks, "Really? Who is giving that lecture at this time of night?"

The man replies, "My wife."

The Value of a Drink

'Sometimes when I reflect back on all the wine I drink
I feel shame. Then I look into the glass and think
about the workers in the vineyards and all of their hopes
and dreams. If I didn't drink this wine, they might be out
of work and their dreams would be shattered.
Then I say to myself, 'It is better that I drink this wine and let their
dreams come true than be selfish and worry about my liver.'
~ *Jack Handy*

WARNING: The consumption of alcohol may
leave you wondering what the hell
happened to your bra and panties.

'I feel sorry for people who don't drink. When they
wake up in the morning, that's as good as they're
going to feel all day.'
~*Frank Sinatra*

WARNING: The consumption of alcohol may create the illusion that
you are tougher, smarter, faster and better looking than most people.

'When I read about the evils of drinking, I gave up reading.'
~ *Henny Youngman*

WARNING: The consumption of alcohol may lead
you to think people are laughing WITH you.

'24 hours in a day, 24 beers in a case. Coincidence? I think not.'
~ *Stephen Wright*

WARNING: The consumption of alcohol may
cause you to think you can sing.

~~~~~~~~

'When we drink, we get drunk. When we get drunk,
we fall asleep. When we fall asleep, we commit no sin.
When we commit no sin, we go to heaven. So, let's all
get drunk and go to heaven!'
~ Brian O'Rourke

WARNING: The consumption of alcohol may cause pregnancy.

~~~~~~

'Beer is proof that God loves us and wants us to be happy.'
~ Benjamin Franklin

WARNING: The consumption of alcohol is a
major factor in dancing like a retard.

~~~~~~~~~~~~~~~~~~~~~~~~~~~~~~~~~~~~~~~

'Without question, the greatest invention in the
history of mankind is beer. Oh, I grant you that the
wheel was also a fine invention, but the wheel does
not go nearly as well with pizza.'
~ Dave Barry

WARNING: The consumption of alcohol may cause you to
tell your friends over and over again that you love them.

~~~~~~

To some ! it's a six-pack, to me it's a Support Group. Salvation in a can!
~ Dave Howell

WARNING: The consumption of alcohol may make you think you can
logically converse with members of the opposite sex without spitting.

~~~~~~

And saving the best for last, as explained by Cliff Clavin, of Cheers.

261

One afternoon at Cheers, Cliff Clavin was explaining
the Buffalo Theory to his buddy Norm.
Here's how it went:

'Well ya see, Norm, it's like this... A herd of buffalo can only move as fast as the slowest buffalo. And when the herd is hunted, it is the slowest and weakest ones at the back that are killed first. This natural selection is good for the herd as a whole, because the general speed and health of the whole group keeps improving by the regular killing of the weakest members. In much the same way, the human brain can only operate as fast as the slowest brain cells. Excessive intake of alcohol, as we know, kills brain cells. But naturally, it attacks the slowest and weakest brain cells first. In this way, regular consumption of beer eliminates the weaker brain cells, making the brain a faster and more efficient machine. That's why you always feel smarter after a few beers.'

WARNING: The consumption of alcohol may make
you think you are whispering when you are not.
After reading all of the above, I have a new personal rule, 'I WILL
NO LONGER WORK DURING DRINKING HOURS.'

At a bar

Having already downed a few power drinks, she turns around, faces him, looks him straight in the eye and says, "Listen here good looking, I screw anybody, anytime, anywhere, your place, my place, in the car, front door, back door, on the ground, standing up, sitting down, naked or with clothes on, it doesn't matter to me. I just love it." Eyes now wide with interest, he responds, "No kidding. I'm in Congress too. What state are you from?"

Do not ask the Lord to guide your footsteps, if you are not willing to move your feet.

Twas the month before Christmas*
When all through our land,
Not a Christian was praying
Nor taking a stand.
See the PC Police had taken away,
The reason for Christmas – no one could say.
The children were told by their schools not to sing,
About Shepherds and Wise Men and Angels and things.
It might hurt people's feelings, the teachers would say
* December 25th is just a ' Holiday '.*
Yet the shoppers were ready with cash, checks and credit
Pushing folks down to the floor just to get it!
CDs from Madonna, an X BOX, an I-pod
*Something was changing, something quite odd! *
Retailers promoted Ramadan and Kwanzaa
In hopes to sell books by Franken & Fonda.
As Targets were hanging their trees upside down
* At Lowe's the word Christmas – was no where to be found.*
At K-Mart and Staples and Penney's and Sears
You won't hear the word Christmas; it won't touch your ears.
Inclusive, sensitive, Di-ver-si-ty
Are words that were used to intimidate me.
Now Daschle, Now Darden, Now Sharpton, Wolf Blitzen
On Boxer, on Rather, on Kerry, on Clinton !
At the top of the Senate, there arose such a clatter
To eliminate Jesus, in all public matter.

And we spoke not a word, as they took away our faith
* Forbidden to speak of salvation and grace*
The true Gift of Christmas was exchanged and discarded
The reason for the season, stopped before it started.
So as you celebrate 'Winter Break' under your 'Dream Tree'
Sipping your Starbucks, listen to me.
Choose your words carefully, choose what you say
*Shout <u>MERRY CHRISTMAS</u> ,
not Happy Holiday !*
Please, all Christians join together and
wish everyone you meet during the holidays a
MERRY CHRISTMAS
Christ is The Reason for the Christ-mas Season!

Note: We are indebted for the above eight pages to Jim Hall and his group.
He can be reached at: murphyplus2@hotmail.com .

A Few Political Short Takes

Nothing Changes in Politics – "The budget should be balanced, the Treasury should be refilled, public debt should be reduced, the arrogance of officialdom should be tempered and controlled, and the assistance to foreign lands should be curtailed lest Rome become bankrupt. People must again learn to work, instead of living on public assistance." – *Cicero* in 55 BC.

"The government's view of the economy could be summed up in a few short phrases: If it moves, tax it. If it keeps moving, regulate it. And if it stops moving, subsidize it." *Ronald Reagan.*

"On my arrival in the United States I was struck by the degree of ability among the governed and the lack of it among the governing." *Alexis de Toqueville.*

"Politics is the art of looking for trouble, finding it everywhere, diagnosing it wrongly, and applying unsuitable remedies." *Sir Ernest Benn.*

"In politics, absurdity is not a handicap." *Napoleon Bonaparte.*

"Although he is regularly asked to do so, God does not take sides in American politics." *George Mitchell.*

"You can fool all of the people all of the time if the advertising is right and the budget is big enough." *Joseph Levine.*

A lie can travel halfway around the world while the truth is putting on its shoes. *Mark Twain.*

When buying and selling are controlled by legislation, the first things to be bought and sold are legislators. *PJ O'Rourke.*

Diplomacy is the art of saying 'Nice doggie' until you can find a rock. *Will Rogers.*

Confucius Say

Confucius Say: When penis become hard, brain become soft.

Confucius Say: When woman fly plane upside down, she have crack up.

Confucius Say: When man urinate in cash register, he finds it runneth into money.

Confucius Say: Better to be pissed off than pissed on.

Confucius Say: People who love sausage and respect the law should never watch either one being made.

Confucius Say: Boss stands for stupid s.o.b. spelled backwards. S.O.B. is a polite way of saying 'son of a bitch'.

Confucius Say: Man who takes umbrage at nothing, becomes nothing. Man who takes umbrage at something, becomes something.

Confucius Say: Socialism starts by pillaging the wealth of the past, continues by re-distributing the wealth of the present, and ends by mortgaging the wealth of the future – until someone calls the mortgage.

Confucius Say: Socialism says: From each according to his abilities, to each according to his needs. I say: Then everyone will have needs, but no one will have abilities.

Confucius Say: Woman who put husband in doghouse soon find him in cathouse.

Confucius Say: Man who fight with wife all day get no piece at night.

Quotes Worth Remembering

Porfirio Diaz (September 15, 1830 – July 2, 1915), the President of Mexico from 1876 to 1911, once said:
"Poor Mexico, so far from God, so near to the United States."

Andrew, the United Kingdom General Manager, was listening to Charles C. Fitzmorris, the President of the Company; explain the capabilities of the World Wide Chain Store system to a group of potential customers in the U.K. As he left the meeting, he whispered to a fellow employee:
"As I listened to Charlie speak, I could feel my dick grow shorter."

Sir Winston Churchill (1874 – 1965) – British politician -
"An appeaser is one who feeds a crocodile, hoping it will eat him last."

Benjamin Franklin (1706 – 1790) – American politician -
"Experience keeps a dear school, but fools will learn in no other."

George Santayana (1863-1952) – Spanish – Philosopher, essayist, poet, and novelist -
"Those who cannot remember the past are condemned to repeat it."

Harry S. Truman (1884-1972) – American politician –
"The *only thing new* in this world is the history that you don't know."

Joseph Goebbels (1897-1947) – German – Reich Minister of Propaganda -
"If you tell a lie long enough, it becomes the truth."

Thomas Jefferson (1743-1826) – American politician -
"To compel a man to furnish contributions of money for the propagation of opinions which he disbelieves and abhors is sinful and tyrannical."

F. Scott Fitzgerald (1896-1940) – American novelist -
"They were careless people, Tom and Daisy – they smashed up things and creatures and then retreated back into their money or their vast carelessness, or whatever it was that kept them together, and let other people clean up the mess they had made." From *The Great Gatsby* via *13 Bankers* by Simon Johnson and James Kwak.

Simon Johnson – American/British economist -
"The basic principle behind any oligarchy is that economic power yields political power."

Alexis De Tocqueville (1805-1859) – French writer who visited and wrote about America -
"The idea of right is simply that of virtue introduced into the political world."

John Milton (1608-1674) – English poet chiefly remembered for his epic poem describing humanity's fall from grace *Paradise Lost* -
"Who overcomes by force hath overcome but half his foe."

One of Dinesh D'Souza's high school teachers –
"If Hitler had been ruling India, Gandhi would be a lamp shade."

James Burnham (1905-1987) – American writer and popular political theorist, best known for his influential work *The Managerial Revolution*. He also wrote *Suicide of the West,* published in 1964 at the height of the Cold War, from which the following quotes are taken -
"It is probable that the West, in shrinking, is also dying." … in a few decades "the West will be finished."

Jean Paul Sartre (1905-1980) – French dramatist and writer. He was also a leading existential philosopher. The following quotes are taken from his introduction to Frantz Fanon, *The Wretched of the Earth* published in 1963. He died prior to the fall of the Berlin Wall and the collapse of the Soviet empire in 1989. Note the exultant tone in these quotes. -
"Europe is at death's door," "Europe is springing leaks everywhere. In the past we made history and now it is being made of us. The ratio of forces has been inverted; decolonization has begun."

Dinesh D'Souza (born April 21, 1961) – American writer -
"America's power had been awesomely displayed as early as World War II, but not until the early 1990s did America begin to enjoy an unrivaled supremacy over the globe that was unprecedented in history."

Voltaire (1694-1778) – The pen name of **François Marie Arouet.**
French philosopher and writer, poet and dramatist whose works epitomize the Age of Enlightenment, often attacking injustice and intolerance. He wrote *Candide* (1759) and the *Philosophical Dictionary* (1764). -
"Where there is one religion, you have tyranny; where there are two, you have religious war; but where there are many, you have freedom."

Samuel Johnson (1709-1784) – English writer -
"There are few ways in which a man is so innocently occupied than in getting money."

Confucius (551-479 BC) – Chinese philosopher – The below quotation is taken from his *Analects*. -
"The gentleman understands what is noble. The small man understands what is profitable."

Dinesh D'Souza (born April 21, 1961) – American writer. Here, he is speaking about his daughter, and the fallacy of accepting full assimilation for her. -
"What are the chances that my effort to thwart full assimilation will succeed? Not very good. But I still intend to try. So wish me luck: I will need it."

One-Liners

Q: Why won't a shark ever attack a lawyer?
A: Professional courtesy.

Q: How can you tell when a lawyer is lying?
A: The lips are moving.

Q: What do you call three thousand lawyers at the bottom of the ocean?
A: A good start.

Q: What's the difference between a dead snake lying in the middle of the road and a dead lawyer lying in the middle of the road?"
A: There are skid marks in front of the snake.

Q: What do you have when you have one lawyer in a town?
A: Too little work.
Q: What do you have when you have two lawyers in a town?
A: Too much work.

Q: What do you get when you cross a rooster and a telephone pole?
A: A twenty-foot cock that wants to reach out and touch someone.

Q: What do you get when you cross a rooster and an owl?
A: A cock that stays up all night.

Q: What do you get when you cross a Mexican and a Japanese?
A: A car thief that can't drive.

Q: What do you get when you cross a prostitute and a computer?
A: A fucking know-it-all.

Q: How can a bartender tell which patrons like Moose Head?
A: They're the ones with antler marks on their hips.

Q: A woman asks a Martian: "Do you smoke after sex?
A: The Martian replies: "I don't know. I've never looked to see."

Q: What is the difference between a woman with PMS and a Rottweiler?
A: Lipstick.

Q: What's the difference between a hobo and a homosexual?
A: A hobo doesn't have any friends, whereas a homosexual has friends up the ass.

Q: Do you know what the masochist said to the sadist?
A: Kill me, kill me.
Q: Do you know what the sadist answered to the masochist?
A: No-o-o-o.

Q: What do an extremely fat woman and a moped have in common?
A: They're both fun to ride until your friend sees you with either one of them.

Q: What does it mean to be Scotch-Irish?
A: It means that you love to drink, but you hate to pay for it.

Q: Do you know what the optimist said to the pessimist?
A: "This is the best of all possible worlds."
Q: Do you know what the pessimist answered?
A: "You're right."

Q: Why was the actor happy?
A: He heard that Leonidas was accompanied by seven hundred Thespians in addition to three hundred Spartans when he entered the pass at Thermopylae.

Note: The story is correct. However, the seven hundred Thespians were inhabitants of a city in Greece called Thespis, which does not exist today. There was no relationship to Thespis, the Greek poet who is said to have originated Greek tragedy (sixth century BC). We can be thankful for the Greek defeat at Thermopylae and the subsequent victory over Xerxes and the Persians at Plataea in 479 B.C. We can also be grateful for the previous Greek victory over the Persians and King Darius at Marathon in 490 B.C. Otherwise, we would probably speak Farsi today.

Q: Did you hear that the Eveready Bunny has died from sexual over-stimulation?
A: Yes, somebody reversed the polarity on his batteries, and he kept coming and coming and coming and coming ...

Q: What is the difference between a bowling ball and black pussy?
A: You could eat a bowling ball if you had to.
Note: See the joke entitled 'Ignorant, Ignorant, Ignorant' for disclaimers concerning this type of one-liner and joke.

Q: Why do Italians have rounded shoulders and sloping foreheads?
A: If you ask a question, an Italian always shrugs the shoulders. When you tell an Italian the answer, they always slap their forehead with the palm of their hand.

Q: Did you hear about the Polish mom who was delighted to hear that her daughter's new boy friend was into oral sex?
A: After all, it's not every young man who's content to just talk about it.

Q: Why do the Scots wear kilts, instead of trousers?
A: Because the sheep can hear the sound of a zipper a half-mile away.
Note: See bestiality definition under vocabulary at the end of this section.

Q: Did you hear about the penis transplant?
A: The hand rejected it.

Q: There are very few golf courses in Italy, do you know why?
A: Because they literally cannot tell the difference between their ass and a hole in the ground.

Q: What did Adam say to Eve when he got his first erection?
A: "Stand back! I'm not sure how big this thing gets!"

Q: What do you get when you cross a computer and a Jewish-American-Princess?
A: A computer system which won't go down on you.

Q: Why does a male dog raise his hind leg when he urinates?
A: To throw his ass out of gear, so he won't shit.

Q: Did you hear about the Hilary Special from KFC?
A: It consists of two small breasts and two large thighs.

Q: How many doctors does it take to change a light bulb?
A: It depends on how much health insurance the light bulb has.

Q: How can you tell if a Pole is at a cockfight?
A: He's the one with a duck.
Q: How can you tell if an Italian is at a cockfight?
A: He's the one betting on the duck.
Q: How can you tell if the Mafia is at a cockfight?
A: The duck wins.

Q: What's the difference between Jell-O and a Jewish-American-Princess?
A: Jell-O moves when you eat it.

Q: What is the Jewish-American-Princess' favorite wine?
A: I wanna go to Miami.

Q: What did the man say to his wife?
A: If only the good die young, you've got to be immortal.

Q: Why do Jewish husbands die young?
A: Because they want to.

Q: Did you hear about the new wine for incontinent seniors developed in California?
A: It's called Pino More.

Q: What do you get when you cross a rooster and M & M's?
A: A cock that melts in your mouth, not in your hands.

Q: What can a Lifesaver do that a man can't do?
A: Come in five flavors.

Q: Why do elephants paint their toenails red?
A: So they can hide in cherry trees without being seen.
Q: Did you ever see an elephant in a cherry tree?
A: No.
Q: There, you see it works, doesn't it?

Q: What do you call four Mexicans drowning?
A: Quatro Sinko.

Q: Why did God create gentiles?
A: Someone has to buy retail.

Q: Did you hear about the Polish actress?
A: She slept with the writer.

Q: How many psychiatrists does it take to change a light bulb?
A: One. But it has to want to be changed.

Q: What do you call a man and woman using the rhythm method of birth control?
A: Parents.

Q: What would one of the best things be about having a woman Vice President?
A: We wouldn't have to pay her as much as we would a man. *With appropriate apologies to all my feminist friends.*

Q: What's the difference between a Cadillac and a porcupine?
A: For a porcupine, all of the pricks are on the outside.

Q: How do porcupines make love?
A: Carefully, very carefully.

Q: What do a meteorologist in a snowstorm and a woman's sex life have in common?
A: They're both concerned with how many inches there are and how long it will last.

Q: What's the difference between a bartender and a proctologist?
A: The proctologist looks at ass-holes one at a time.

Q: What kind of murderer has moral fiber?
A: A cereal killer.

Q: What is the difference between leaves and a car?
A: One you brush and rake, the other you rush and brake.

Q: What do you call a strange market?
A: A bizarre bazaar.

Q: Did you hear about the guy who went out every Saturday evening to sow wild oats?
A: Every Sunday, he went to church and prayed for a crop failure.

Q: What is German for brassiere?
A: Ein stoppenfloppen.

Q: What do Italians call suppositories?
A: Innuendoes.

Q: What is the epitome of conceit?
A: A flea floating down the river on his back with a hard-on yelling: "Raise the drawbridge."

Q: What is this: 10, 9, 8, 7, 6, 5, 4, 3, 2, 1?
A: Bo Derek getting older.

Q: Did you hear about the two gay Irishmen?
A: Gerald Fitzpatrick and Patrick Fitzgerald.

Q: What are a Jewish-American-Princess' first words?
A: Gucci, Gucci, Gucci.

Q: What is six inches long that women love?
A: Money.

Q: Why didn't the Polish man enjoy his honeymoon?
A: He kept waiting for the swelling to go down.

Q: What's the difference between a dog and a fox?
A: About six drinks at the bar.

Q: Why do the Irish have potatoes, and the Arabs have oil?
A: The Irish had first choice.

Q: What's the definition of eternity?
A: The length of time between when you come and she leaves.

Q: What do you get when you cross an onion and a donkey?
A: Ordinarily, you just get an onion with a little fur on it – but every once in a while, you get a piece of ass that brings tears to your eyes.

Q: Why don't women blink during foreplay?
A: They don't have time.

Q: Why is wonton soup a Jewish-American-Princess's favorite soup?
A: Because it is "not now" spelled backwards.

Q: What do peroxide blondes and Boeing 747s have in common?
A: They both have black boxes.

Q: Why is air like sex?
A: Because it's no big deal unless you're not getting any.

Q: What do toy train sets and a woman's breasts have in common?
A: They were both originally intended for children, but it's the fathers that actually play with them.

Q: What is the difference between worry and panic?
A: About twenty-eight days.

Q: What is the first thing a blonde does in the morning?
A: She puts on her clothes and goes home.

Q: What is the difference between a penis and a prick?
A: A penis is the male sexual organ, and a prick is the owner.

Q: What is the definition of "vagina"?
A: It's the box a penis comes in.
Q: What do you call a blonde with pigtails?
A: A blowjob with handlebars.

Q: What is the last thing that goes through a mosquito's brain just before he hits your windshield?
A: His asshole.

Q: What two words will clear out a men's room faster than anything else?
A: Nice dick.

Q: Did you hear about the new Playboy magazine for married men?
A: Every month, it has the same centerfold.

Q: What is the mating call of a blonde?
A: Boy, am I drunk!
Q: What is the mating call of a brunette?
A: Has that drunk blonde left yet?

Q: Why do doctors slap babies' butts right after they're born?
A: To knock the penises off the dumb ones.

Q: What is the speed limit outside Billie Jean King's house?
A: Lickety-split.

Q: What's the difference between erotic and kinky?
A: Erotic, you use a feather – kinky, you use the whole chicken.

Q: Why do blondes like cars with sun roofs?
A: More legroom.

Q: What do you call a lesbian with fat fingers?
A: Well hung.

Q: How many perverts does it take to screw in a light bulb?
A: Just one, but it takes the whole emergency room to get it out.

Q: Why don't blondes use vibrators?
A: Because they chip their teeth.

Q: What do women and condoms have in common?
A: They both spend more time in your wallet than they do on your dick.

Q: What's the smartest thing ever to come out of a woman's mouth?
A: Einstein's dick.

Q: What does a man do standing up, that a woman does sitting down, that a dog does standing on three legs?
A: Shake hands.

Q: What goes in hard, stiff, and dry, and comes out soft, wet, and sticky?
A: Chewing gum.

Q: Do you know what the sadist said to the masochist?
A: Absolutely nothing.

Q: Why did the Polish grandmother have her tubes tied?
A: She didn't want any more grandchildren.

Q: Why did the Polish man return his necktie?
A: It was too tight.

Q: What's the difference between a rooster and a prostitute?
A: A rooster says: "Cock a doodle do." A prostitute says: "Any cock'll do."

Q: What kind of shirt did General George A. Custer wear at the Battle of Little Bighorn?
A: An Arrow Shirt.

Q: What do you need when you have three lawyers up to their necks in cement?
A: More cement.

Q: What's the difference between a pregnant woman and a light bulb?
A: You can unscrew the light bulb.

Q: How do you say "Fuck You" in Yiddish?
A: "Trust Me".

Q: How many feminists does it take to change a light bulb?
A: One. And there's nothing funny about this.

Q: In the Jewish faith, when does a fetus become human?
A: When he or she graduates from medical school.

Q: How are women and tornadoes alike?
A: They both moan like hell when they come, and take the house when they leave.

Q: What's the definition of a lawyer?
A: A mouth with a life support system.

Q: What's the definition of mixed emotions?
A: Watching your attorney drive over a cliff in your new car.

Q: Have you heard about the lawyers' word processor?
A: No matter what font you select, everything comes out in fine print.

Q: What do honest lawyers and UFOs have in common?
A: You always hear about them, but you never see them.

Q: What's the difference between a lawyer and a terrorist?
A: You can negotiate with a terrorist.

Q: What's the difference between a lawyer and a vulture?
A: Lawyers accumulate frequent flyer points.

Q: What can suffer from constipation and diarrhea simultaneously?
A: Your spouse – constipation of the brain and diarrhea of the mouth.

Q: What is a synchronization problem?
A: Having a 90-mile-per-hour mouth and a 10-mile-per-hour brain.

Q: What is a crania-rectal-inversion?
A: A polite way of saying that you've got your head up your ass.

Q: What is height of incongruity?
A: Having an alligator mouth and a canary brain.

Q: What is asking for trouble?
A: Having a paper ass-hole in a raging forest fire.

Q: What does RINO stand for?
A: Republican in name only.

Q: What does Oreo stand for?
A: Someone who is black on the outside, but white on the inside. Not a true black, but an Uncle Tom.

Q: What's the difference between rape and seduction?
A: Salesmanship.

Q: What's the difference between a recession and a depression?
A: A recession is when your neighbor loses his job; a depression is when you lose your job.

Vocabulary (One-Liners):

Abdominal – Relating to the abdomen, the belly, that part of the body that contains all of the structures between the chest and the pelvis.

AC/DC – Someone who has sex with both men and women.

Acronym – A word formed from the initial letters of a name, such as WAC for Women's Army Corps.

A.D. – Is Latin and stands for Anno Domini (In the year of our Lord). It means after the birth of Jesus Christ. The birth of Christ is the dividing line between B.C. and A.D.

Adolescence – The period of physical and psychological development from the onset of puberty to maturity. Generally considered to be synonymous with teen-ager. It terminates legally at the age of majority. This is usually 18 years-of-age, but varies according to state law.

Adulthood – The period of time in your life after your physical growth has stopped and you are fully developed. In the Jewish religion, a 13-year-old boy is considered adult, and this is celebrated by a Bar Mitzvah ceremony.

Age of majority – The legally defined age at which a person is considered an adult, with all the attendant rights and responsibilities of adulthood. The end of adolescence. The age of majority is defined by state laws, which vary by state, but is 18 in most states.

American Indian – A member of the race of people living in America when Europeans arrived. When Columbus landed, he thought he had arrived in India.

Anglican – Of or characteristic of the Church of England or any of the churches related to it in origin and communion, such as the Protestant Episcopal Church.

Anterior – The front, as opposed to the posterior.

Anthropoids – Resembling a human, especially in shape or outward appearance.

281

Arboreal – Living in trees or adapted for living in trees.

Arrow Shirt – Trade name for a famous line of shirts by Phillips/Van Heusen.

Ass – Slang for backside or buttocks: the fleshy part of the human body that you sit on. It can also mean a donkey-like animal which is a long-eared, slow, patient, sure-footed domesticated mammal, Equus asinus, related to the horse, used chiefly as a beast of burden.

Assassin – A murderer (especially one who kills a prominent political figure) who kills by a surprise attack and often is hired to do the deed.

Assassinated – Murdered by surprise attack for political reasons.

Austin – A sports motor car manufactured in Longbridge, Birmingham in England.

Automotive – Of or relating to motor vehicles.

B.C. – Before the birth of Jesus Christ. See A.D. above for a description of after the birth of Christ.

Bar Mitzvah – (Judaism) an initiation ceremony marking the 13th birthday of a Jewish boy and signifying the beginning of religious responsibility. A bar mitzvah is an important social event in the life of a Jewish man.

Bartender – One who mixes and serves alcoholic drinks at a bar. Also called a barkeeper.

Bastard – Some one born outside of wedlock. Someone whose parents were never married. Also, a term for someone you hate.

Battle Of Little Bighorn – See Little Bighorn below.

Bazaar – A market consisting of a street lined with shops and stalls, especially one in the Middle East. Also, a shop or a part of a store in which miscellaneous articles are sold.

Benn – *Antony (Neil) Wedgwood*, known as *Tony Benn*. Born in 1925, British Labour politician, a leading figure on the party's left wing. He renounced (1963) the title of Viscount Stansgate and also renounced his seat in the House of Lords.

Bestiality – Sexual relations between a human being and an animal. At Common Law, bestiality was considered a crime against nature and was punishable by death. Example: American farmers are infamous for having sexual relations with female sheep (Ewes).

Bitch – A female dog. Listed on the papers of a pure-bred dog. To call someone a son of a bitch implies that his mother was a female dog. This (along with bastard) is an insult reserved for people you hate. See S.O.B. below.

Bizarre – Strange, conspicuously or grossly unconventional or unusual.

Billie Jean King – Billie Jean King dominated women's tennis for nearly two decades, retiring from professional play in 1984. In 1981 her longtime secretary, Marilyn Barnett, brought a palimony lawsuit against King and their love affair became public.

Bo Derek – A slang term used to describe a perfect stock or investment. In the 1979 hit movie "10", actress Bo Derek portrayed the "perfect woman", or "the perfect 10".

Bonaparte – Napoleon: French general who became emperor of the French (1769-1821).

Bowling Ball – A large ball with finger holes used in the sport of bowling. It is quite inedible.

Bowling – A game that uses ten pins and a ball which is thrown down an alley towards the pins. Complete knocking down of all ten pins is called a strike. One pin left standing is called a spare.

Brassiere – A woman's undergarment worn to support and give contour to the breasts.

Breast – The upper ventral region of an animal's torso, particularly that of mammals, including human beings. Either of two milk-secreting, glandular organs on the chest of a woman; the human mammary gland. In a chicken, this is a part of the body and does not include the wing or the thigh.

Buffalo – American bison: large shaggy-haired brown bison of North American plains.

Bush Baby – Name for several small, active nocturnal primates of the loris family, found in forested parts of Africa. Bush babies, also called galagos, form the subfamily Galaginae. The smallest are about 1 ft (30 cm) long, including the long, furry tail. All have fluffy fur, small pointed faces with large eyes, and naked, highly mobile ears.

Butt – In this case, *Informal* the buttocks; the rear end.

Buttocks – The fleshy part of the human body that you sit on.

Cadaver – The dead body of a human being. Also, a dead body used for medical purposes.

Calcined – To heat (a substance) to a high temperature but below the melting or fusing point. This is done as part of the process of making cement. See cement below.

Capone, Al – Nicknamed Scarface, he was a leading gangster in Chicago.

Carpe Diem – Seize the day. Make the most of the time we have.

Cathouse – Slang term for a whorehouse: a building where prostitutes are available.

Cavity – A hollow place or space, or a potential space, within the body or one of its organs.

Cement – A building material made by grinding calcined limestone and clay to a fine powder, which can be mixed with water and poured to set as a solid mass or used as an ingredient in making mortar or concrete.

Cervix – The lower, narrow part of the uterus (womb). The word *cervix* comes straight from Latin for *neck*.

Chain – In this case, a number of similar establishments (stores or restaurants or banks or hotels or theaters) under one ownership.

Cherry – Slang for hymen or maidenhead.

Cicero – Cicero, (Marcus Tullius) 106-43 BC; Roman statesman, orator, & philosopher.

Clitoris – A small elongated erectile organ at the anterior part of the vulva. Homologous with the penis in the male. Sometimes referred to as the clit.

Clue In – Provide someone with a clue. Inform of the situation.

Cock – Slang term for penis. It can also mean a male chicken, or rooster.

Cockfight – A fight between gamecocks, usually wearing metal spurs on the legs, with informal betting on the outcome and with prize money awarded to the owner of the winner. Cockfights are illegal in the U.S.

Cocktail – An iced drink of wine or distilled liquor mixed with flavoring ingredients. This expression has come to mean any mixed drink.

Colleague – A fellow member of a profession, staff, or academic faculty; an associate.

Colloquialism – Characteristic of or appropriate to ordinary or familiar conversation rather than formal speech or writing – informal.

Conceit – A favorable and especially unduly high opinion of one's own abilities or worth.

Consists Of – To be made up of or composed of.

Contrary – Very opposed in nature or character or purpose. Examples would be: Acts contrary to our code of ethics, and the facts point to a contrary conclusion.

Corpse – Cadaver: the dead body of a human being.

Counterbalance – A force or influence equally counteracting another.

Cranium – The portion of the skull enclosing the brain; the braincase.

Crop Failure – Reduction in crop yield to a level that there is no marketable surplus or the nutritional needs of the community cannot be met.

Cuckold – A man married to an unfaithful wife. Also to cuckold a man by cheating on him.

Cunnilingus – Oral stimulation of the vulva or clitoris. During cunnilingus, one tries to 'Kick the little man out of the sailboat.' The clitoris is the <u>little man</u>.

Custer (1839-1876) – General George Armstrong Custer, commanding general of the U.S. Cavalry. He was killed along with all his command by the Sioux Indians at the Battle of Little Bighorn in 1876.

Darius – King of Persia at the time of the battle of Marathon in Greece in 490 B.C., and father of King Xerxes the Great of Persia.

Debris – Dust, junk, rubble, detritus.

Department – A distinct, usually specialized division of a large organization.

Department Store – A large retail store offering a variety of merchandise and services and organized in separate departments.

Derriere – The buttocks; the rear; the ass. (French, behind).

Detritus – The remains of something that has been destroyed or broken up.

Devout – Devoted to religion or to the fulfillment of religious obligations.

Diaper – A garment consisting of a folded cloth drawn up between the legs and fastened at the waist; worn by infants to catch excrement.

Dick – Slang term for penis.

Dinghy – A small open boat carried as a tender, lifeboat, or pleasure craft on a larger boat.

Ditties – Short simple songs (or the words of poems intended to be sung).

Dog – Slang for a person regarded as unattractive or uninteresting.

Dollar – It literally means one twentieth of an ounce of gold.

Dork – *Slang:* A stupid, inept, or foolish person. *Vulgar Slang:* The penis.

Drawbridge – A bridge that can be raised or drawn aside either to prevent access or to permit passage beneath it.

Dyke – Slang term for the person who plays the male role in Lesbian female sex. See lesbian below.

Eateries – A restaurant which prepares and serves food, drink and dessert to customers. Meals are generally served and eaten on premises, but many restaurants also offer take-out and food delivery services.

Einstein – Physicist born in Germany who formulated the special theory of relativity and the general theory of relativity; Einstein also proposed that light consists of discrete quantized bundles of energy (later called photons)

(1879-1955). Also: a genius, someone who has exceptional intellectual ability and originality.

Elephant – Either of two very large herbivorous mammals, *Elephas maximus* of south-central Asia or *Loxodonta africana* of Africa, having thick, almost hairless skin, a long, flexible, prehensile trunk, upper incisors forming long curved tusks of ivory, and, in the African species, large fan-shaped ears. The **African elephant** (*Loxodonta africana*) is the larger species, with large flapping ears and a less humped back than the **Indian elephant** (*Elephas maximus*), of S and SE Asia.

Elongated – Having notably more length than width; being long and slender. An example would be: 'An *elongate* tail tapering to a point'.

Embarrassing – Awkward: hard to deal with; especially causing pain or embarrassment.

Embryo – The organism in the early stages of growth and differentiation from fertilization to, in humans, the beginning of the third month of pregnancy. After that point in time, it is termed a fetus. See fetus below.

Endometrial – The uterine lining. The cells that line the uterus (the womb). The inner layer of the uterus. This tissue is shed monthly in response to the hormonal changes of the menstrual period. The endometrium then grows back and slowly gets thicker and thicker until the next period when it is once again sloughed off.

Epitome – A person or thing that is typical of or possesses to a high degree the features of a whole class.

Erectile – Capable of being raised to an upright position. Usually, the organ becomes erect due to blood flowing to it, which in turn is caused by sexual excitement or stimulation.

Erectile Dysfunction – Sometimes referred to as ED. Impotence resulting from a man's inability to have or maintain an erection of his penis.

Erection – An erect penis. A slang term is hard on.

Erotic – Of, devoted to, or tending to arouse sexual love or desire.

Estrogen – A female hormone produced by the ovaries.

Ewe – A female sheep. This word is pronounced the same as <u>you</u>.

Fairway – On a golf course, the area between the tee and putting green where the grass is cut short.

Fallopian Tubes – Either of a pair of slender ducts through which ova (eggs) pass from the ovaries to the uterus in the female. Tying the Fallopian Tubes is a popular way of sterilization in women.

Famous – Well or widely known. See also infamous below.

Farsi – The language spoken both by the ancient Persians and the modern Iranians.

Fellatio – Oral stimulation of the penis.

Feminism – The doctrine advocating social, political, and all other rights of women equal to those of men. Equal pay for equal work, etc.

Feminist – A person whose beliefs and behavior are based on feminism.

Ferocity – A ferocious quality or state; savage fierceness.

Fertile – Capable of reproducing.

Fetus – The unborn offspring from the end of the 8th week after conception (when the major structures have formed) until birth. Up until the eighth week, the developing offspring is called an embryo. See embryo above.

Fibula – The lateral (outside) and smaller of the two bones in the lower leg.

Flea – Any of various small, wingless, bloodsucking insects of the order Siphonaptera that have legs adapted for jumping and are parasitic on warm-blooded animals.

Floating – Being buoyed up on water or other liquid.

Fly – The zipper on bottom-wear. Example: Your fly is open, which is embarrassing.

Follicle – A small bodily cavity or sac.

Fox – *Slang* for a sexually attractive person.

Galagos – A type of monkey. See bush baby above.

Gashie – Slang for a woman's genitalia.

Gay – See homosexual below.

Genitalia – The male and female reproductive organs. The genitalia include internal structures such as the ovary, and external structures such as the penis.

Gentiles – People who are not Jewish. Sometimes referred to as an insult as Goyim by Jewish people.

Gigolo – A male who accepts money or other favors from women. This is normally a young man accepting favors from an older woman.

Golf – A game played on a large outdoor course with a series of 9 or 18 holes spaced far apart, the object being to propel a small, hard ball with the use of various clubs into each hole with as few strokes as possible.

Goy – Plural Goyim – Offensive. Used as a disparaging term for one who is not a Jew. Also, a Jew ignorant of the Jewish religion.

Heifer – A young female bovine (cow) that has not yet had a calf. Also, an ugly or objectionable woman; a cow.

Hind – Located at or forming the back or rear; posterior: an animal's hind legs; the hinder part of a steer.

Hobo – One who wanders from place to place without a permanent home or a means of livelihood. A tramp: a disreputable vagrant; 'a homeless tramp'; 'he tried to help the really down-and-out bums.'

Homologous – Corresponding or similar in position, value, structure, or function.

Homosexual – Sometimes referred to as gay. A man who prefers other men as sexual partners rather than women. A typical question is: Are you gay or straight?

Hormone – A chemical substance produced in the body that controls and regulates the activity of certain cells or organs.

Hymen – A fold of mucous membrane that surrounds or partially covers the external vaginal opening. It forms part of the vulva, or external genitalia. The presence of a hymen is considered proof of virginity

Immortal – Not subject to death. Examples would be: **immortal** deities and the **immortal** soul.

Impregnate – To make pregnant; inseminate. To fertilize (an ovum, for example).

Incontinent – Not having control over urination and defecation. Going in your pants.

In Doghouse – Informal; disfavor (as in the phrase: "in the **doghouse**").

Inedible – Not fit to be eaten; uneatable.

Infamous – Famous in a bad way. Hitler is considered infamous, while Churchill is considered famous.

Inhabitants – People or animals that live in a place, especially as permanent residents.

Innuendoes – Indirect or subtle, usually derogatory implications in an expression; insinuations.

Inseminate – The introduction of sperm into the vagina.

Internecine – (Of conflict) within a group or organization.

Irredentism – A national policy advocating the acquisition of some region in another country by reason of common linguistic, cultural, historical, ethnic, or racial ties.

Jack Off – Slang for masturbate in the male.

Jell-O – A fruit-flavored dessert (trade mark Jell-O) made from a commercially prepared gelatin powder.

Jewish-American-Princess – Sometimes referred to as a JAP. A bitchy, spoiled, gold-digging Jewish female; raised in a wealthy household, selfish, high-maintenance to the point of sheer insanity, stuck-up, the worst woman to date/marry on planet earth, yet deemed the most desirable by Jewish mothers, who attempt to force them down the throats of their unsuspecting sons (all for the sake of preserving "Jewish Heritage.") A female who collects designer fashion items and status symbols (including men). Bane to the existence of dating men. The key to an unhappy relationship for the rest of your life. Large-breasted, outwardly attractive, internally spoiled, greedy, complicated, self-righteous, and obnoxiously difficult and overbearing Jewish female. Before marriage, you can't get a JAP out of bed – after marriage, you can't get her into it.

Jimi Hendrix – United States guitarist whose innovative style with electric guitars influenced the development of rock music (1942-1970).

Keister – Slang for the buttocks: the fleshy part of the human body that you sit on.

KFC – The Kentucky Fried Chicken chain of fried chicken eateries.

Kilt – A knee-length skirt with deep pleats, usually of tartan wool, worn as part of the dress for men in the Scottish Highlands.

Kinky – Slang: Showing or appealing to bizarre or deviant tastes, especially of a sexual or erotic nature.

Kosher – Separating meat and milk dishes. Maintaining two separate sets of dishes – one for meat dishes, and the other for milk and dairy dishes. The word kosher has become a part of English slang, a colloquialism meaning proper, legitimate, genuine, fair, or acceptable.

Lamb – A baby sheep.

Legal Tender – Something that can be used as an official medium of payment.

Lemur – Any of various small, arboreal, chiefly nocturnal mammals of the family Lemuridae, of Madagascar and the Comoro Islands, especially of the genus Lemur, usually having large eyes, a fox like face, and woolly fur. Most lemurs are endangered.

Leonidas – King of the Greek City of Sparta. He was the defender of the pass at Thermopylae, where three hundred Spartans (and 700 Thespians) held up a Persian force many times its size. The Spartans were fierce warriors. According to legend, the saying: 'Come back with your shield or on it' originated with the Spartans. Although they were annihilated to the last man at Thermopylae, they succeeded in holding the Persian army under King Xerxes the Great at bay and inflicting many casualties on them.

Lesbian – A female homosexual. Someone who prefers other women as sexual partners rather than men. The person who plays the male role is sometimes referred to as a dyke.

Levine – Joseph E. Levine (September 9, 1905 – July 31, 1987) was an American film producer.

Lewinsky, Monica – In 1995, a graduate of Lewis & Clark College, was hired to work as an intern at the White House during Clinton's first term, and began a personal relationship with him including blow jobs.

Liberace – Wladziu Valentino Liberace (May 16, 1919 – February 4, 1987), better known by only his last name Liberace, was a famous American entertainer and pianist. During the 1950s–1970s he was the highest paid entertainer in the world.

Lifesaver – In this case, a roll of hard candy, the pieces of which come in five flavors.

Little Bighorn – A river in the West Central US, rising in Northern Wyoming and flowing north to the Bighorn River. Its banks were the scene of the defeat (1876) and killing of General George A. Custer and his command by Sioux Indians.

Livelihood – Way of making a living.

Loris – Any of three species of nocturnal, arboreal primates in the family Lorisidae. Lorises have soft gray or brown fur, huge eyes encircled by dark patches, and no tail. They move slowly and often hang by their feet, leaving their hands free to grasp branches or food. The slender loris (*Loris tardigradus*) of India and Sri Lanka is 8 – 10 in. (20 – 25 cm) long; it eats insects and small animals. The slow lorises (genus *Nycticebus*) of South Asia and the Malay Peninsula eat insects, small animals, fruit, and vegetation. *Nycticebus pygmaeus* is about 8 in. (20 cm) long; *N. coucang* is 10.5 – 15 in. (27 – 38 cm) long. Habitat degradation and hunting have seriously depleted loris populations.

M & M's – A chocolate assortment of candy encased in a sugar-coated shell.

Machiavelli (1469-1527) – Niccolò di Bernardo dei **Machiavelli** was an Italian philosopher, humanist, and writer based in Florence during the Renaissance. Although not a prince, he wrote *The Prince*. To this day, Machiavellian is synonymous with deviousness and evil.

Magic Johnson – Earvin "Magic" Johnson Jr. (born August 14, 1959) is a retired American professional basketball player who played point guard for the Los Angeles Lakers of the National Basketball Association (NBA). He also contracted AIDS (was HIV positive in 1990-1991).

Maidenhead – The quality or state of being a maiden: virginity. See hymen above.

Male Prostitute – A gay (homosexual) or AC/DC male, usually young, who accepts money to perform sexual favors, usually to older men.

Mammal – Any of various warm-blooded vertebrate animals of the class Mammalia, including humans, characterized by a covering of hair on the skin and, in the female, milk-producing mammary glands for nourishing the young.

Mammary Glands – Milk-producing glands of the female. Known vulgarly as tits in a young woman. Known politely as breasts.

Manichean – A believer in religious or philosophical dualism.

Marathon – A village and plain of ancient Greece northeast of Athens. It was the site of a major Athenian victory over the Persians commanded by Darius in 490 B.C. It is also the name of any race of 26 miles and 385 yards, because of the soldier messenger who ran to inform the Athenians of the victory.

Mark Twain (1835-1910) – Pen name for Samuel J. Clemens: United States writer and humorist best known for his novels about Tom Sawyer and Huckleberry Finn.

Marketable Surplus – Depends on the availability of cultivated land under the crop. Besides this, among the factors that permit the farmer to increase his marketable surplus the most important one is his family size. If the family size is big, the marketable surplus will be relatively lower, even for the big-sized farms. Per capita availability of cultivated land among the larger farms is certainly higher compared to the smaller ones, but per capita availability of land under a specific crop need not be higher in the larger size groups than the smaller farms. The phenomenon of marketable surplus should be examined not in terms of size-classes of holdings but with the acreage of individual crops separately against each size-class.

Mashie – In golf, a middle-distance iron.

Masochist – Some one who likes to take punishment on him self. He is the opposite of a sadist. In other words, he wants to be whipped. See sadist below.

Menarche – The first occurrence of menstruation in a woman.

Menopause – The permanent cessation of menstruation, occurring usually between the ages of 45 and 55. It marks the completion of a woman's childbearing years and the cessation of menses (menstrual cycles). Women can become quite moody during this part of their lives.

Menses – The monthly flow of blood and cellular debris from the uterus that begins at puberty in women and the females of other primates. In women, menses ceases at menopause. It is also called catamenia. See menstruation below.

Menstruation – The monthly discharge of blood from the uterus of nonpregnant women from puberty to menopause. A slang term is a woman's period.

Menstrual Cycle – Recurring cycle (beginning at menarche and ending at menopause) in which the endometrial lining of the uterus prepares for pregnancy. If pregnancy does not occur, the lining along with blood is shed at menstruation. The average menstrual cycle is 28 days in a human female.

Meteorologist – A specialist who studies processes in the earth's atmosphere that cause weather conditions.

Meteorology – The science that deals with the phenomena of the atmosphere, especially weather and weather conditions.

Mirabeau (1749-1791) – Short for Comte (Count) Honoré Gabriel Riqueti de Mirabeau. He was an orator and statesman prominent during the French revolution.

Mitchell – George J. Mitchell (born 1933), former Senator from Maine, special envoy to the Middle East for the Obama administration, former Senate majority leader.

Money – A medium of exchange. It functions as legal tender. Paper money depends for its validity upon the validity of the government issuing the paper money. Incidentally, dollar literally means one twentieth of an ounce of gold.

Moped – A type of motorcycle without much power.

Mortgaging – A temporary, conditional pledge of property to a creditor as security for performance of an obligation or repayment of a debt.

Neo-Pagan – An umbrella term used to identify a wide variety of modern religious movements, particularly those influenced by pre-Christian pagan beliefs of Europe.

Ness, Elliott – Head of a federal crime-fighting unit in Chicago.

Nimby – Stands for Not In My Backyard. Someone who objects to siting something in their own neighborhood but does not object to it being sited elsewhere; an acronym for not in my backyard.

Nocturnal – Belonging to or active during the night.

Noumenal – In the philosophy of Kant, an object as it is in itself independent of the mind, as opposed to a phenomenon. It is sometimes considered to be another world.

Nude – Completely unclothed or uncovered; naked; bare.

Obama – Barack Hussein Obama II (born August 4, 1961) is the 44th and current President of the United States.

Optimist – Some one who always looks on the bright side of things. To an optimist, the glass is always half full.

O'Rourke – Patrick Jake O'Rourke (born November 14, 1947 in Toledo, Ohio) is an American political satirist, journalist, writer and author.

Oral Sex – Sexual activity involving the stimulation of the genitalia of a sex partner by the use of the mouth, tongue, teeth or throat.

Out Of Gear – In neutral. In any other position, the machinery will move either backwards or forwards.

Ova – Eggs. An ovum (plural ova) is a mature egg released at ovulation. In humans only one egg is normally shed, from one of the ovaries, about 14 days after the start of each 28-day menstrual cycle. This contrasts with the massive output of sperm from the testes (testicles), which begins at puberty and continues throughout life. Thus females have a different approach to processing germ cells for fertilization. In the case of the use of birth control pills and cessation of use, the ovaries can release multiple eggs at one time, leading to multiple pregnancies at one time. In other words, when women stop using birth-control pills, they run a much greater risk of paternal twins or paternal triplets. There are two types of twins or triplets – identical and paternal. Paternal siblings come from separate eggs, while identical siblings come from the same egg.

Ovaries – The paired female reproductive organ that produces ova (Eggs) and, in vertebrates, estrogen and progesterone.

Ovulation – The release of the ripe egg from the ovary. The egg is released when the cavity surrounding it (the follicle) breaks open in response to a hormonal signal. Ovulation occurs around fourteen or fifteen days from the first day of the woman's last menstrual cycle. When ovulation occurs, the ovum moves into the fallopian tube and becomes available for fertilization.

Ovum – An egg.

Par – In golf, the standard number of strokes set for each hole on a golf course, or for the entire course.

Paraprosdokian – A figure of speech in which the latter part of a sentence or phrase is surprising or unexpected in a way that causes the reader or listener to reframe or reinterpret the first part. It is frequently used for humorous or dramatic effect, sometimes producing an anticlimax.

Pate – Slang for the human head, especially the top of the head: a bald *pate.* *Pelosi* – Nancy Patricia D'Alesandro Pelosi (born March 26, 1940) is the 60th and current Speaker of the United States House of Representatives. She is the Democratic Leader of the House of Representatives, and a member of Congress elected from the state of California.

Penis – Male sexual organ. The male organ of copulation in higher vertebrates, homologous with the clitoris in the female. In mammals, it also serves as the male organ of urinary excretion. When sexually excited, this organ fills with blood, and becomes hard and stiff or erectile. Erectile dysfunction is the inability for the penis to become full of blood. Slang synonyms are cock, dick, tallywacker, etc. *Period* – Slang term for menstruation.

Peroxide – Hydrogen peroxide: a viscous liquid with strong oxidizing properties; a powerful bleaching agent; also used (in aqueous solutions) as a mild disinfectant.

Pervert – A corrupt person: corrupt morally or by intemperance or sensuality.

Pervert – To cause to turn aside or away from what is good or true or morally right: to corrupt.

Pessimist – Some one who always looks on the dark side of things. The glass is always half empty.

Phallus – A symbol or representation of the penis.

Phenomenal – Of, relating to, or constituting phenomena or a phenomenon.

Physiologically – Characteristic of or promoting normal, or healthy, functioning.

Pill – Sometimes referred to as the pill, it means the <u>birth control pill</u>. Upon stopping to take it, it frequently leads to multiple pregnancies. Twins or triplets are common after stopping taking the pill.

Pillaging – Plundering: the act of stealing valuable things from a place.

Plataea – An ancient city of central Greece southwest of Thebes. It was the site of a major Greek victory over the Persians in 479 B.C.

Pleats – Folds in cloth made by doubling the material upon itself and then pressing or stitching it into place

Plundering – The act of stealing valuable things from a place.

PMS – Pre-Menstrual-Syndrome. Occurs just before the menstrual period. Women are usually moody during this period, some to the point of violence.

Porcupine – A relatively large rodent with sharp erectile bristles mingled with the fur.

Posh – Classy: elegant and fashionable. This is a steamship liner term. On ships, even on the first class cabins there was only room to pass in one direction. Posh literally stands for *port out starboard home*. Port is a nautical term meaning the left of a ship as the captain faces on the bridge. Starboard means to the right.

Posterior – The back or behind, as opposed to the anterior.

Prick – Slang term for a penis. Also, a slang term for an unpleasant person, an insult.

Primate – A mammal of the order Primates, which includes the anthropoids and prosimians, characterized by refined development of the hands and feet.

Proctologist – A doctor specializing in diseases of the rectum and anus.

Procreation – To beget and conceive (offspring).

Progesterone -A steroid hormone produced in the ovary; prepares and maintains the uterus for pregnancy.

Polarity – In batteries, this indicates what is plus and what is minus. Reversing the polarity means to make the plus minus and vice versa.

Prosimians – Any of a suborder (Strepsirhini) of small, arboreal primates, including lemurs, lorises, and bush babies.

Prostitute – A woman (or man) who plays for pay. She (or he) exchanges sexual favors for money. Sometimes referred to as the world's oldest profession. See gigolo and male prostitute above.

Puberty – The stage of adolescence in which an individual becomes

physiologically capable of sexual reproduction.

Quandary – Predicament: a situation from which extrication is difficult, especially an unpleasant or trying one.

Queer – Slang for gay or homosexual. It also means not normal.

Ram – A male sheep.

Rape – In criminal law, **rape** is an assault by a person involving sexual intercourse with another person without that person's consent.

Reagan – Ronald (Wilson) 1911-2004; 40th president of the U.S. (1981-89).

Redistribution – The act or process of redistributing. An economic theory or policy that advocates reducing inequalities in the distribution of wealth. This is also known in the vernacular as 'Robbing Peter to pay Paul.'

Reid – **Harry Mason Reid** (born December 2, 1939) is the senior United States Senator from Nevada and a member of the Democratic Party, for which he serves as Majority Leader.

Remedies – Cures. Actions by a court of law to impose its will.

Reproduction – The sexual or asexual process by which organisms generate new individuals of the same kind. Also known as procreation.

Rhythm Method Of Birth Control – Natural family planning in which ovulation is assumed to occur 14 days before the onset of a period (the fertile period would be assumed to extend from day 10 through day 18 of her cycle). It doesn't work very well, as evidenced by the large number of pregnancies experienced by the couples practicing this method.

Rodgers – Will Rodgers – United States humorist remembered for his homespun commentary on politics and American society (1879-1935).

Rooster – Male chicken. Responsible for excreting sperm to impregnate hens (Female chickens). Also known as a cock.

Rowboat – Dinghy: a small boat of shallow draft with cross thwarts for seats and rowlocks for oars with which it is propelled.

Sadist – Some one who takes pleasure in inflicting pain on someone else. They are the opposite of a masochist. In other words, they want to be the one wielding the whip. See masochist above.

Salamis – An island of Greece in the Saronic Gulf east of Athens. In an important naval battle off the island's northeast coast the Greek naval ships, led by Themistocles, defeated the Persian fleet in 480 B.C.

Salesmanship – Skill in selling; skill in persuading people to buy.

Sausage – Pork or other meat, chopped fine, highly seasoned, and either stuffed into membranous casings of varying size, as bologna or salami, or made into patties or links for cooking. Kosher meats are prepared under the supervision of a Rabbi. The Rabbi doesn't allow anything impure or waste products to go into sausage. The pareve (Also called parve, A U-shaped symbol) is the sign put on all kosher products. Since Jewish sausage contains no milk, it can be eaten with meat dishes by orthodox Jews.

Screwed – *Vulgar Slang:* The act or an instance of having sexual intercourse.

Seduction – Enticing someone astray from right behavior. Convincing someone to have sex with you,

Segment – Any of the parts into which something can be divided.

Segmented – Divided into or made up of distinct segments.

Senior – A senior citizen. Also, one that is of a higher position, rank, or grade than another in the same set or class. Also in the *US*, of or designating students in the fourth and final year at college or high school.

Shrug – To raise the shoulders, especially as a gesture of doubt, disdain, or indifference.

Sibling – Brother or sister. Sibling rivalry means competition between siblings.

Simian – Relating to, characteristic of, or resembling an ape or a monkey.

Slang – A kind of language occurring chiefly in casual and playful speech, made up typically of short-lived coinages and figures of speech that are deliberately used in place of standard terms for added raciness, humor, irreverence, or other effect.

S.O.B. – A polite way of saying 'son of a bitch'.

Socialism – An economic and political theory advocating public or common ownership and cooperative management of the means of production and allocation of resources.

Sorcery – The belief in magical spells that harness occult forces or evil spirits to produce unnatural effects in the world.

Sow Wild Oats – To do wild and foolish things in one's youth (often assumed to have some sort of sexual meaning).

Spare – In bowling, this means a single pin was left standing.

Spartan – A member of the city-state of Sparta in Greece. They were professional warriors, known for their ferocity in battle. Even today, Spartan stands for without frills, or reduced to the bare necessities. They are credited with originating the saying: <u>Come back with your shield or on it</u>. During a battle, the first thing to be tossed aside in a rout was the shield to enable someone to run faster without it. See Leonidas above.

Strike – In bowling, this means that no pins were left standing.

Subsidize – Monetary assistance granted by a government to a person or group in support of an enterprise regarded as being in the public interest.

Suppositories – Small plugs of medication designed to melt at body temperature within a body cavity other than the mouth.

Synchronization – The maintenance of one operation in step with another.

Precisely coordinating or matching two or more activities, devices, or processes in time.

Talleyrand (1754-1838) – He was born Charles Maurice de Talleyrand-Périgord. He was Prince of Benevento, and a statesman and diplomat during the French revolution.

Tallywacker – Slang term for penis.

Tapering – Tapered: becoming gradually narrower. Also, a very old name for a candle is a taper.

Tartan – Any of numerous textile patterns consisting of stripes of varying widths and colors crossed at right angles against a solid background, each forming a distinctive design worn by the members of a Scottish clan.

Telephone Pole – Normally made of wood, it is about 20-feet tall and has telephone lines connected to it.

Themistocles – Around 525–462 B.C., Athenian statesman and naval commander. He was elected one of the three archons in 493 B.C. In succeeding years, he became the chief figure of Athenian politics. He persuaded the Athenians to build up their navy, foreseeing that the Persians, defeated at Marathon in 490 B.C., would send another and stronger force against Greece.

Thespian – Person who lived in the city-state of Thespis in Greece. Also, an actor or actress.

Thighs – In humans the thigh is the area between the pelvis and the knee. Anatomically, it is part of the lower limb. In a chicken, it is the true femoral region that is hidden by the skin or feathers of the body.

The segment below, containing the fibula and tibia.

Tibia – The larger of the two bones in the leg (the smaller one being the fibula).

Tomb – Grave: a place for the burial of a corpse (especially beneath the ground and marked by a tombstone).

Tocqueville – **Alexis Charles Henri Maurice Clérel de**. 1805-59, French politician and political writer. His chief works are *De la Démocratie en Amérique* (1835-40) and *L'Ancien régime et la révolution* (1856).

Trabant – Was an automobile manufacturer from the former East Germany. Trabant cars have a bad reputation and are often regarded to be amongst the worst ever produced. They were, however, quite reliable, and Trabants were the most popular vehicles in use in the area of former communist countries, and they are still affectionately regarded by many. *Trabant* means "escort" in German.

Transplant – Transplant surgery is the division of medicine that surgically replaces an organ that is no longer functioning with an organ from a donor that does function. Organs are donated by living and deceased donors.

Transvestite – A person who dresses and acts in a style or manner traditionally associated with the opposite sex Especially, a male who adopts the dress and often the behavior typical of the opposite sex especially for purposes of emotional or sexual gratification.

Tubes – See fallopian tubes above.

Tune-Up – An adjustment, as of a motor or engine, made to improve working order or efficiency.

Umbrage – Offense; resentment. Example: He took umbrage at their rudeness.

Unperturbed – Calm and serene; unruffled.

Urethra – The tube which comes out of the bladder. It extends to the head of the penis in the male, and comes out in the vulva of the female.

Urinary excretion – Of or relating to the organs involved in the formation and excretion of urine. Urine originates in the kidneys, is stored in the bladder, and is finally excreted through the urethra. This takes place at the tip of the penis in the male, and in the vulva of the female. Although the man can stand to urinate, the woman is forced to squat on a toilet.

Uterus – A hollow muscular organ in the pelvic cavity of females. It contains the developing fetus. Also known as the womb, it is a hollow, pear-shaped organ located in a woman's lower abdomen between the bladder and the rectum. The narrow, lower portion of the uterus is the cervix; the broader, upper part is the corpus. The corpus is made up of two layers of tissue.

Uxorious – Excessively submissive or devoted to one's wife.

Vernacular – The standard native language of a country or locality. The everyday language spoken by a people as distinguished from the literary language. A variety of such everyday language specific to a social group or region: an example would be *the vernaculars of New York City*. The idiom of a particular trade or profession: an example would be *in the legal vernacular*. An idiomatic word, phrase, or expression. The common, nonscientific name of a plant or animal. See slang above.

Vertebrates – Animals having a bony or cartilaginous skeleton with a segmented spinal column and a large brain enclosed in a skull or cranium.

Vibrator – A device used for sexual stimulation of the clitoris and vagina. An electrically operated device used for massage.

Vice Versa – With the order or meaning reversed; conversely.

Vulgar – Coarse: lacking refinement or cultivation or taste.

Vulva – The external genital organs of the female, including the labia majora, labia minora, clitoris, and vestibule of the vagina. When a female is sexually excited, this area becomes wet.

Wealth – An abundance of valuable material possessions or resources; riches. Not to be confused with money, which is a medium of exchange. Money can be exchanged for wealth (Something can be bought) only as long as the person or government backing the money is good for it. As an example, people who fled Saigon in 1975 sometimes took with them suitcases of piasters, which became worthless with the fall of the government of South Vietnam.

Whereas –Has two different meanings: 1. While at the same time. 2. While on the contrary.

Wiccan – A Neopagan religion and a form of modern witchcraft.

Windshield – A framed pane of usually curved glass or other transparent shielding located in front of the occupants of a vehicle to protect them from the wind.

Witchcraft – The use of sorcery or magic.

Womb – The place where a person is nurtured inside the female body before birth. From womb to tomb means from conception to death. Another name for uterus. See uterus above.

Wooed – To seek the affection of with intent to romance. Example: He wooed her and won her.

Xerxes I – He succeeded his father, Darius. Also known as King Xerxes the Great. He was the King of Persia (486-465 B.C.) who organized a vast army that defeated King Leonidas and the Greeks at Thermopylae pass and destroyed Athens (480). After the defeat of his navy at Salamis (480) and of his army at Plataea (479), he retreated to Persia, where he was later assassinated.

Yiddish – A language spoken as a vernacular by Jews in Europe and elsewhere by Jewish emigrants, usually written in the Hebrew alphabet. Historically, it is a dialect of High German with an admixture of words of Hebrew, Romance, and Slavonic origins, developed in central and Eastern Europe during the Middle Ages.

Yugo – A car made in the former Yugoslavia. It is not considered reliable by modern western standards. The Zastava Koral (Serbian Cyrillic: Застава Корал), also known simply as the Yugo, was a subcompact vehicle built by Zastava corporation. The first Yugo 45 was handmade on 2 October 1978.

Zipper – A fastening device consisting of parallel rows of metal, plastic, or nylon teeth on adjacent edges of an opening that are interlocked by a sliding tab. Used on the fly on most trousers instead of buttons.

Conclusion

We hope that the serious student of language and linguistics will continue his or her studies with other works. We hope you will always be armed with a good dictionary when you do this. This dictionary should always be in your native language and English. In the event that English is already your native tongue, please use a dictionary such as Webster's. No one's vocabulary is perfect, so you never know when you will encounter a word whose meaning is unclear to you. When you encounter such a word, look it up in your dictionary!

If you have access to a computer, you may choose to jot down words you do not know and look them up later.

Appendix I:
French Expressions and Words

Throughout this book, the reader will encounter some words and expressions which are French. This appendix is an attempt to give definitions to some common French expressions in English. We owe a Google search based on the use of *French terms in English* and the subsequent reference to the web site "About.com" and Laura K. Lawless for the following definitions.

Adieu – Used like "farewell": when you don't expect to see the person again until God (when you die and go to Heaven). It literally means *until God*.

Agent provocateur – A person who attempts to provoke suspected individuals or groups into committing unlawful acts. It literally means *provocative agent*.

Aide-de-camp – A military officer who serves as a personal assistant to a higher-ranking officer. It literally means *camp assistant*.

Aide-mémoire – A position paper or something else that acts as an aid to memory, such as crib notes or mnemonic devices. It literally means *memory aid*.

A la carte – By itself price. French restaurants usually offer a *menu* with choices for each of the several courses at a fixed price. If you want something else (e.g. – a side order), you order from the *carte* or menu. It literally means *on the menu*.

A la mode – In English, this means "with ice cream" – apparently someone decided that having ice cream on pie was the fashionable way to eat it. It literally means *in fashion* or *in style*.

Amour-propre – Self respect. It literally means *self love*.

Apropos – In English, there are four ways to use *apropos*:

1. Adjective – A*ppropriate, to the point*: "That's true, but it's not apropos."

2. Adverb – A*t an appropriate time, opportunely*: "Fortunately, he arrived apropos."

3. Adverb/Interjection – B*y the way, incidentally*: "Apropos, what happened yesterday?"

4. Preposition (may or may not be followed by *of*) – W*ith regard to or speaking of*: "Apropos our meeting, I'll be late"; "He told a funny story apropos of the new president."

This is taken from the French **à propos (de).**

In French, *à propos* must be followed by the preposition *de*. It literally means *on the subject of.*

Art deco – Decorative art. In French, this is short for *art decorative*.

Attaché – A person assigned to a diplomatic post. It literally means *attached*.

Au contraire – On the contrary. It is usually used playfully in English. It literally means *on the contrary* in French.

Au courant – Informed on current affairs; up-to-date. Fully familiar; knowledgeable. It literally means *in the current*.

Au fait – Used in British English to mean "familiar" or "conversant": She's not really *au fait* with my ideas. It literally means *conversant* or *informed*.

Au gratin – With cheese. In French, *au gratin* refers to anything that is grated and put on top of a dish, like breadcrumbs or cheese. It literally means *with gratings*.

Au jus – Served with the meat's natural juices. It literally means *in the juice*.

Au naturel – In French, *au naturel* can mean either "in reality" or the literal meaning of "unseasoned" (in cooking). In English, we picked up the latter, less common usage and used it figuratively, to mean natural, untouched, pure, real. It literally means *in reality* or *unseasoned*.

Au pair – A person who works for a family (cleaning and/or teaching the children) in exchange for room and board. It literally means at par. See the joke *My Dad Has Two Of Those*.

Avant-garde – Innovative, especially in the arts. It literally means *before guard*.

Avoirdupois – Goods of weight. It literally means *goods of weight* or *having of weight*. It was originally spelled *averdepois* in French.

Bas-relief – Sculpture that is only slightly more prominent than its background. It literally means *low relief/design*.

Beau – A handsome young man. It also means a girl's boyfriend. It literally means *beautiful*.

Belle – A beautiful young lady. It literally means *beautiful*.

Belle époque – The golden age of art and culture in France in the early 20th century. It literally means *beautiful era*.

Bête noire – Similar to a pet peeve: something that is particularly distasteful or difficult and to be avoided. It literally means *black beast*.

Billet-doux – A love letter. It literally means a *sweet note*.

Blond, blonde – This is the only adjective in English which agrees in gender with the person it modifies: *blond* is for a man and *blonde* for a woman. Note that these can also be nouns. It literally means *fair-haired*.

Bon appétit – The closest English equivalent is "Enjoy your meal." It literally means *good appetite*.

Bon mot, bons mots – A joke, clever remark, or witticism. It literally means *good word(s)*.

Bon vivant – Someone who lives well, who knows how to enjoy life. It literally means *good 'liver'*.

Bon voyage – English has "Have a good trip," but *Bon voyage* is more elegant. It literally means *good trip*.

Brunette – The French word *brun (brown)*, dark-haired, is what English really means by "brunette." The *-ette* suffix indicates that the subject is small and female. It literally means *small, dark-haired female*.

Café au lait – It is the same thing as the Spanish term *café con leche*. It literally means *coffee with milk*.

Carte blanche – A free hand, the ability to do whatever you want/need. It literally means *blank card*.

Cause célèbre – A famous, controversial issue, trial, or case. It literally means *famous* or *celebrated cause*.

Cerise – The French word for the fruit gives us the English word for the color. It literally means *cherry*.

C'est la vie – That's life. It has the same meaning and usage in both languages. It literally means *that's life*.

Chaise longue – In English, this is often mistakenly written as "chaise lounge" – which actually makes perfect sense. It literally means *long chair*.

Chargé d'affaires – A substitute or replacement diplomat. It literally means *charged with business*.

Chic – In style. *Chic* sounds more *chic* than "stylish." It literally means *stylish*.

Cinéma vérité – Unbiased, realistic documentary filmmaking. It literally means *cinema truth*.

Comme il faut – The proper way, as it should be. It literally means *as it must*.

Cordon bleu – A master chef. It literally means *blue ribbon*.

Cordon sanitaire – Quarantine, buffer zone for political or medical reasons. It literally means *sanitary line*.

Corps – Body of men and women. An army unit usually consisting of two or more divisions and their support. The Marine Corps is actually part of the U.S. Navy. It literally means *body*.

Coup de foudre – Love at first sight. It literally means *bolt of lightning*.

Coup de grace – Deathblow, final blow, decisive stroke. It literally means *mercy blow*.

Coup d'état – A change of government, from one group to another. A sudden and decisive change of government illegally or by force. A bloodless coup is a change of government without bloodshed or violence.
It literally means *blow of state*.
Counting coup refers to the winning of prestige in battle by the Plains Indians of North America. Warriors won prestige by acts of bravery in the face of the enemy, and these acts could be recorded in various ways and retold as stories. Also, the Sioux ritual of striking an enemy who has fallen, wounded or dead; the first person to count coup is considered bravest of the group, almost as brave as the one who has brought the enemy down.

Crème brûlée – Baked custard with a caramelized crust. It literally means *burnt cream*.

Crème caramel – Synonym of flan – custard lined with caramel. It literally means *caramel cream*.

Crème de cacao – A chocolate-flavored liqueur. The cacao plant is grown primarily in South America, and the liqueur is from that region. It literally means *cream of cacao*.

Crème de la crème – It is synonymous with the English expression "cream of the crop" and refers to the best of the best. It literally means *cream of the cream*.

Crème de menthe – A mint-flavored liqueur. It literally means *cream of mint*.

Crème fraîche – This is a funny term. Despite its meaning, crème fraîche is in fact slightly fermented, thickened cream. It literally means *fresh cream*.

Crime passionnel – A crime of passion. It literally means *passionate crime*.

Critique – Critique is an adjective and noun in French, but a noun and verb in English; it refers to a critical review of something or the act of performing such a review. It literally means *critical judgment*.

Cuisine – In English, *cuisine* refers only to a particular type of food/cooking, such as French cuisine, Southern cuisine, etc. It literally means *kitchen, food style.*

Cul-de-sac – A dead-end street. It literally means *bottom (butt) of the bag.*

Debutante – In French, *débutante* is the feminine form of *débutant* – beginner (noun) or beginning (adj). In both languages, it also refers to a young girl making her formal début into society. Interestingly, this usage is not original in French; it was adopted back from English. It literally means *beginner.*

Décolletage, décolleté – The first is a noun, the second an adjective, but both refer to low necklines on women's clothing. It literally means *low neckline, lowered neckline.*

Dégustation – The French word simply refers to the act of tasting, while in English "degustation" is used for a tasting event or party, as in wine or cheese tasting. It literally means *tasting.*

Déjà vu – This is a grammatical structure in French, as in *Je l'ai déjà vu*=> I've already seen it. It can also disparage a style or technique that has already been done, as in *Son style est déjà vu*=> His style is not original.
In English, *déjà vu* refers to the scientific phenomenon of feeling like you have already seen or done something when you're sure that you haven't: a feeling of déjà vu = *une impression de déjà vu.* It literally means *already seen.*

Demimonde –
1. A marginal or disrespectful group.
2. Prostitutes and/or kept women.
It literally means *half world.*

Demitasse – Refers to a small cup of espresso or other strong coffee. It literally means *half cup.*

Démodé – Has the same meaning in both languages: outmoded, out of fashion. It literally means *out of fashion.*

De rigueur – Required, mandatory. It literally means *of rigueur.*

Dernier cri – The newest fashion or trend. It literally means *last cry.*

De trop – Excessive, superfluous. It literally means *of too much.*

Derriere – Backside. Sometimes used as a polite expression for buttocks. The slang term in English is ass. It literally means *behind* or *in back of.*

Double entendre – A word or phrase which can be taken more than one way. A word play or pun. For example, you're looking at a field of sheep and you say "How are you (ewe)?" It literally means *double hearing.*

Du jour – "Soup *du jour*" is nothing more than an elegant-sounding version of "soup of the day." It literally means *of the day.*

Droit du seigneur – The feudal lord's right to deflower his vassal's bride. It literally means *right of the lord of the manor.*

Eau de Cologne – This is often cut down to simply "cologne" in English. Cologne is the French and English name for the German city of Köln. It literally means *water from Cologne.*

Eau de toilette – Toilet here does not refer to a commode. It is a very weak perfume. It literally means *toilet water.*

En bloc – In a group, all together. It literally means *in a block.*

En brochette – It is also known by the Turkish name: *shish kebab.* It literally means *on* (a) *skewer.*

Encore – A simple adverb in French, "encore" in English refers to an additional performance, usually requested with audience applause. It literally means *again.*

Enfant terrible – Refers to a troublesome or embarrassing person within a group (of artists, thinkers, etc). It literally means *terrible child.*

En garde – Warning that one should be on his/her guard, ready for an attack (originally in fencing). It literally means *on guard.*

En masse – In a group, all together. It literally means *in mass.*

En passant – In passing, by the way; (chess) the capturing of a pawn after a specific move. It literally means *in passing.*

En prise – In the game of chess, exposed to capture. It literally means *in grasp*.

En rapport – Agreeable, harmonious. It literally means *in agreement*.

En route – On the way. It literally means *on route*.

En suite – Part of a set, together. It literally means *in sequence*.

Entente cordiale – Friendly agreements between countries, especially those signed in 1904 between France and the UK. It literally means *cordial agreement*.

Entrez (vous) – English speakers often say this, but it's wrong – the correct way to say "come in" in French is simply *entrez*. Entrez literally means *come in*.

Esprit de corps – Similar to team spirit or morale. It literally means *group spirit*.

Esprit d'escalier – Thinking of an answer or comeback too late. It literally means *stairway spirit*.

Fait accompli – *Fait accompli* seems more fatalistic to me than done deed, which is so factual. It literally means *done deed*.

Faux – False, fake. I once saw an ad for "genuine faux pearls." No worries that those pearls might be real, I guess – you were guaranteed fake ones. It literally means *false, fake*.

Faux pas – Stands for false step. It means to make a mistake or to open your mouth and say something wrong. It literally means *false step*.

Femme fatale – An alluring, mysterious woman who seduces men into compromising situations. It literally means *deadly woman*.

Fiancé, fiancée – An engaged person, betrothed. Note that *fiancé* refers to a man and *fiancée* to a woman. It literally means *engaged person, betrothed*.

Film noir – Black is a literal reference to the stark black-and-white cinematography style, though *films noirs* tend to be figuratively dark as well (e.g., morbid, bleak, depressing, etc). It literally means *black movie*.

Fin-de-siècle – Hyphenated in English, *fin-de-siècle* refers to the end of the 19th century. It literally means *end of the century*.

Fleur-de-lis, fleur-de-lys – A type of iris or an emblem in the shape of an iris with three petals. It literally means *flower of lily*.

Foie gras – The liver of a force-fed goose, considered a delicacy. It literally means *fat liver*.

Folie à deux – Mental disorder which occurs simultaneously in two people with a close relationship or association. It literally means *craziness for two*.

Force majeure – Refers to superior/greater force, or to an unexpected or uncontrollable event, such as "an act of God" like a tornado or earthquake. It literally means *greater force*.

Gamine – Refers to an impish or playful girl/woman. It literally means *playful, little girl*.

Gauche – Awkward, tactless, lacking in social grace. It literally means *left, awkward*.

Genre – Used mostly in literature, art and film – "I really like this *genre*..." It literally means *type*.

Grand mal – Severe epilepsy. Also see *petit mal*. It literally means *great illness*.

Haute couture – High-class, fancy (and expensive) clothing styles. It literally means *high sewing*.

Haute cuisine – High-class, fancy (and expensive) cooking or food. It literally means *high cuisine*.

Honi soit qui mal y pense – Evil be to him whom evil thinks. Motto for the Knights of the Garter. Supposedly said by King Louis XIV of France when a courtier made an obscene remark about a lady who raised her skirt too high in the French court.

Hors de combat – Out of action. It literally means *out of combat.*

Hors d'œuvre – An appetizer. *Œuvre* here refers to the main work (course), so *hors d'œuvre* simply means something besides the main course. It literally means *outside of work.*

Idée fixe – Fixation, obsession. It literally means *set idea.*

Je ne sais quoi – Used to indicate a "certain something," as in "I really like Ann. She has a certain *je ne sais quoi* that I find very appealing." It literally means *I don't know what.*

Joie de vivre – The quality in people who live life to the fullest. It literally means *joy of living.*

Laissez-faire – A policy of non-interference. Note that the expression in French is *laisser-faire.* It literally means *let it be.*

Maître d', maître d'hôtel – The former is more common in English, which is strange since it is incomplete: "The 'master of' will show you to your table." It literally means *master of, master of hotel.*

Mal de mer – Seasickness. It literally means *sickness of sea.*

Mardi gras – Celebration in New Orleans (and other former French colonies) before Lent. It literally means *fat Tuesday.*

Matinée – In English, indicates the day's first showing of a movie or play. Can also refer to a midday romp with one's lover. It literally means *morning.*

Ménage à trois – Sexual threesome. It literally means *household of three.*

Mot juste – Exactly the right word or expression. It literally means *right word.*

Née – Used in genealogy to refer to a woman's maiden name: Anne Miller *née* (or nee) Smith. It literally means *born.*

Noblesse oblige – The idea that those who are noble are obliged to act noble. It literally means *nobility obligates.*

Nom de Guerre – Name used in a war. For example, they were frequently adopted by recruits in the French Foreign Legion as part of the break with their past lives. It literally means *war name.*

Nom de Plume – Name used for writing; a pen-name. For example, the pen-name for Samuel Clemens is Mark Twain (This is a river pilot's term meaning that the water is two fathoms deep). The French phrase was coined by English speakers in imitation of *nom de guerre.* It literally means *pen name.*

Nouveau riche – Disparaging term for someone who has recently come into money. It literally means *new rich.*

Nouvelle cuisine – Cooking style developed in the 1960's and 70's that emphasized lightness and freshness. It literally means *new cooking.*

Objet d'art – Art object, such as a painting or sculpture. Note that the French word *objet* does not have a c – you should never write "object d'art." It literally means *art object.*

Oh là là – Oh dear. Note: It is usually misspelled and mispronounced «ooh la la» in English. It literally means *oh dear.*

Papier mâché – Used for art. It literally means *mashed paper.*

Par excellence – By excellence. By preeminence. Superior to or notable above all others; outstanding. It literally means *by excellence.*

Pas de deux – Dance with two people. It literally means *step of two.*

Passé – Old-fashioned, out-of-date, past its prime. It literally means *past.*

Passe-partout:
1. Master key.
2. (In art) a mat, paper, or tape used to frame a picture.
It literally means *pass everywhere.*

Peau de soie – Soft, silky fabric with a dull finish. It literally means *skin of silk.*

Petit – (law) lesser, minor. It literally means *small.*

Petite – It may sound *chic*, but *petite* is simply the feminine French adjective meaning "short" or "small." It literally means *small, short.*

Petit four – Small dessert, especially cake. It literally means *little oven.*

Petit mal – Relatively mild epilepsy. Also see *grand mal.* It literally means *small illness.*

Petit point – Small stitch used in needlepoint. It literally means *little stitch.*

Pièce de résistance – In French, this originally referred to the main course – the test of your stomach's stamina. In both languages, it now refers to an outstanding accomplishment or the final part of something – a project, a meal, etc. It literally means *piece of stamina.*

Pied-à-terre – A temporary or secondary place of residence. It literally means *foot on ground.*

Pince-nez – Eyeglasses clipped to the nose. It literally means *pinch-nose.*

Plus ça change – The more things change (the more they stay the same). It literally means *More it changes.*

Potpourri – A scented mixture of dried flowers and spices; a miscellaneous group or collection. It literally means *rotten pot.*

Prêt-à-porter – Originally referred to clothing, now sometimes used for food. It literally means *ready to wear.*

Protégé – Someone whose training is sponsored by an influential person. It literally means *protected.*

Raconteur – Someone who tells stories or jokes. One who tells stories and anecdotes with skill and wit. This is taken from the French verb *raconter* meaning *to tell* or *to relate.*

Raison d'être – Purpose, justification for existing. It literally means *reason for being.*

Rendez-vous – In French, this refers to a date or an appointment (literally, it is the verb *se rendre* [to go] in the imperative); in English we can use it as a noun or a verb (let's *rendez-vous* at 8pm). It literally means *go to*.

Repartee – The French *repartie* gives us the English "repartee," with the same meaning of a swift, witty, and "right on" retort. It literally means *quick, accurate response*.

Risqué – Suggestive, overly provocative. It literally means *risked*.

Roche moutonnée – Mound of bedrock smoothed and rounded by erosion. Incidentally, *mouton* means "sheep." It literally means *rolled rock*.

Roman à clés – Novel with real people appearing as fictional characters. It literally means *novel with keys*.

Roman-fleuve – A long, multi-volume novel which presents the history of several generations of a family or community. In both French and English, *saga* tends to be used more. It literally means *novel river*.

Rouge – The English refers to a reddish cosmetic or metal/glass-polishing powder, and can be a noun or a verb. It literally means *red*.

R.S.V.P. – This stands for *Repondez, S'il Vous Plait*. Answer If It Pleases You. It means that an answer is expected – either affirmatively or negatively. It literally means *respond please*.

Sang-froid – The ability to maintain one's composure. In cold blood. It literally means *cold blood*.

Sans – Without – used mainly in academia, although it's also seen in the font style "sans serif" => without decorative flourishes. It literally means *without*.

Savoir-faire – To know how to do or make. This phrase is used to identify someone who is sophisticated and never taken off guard. See the joke labeled *Savoir Faire*. It literally means knowing how to do.

Savoir-vivre – To know how to live. It literally means *to know how to live*.

Soi-disant – Self-styled: as claimed by and for yourself often without justification. What one claims about oneself; so-called, alleged. It literally means *self saying*.

Soigné –
1. Sophisticated, elegant, fashionable.
2. Well-groomed, polished, refined.
It literally means *taken care of*.

Soirée – In English, refers to an elegant party. It literally means *evening*.

Soupçon – Used figuratively like hint: There's just a *soupçon* of garlic in the soup. It literally means *suspicion*.

Souvenir – A memento. It literally means *memory, keepsake*.

Succès d'estime – Important but unpopular success or achievement. It literally means *success of estimate*.

Succès fou – Wild success. It literally means *crazy success*.

Tableau vivant – A scene made up of silent, motionless actors. It literally means *living picture*.

Table d'hôte:
1. A table for all guests to sit together.
2. A fixed-price meal with multiple courses.
It literally means *host table*.

Tête-à-tête – A private talk or visit with another person. It literally means *head to head*.

Toilette – In French, this refers both to the toilet itself and anything related to toiletries; thus the expression "to do one's toilette" – brush hair, do makeup, etc. See *eau de toilette* above. It literally means *toilet*.

Touché – Originally used in fencing, now equivalent to "you got me." It literally means *touched*.

Tour de force – Something which takes a great deal of strength or skill to accomplish. It literally means *turn of strength*.

Trompe l'œil – A painting style which uses perspective to trick the eye into thinking it is real. In French, trompe l'œil can also refer in general to artifice and trickery. It literally means *trick the eye*.

Vis-à-vis (de) – In French, when *vis-à-vis* precedes a noun and means facing, next to, or towards, it must be followed by the preposition *de*. In English it means "compared to" or "in relation with": vis-à-vis this decision=> vis-à-vis de cette décision. It literally means *face to face*.

Voilà! – There it is! Nearly every time I see this in English, it is misspelled as "voilá" or "violà. It literally means *There it is!*

Vol-au-vent – In both French and English, a *vol-au-vent* is a very light pastry shell filled with meat or fish with sauce. It literally means *flight of the wind*.

Volte-face – A turnabout, especially a reversal of opinion or policy. It literally means *about face* in military terminology.

Appendix II:
American / British Expressions and Words

This work is American. However, the student may also travel in England and encounter a British version of the language. Indeed, it was George Bernard Shaw who famously said: "England and America are two countries separated by the same language." The differences are cultural as well as linguistic. Here are a few of the more common words which are different in American and British English. This is only meant to highlight some of the variety which exists within English, and is not a complete list by any means. It also does not address different vocabulary which is used in Australia, Canada, South Africa and India as well as the Caribbean, Africa, and the many other places in the world which use English as the language of commerce or government.

This appendix is designed to detail some of these differences in terminology.

American	British
Apartment	Flat
Ale	Beer – American beer is considered to be a light lager
Argument	Row
Bar	Pub (Sometimes known as "your local" in England)
Baby Carriage	Pram (Short for perambulator)
Band-aid	Plaster
Bathroom	Loo or WC (Water Closet)
Beer	Light Lager
Can	Tin
Chopped Beef	Mince
Cookie	Biscuit
Corn	Maize
Cured	Sorted Out
Diaper	Nappy

Elevator	Lift
Eraser	Rubber
Fanny (The expression means backside)	Fanny (This is a very rude expression in England. It means a woman's vagina)
Figures out, infers or discovers	Susses
Flashlight	Torch
Fries	Chips – Fish and chips is a favorite English dish.
Gas	Petrol
Guy	Bloke or Chap
Highway	Motorway
Hood (of a car)	Bonnet (of a car)
Jell-O	Jelly
Jelly	Jam
Kerosene	Paraffin
Ladies' garter belt	Suspenders
Lawyer	Solicitor or Barrister
Looked at; observed, saw, understood	Twigged
License Plate	Number Plate
Line	Queue
Man	Bloke
Mail	Post
Mistake	Cock up (Sometimes used by women as well as men in England)
Motor Home	Caravan
Movie Theatre	Cinema
Muffler	Silencer
Napkin	Serviette
Nothing	Nought
Overpass	Flyover
Pacifier	Dummy
Pants	Trousers (Pants are worn by women)
Parking Lot	Car Park

Period	Full Stop
Pharmacist	Chemist
Potato Chips	Crisps
Raisin Pudding	Spotted Dick
Rent	Hire
Rubber – Slang term for condom	Condom (Rubber means eraser)
Sausage	Banger
Shut the door	Put the wood in the hole
Sidewalk	Pavement
Soccer	Football
Straightened out	Sorted out
Suspenders	Braces (Suspenders are a ladies foundation garment which is used to hold up her stockings. See Ladies' garter belt above)
Sweater	Jumper
Take off	Do a runner
Trash Can	Bin
Truck	Lorry
Trunk (of a car)	Boot (of a car)
Undershirt	Vest (This is on laundry lists)
Vacation	Holiday
Vest	Waistcoat (A vest is an undershirt)
Vulgar	Rude
Windshield (Of a car)	Windscreen
Zip Code	Postal Code
Zucchini	Courgettes (The English use the French rather than the Italian term)

Appendix III:
Colloquialisms

Spoken or colloquial English is somewhat different than formal or written English. We are indebted to the internet for a list of these terms. They are grouped by their purpose.

Miscellaneous:
Sweating like a whore in church.
Nervous as a whore in church.
Nervous as a long-tailed cat in a roomful of rocking chairs.
Off like a prom dress.
Like pissing up a rope.
In and out like a fiddler's elbow.
Up and down like a bride's nightie.
Going up and down like a whore's panties.
Shivering like a dog shitting razor blades.
Shaking like a dog passing peach seeds.
You're so green if I stuck you in the ground you'd grow.
Raining like a cow pissing on a flat rock.
Make you want to slap your Granny.
You look like the syphilitic afterbirth of a Lower Slobovian gang bang.
It ain't what you want, but what you get that makes you fat.
Hotter than two rats fucking in a wool sock.
Hotter than a fresh fucked fox in a forest fire.
Slicker than snot on a doorknob (owl shit through a tin horn).
Shut up tighter'n a bull's ass in fly season.
Couldn't hit a bull's ass with a bass fiddle.
Lower than a well digger's ass.
Nuttier than a squirrel turd.
Happier than a dog with two dicks.
Busier than a one-legged man in an ass kicking contest.
Busier than a two-peckered fox in mating season.
Went through here like fat through a goose.
Bleeding like a stuck pig.
You can't put a square peg in a round hole.

Usefulness:
Useful as tits on a warthog.
Useful as tits on a bull.
Useful as tits on a boar hog.

Dumb or crazy (not intelligent):
Not too smart.
Stupid as a fried Popsicle.
A few kangaroos short in the top paddock.
Two sandwiches short of a picnic.
One brick shy of a full load.
Toys in the attic.
The lights are on but there's nobody home.
Not the sharpest tool in the shed.
Not the sharpest knife in the drawer.
Not the brightest bulb on the string.
One French fry short of a Happy Meal.
One donut short of a dozen.
He couldn't make a noun and a verb agree if his life depended on it.
If brains were dynamite, he'd be dangerous!
If you had a brain, you'd be dangerous!
If brains were gasoline, yours wouldn't be enough to make a piss-ant's go-cart go around the inside of a Cheerio.
Balancing your brain on a razor blade would be like bouncing a BB down a four lane highway.
He's a quart low in the crankcase.
A day late and a dollar short.
Dumber than a sled rack.
Dumber than a sledge hammer.
Dumber than dirt.
Dumber than a June bug on a string.
Dumber than a box of rocks.
Dumber than a sack of hammers.
Too dumb to pound sand in a rat hole.
Too dumb to pour piss out of a boot with instructions written on the heel.
So dumb he couldn't hit the broad side of the barn.
Dumb as a rock.
Dumb as a post.
Dumb as a stump.
Dumb as a load of coal.
Slow as mud.

Hasn't got both oars in the water.

Porch light is on, but there's nobody home.

So confused he don't know whether to scratch his watch or wind his behind.

If you were twice as smart, you would be a half-wit.

The engine's running, but nobody's driving.

Two bricks shy of a full load.

If all his brains were dynamite, he couldn't blow his nose.

You're about as bright as a burnt out lantern, covered in tar, buried in the storm cellar of a coal mine.

He's crazier than a road-running lizard.

Crazy as a loon.

Crazy as a soup sandwich.

Blind:

Blind as a bat"

A blind man could see that with his cane.

Ray Charles could see that.

If it were a snake, it would've bit me.

Exclamation – Excitement:

Great day in the morning!

Well, I'll swan!

Slick as a whistle! – said when something went well.

Hell in a hand basket – going to pot.

Going to pot – going to hell.

I'll be cow kicked by a mule!

Wouldn't that just dill your pickle? – Used to express dismay over something that has happened or might happen.

Wicked awesome!

Wicked cool.

Wicked awful good.

Some wicked awful good.

Bless her heart – You can say anything about someone, however unkind, as long as you bless her when you're done. "She's dumb as a bag o' hammers, bless her heart."

Experienced or smart – Not dumb:

I like to think that I've 'been around the block few times, just so I don't look that way.

Do I look like I just fell off a turnip truck?

329

Well, don't that just beat all?
This ain't my first rodeo.
Smart as a whip.
Sharper than a tack.
Sly as a fox.

Ugly, Pretty:
Ugly enough to knock a buzzard off a shit wagon.
Ugly enough to scare a buzzard off a meat wagon.
Ugly enough to scare a pit bull up a plate glass window.
Ugly as the south end of a northbound dog (or hog or cow).
Ugly as an unwiped asshole.
Uglier than the south bound end of a north bound donkey.
Uglier than a burnt stump.
Uglier than the east end of a horse headed west.
You're prettier than a glob of butter melting on a stack of wheat cakes.
Prettier than a blue-nosed mule.
Cuter than a speckled pup.
He looks like the dog's been keeping him under the porch – Not handsome.
When I was a kid, I was so ugly that my mother had to tie pork chops to my
ears so the dog would play with me.
Ugly as sin.

Comments made about people:
You could grow potatoes in those dirty ears.
Sweet as honey.
Got off like a fat rat with cheese.
As full of wind as a corn-eating horse – prone to boasting.
He's got a ten-gallon mouth – talkative.
Low man on the totem pole.
Cool as a cucumber.
Flat as a pancake.
Working like a dog.
Meaner 'n a rattlesnake.
Old as Moses' toes.
Older than dirt.
Hair as black as coal.
Deaf as a doorknob / blind as a bat.
So skinny they have to stand up twice to make a shadow.
Couldn't hit a barn if you were on the inside, with the door closed.
Ants in her pants.

So windy he could blow up an onion sack.
So useless that if he had a third hand he would need another pocket to put
it in.
Lower than a snake in a wagon track.
Strong as an ox.
Dishwater blond.
He/she sure has hay on his/her horns today.
Sat there like a bump on a log.
Acting like he/she's got bees in his/her bonnet.
You look like you have been drug through a knot hole backwards.
Ugly as sin.
Straight as an arrow.
As sweet as pie.
Skinny as a bean pole.
Can't carry a tune in a bucket – can't sing.
Butter wouldn't melt in her mouth – cold woman.
As loose as a goose.
Just ignore him and he'll die quietly in a corner. – said when really annoyed
with someone.
Over the hill.
Can't burn both ends of a stick (or a candle) at the same time.
Stubborn as a mule.
Naked as a jaybird.
I hope she lives to a 150 and looks it.
She should get some shoes to go with those bags – said when someone looks
really tired.
Do you have shoes to go with my bags? – If I am looking really tired.
Up & down like a whore's drawers – refers to a nervous person, up & down.
Doesn't know his behind (or ass) from a hole in the ground.
Slicker (or cleaner) than a hounds tooth.
Slipperier than snot on a glass doorknob.
Colder than a well-digger's feet in Alaska.
Dead as a doornail.
Fit as a fiddle.
Quiet as a mouse.
Looks like the cat that swallowed the canary.
Two ax handles wide across the behind – fat.
Two ax handles and a rain barrel – fat.
Like a fish out of water.
Lying like a snake in the grass.
Lies like an old rug.

Dating:
Sure you can date; in fact I'll be waiting for him in the front yard while I sharpen my machete.
Yes, he has to come to the door and pick you up… how else will I get the chance to interrogate him?
If he wants to date you, he has to get through me first!! – referring to a date who blows the car horn for you
Now just wait a minute, you're moving so fast you look like one of Pavlov's dogs running for the bell.
Well, that is rude. How rude? I'll tell you how rude.
Well, he can just stay out there and blow his horn, and maybe he'll get some cows to come home.
Don't stay out later than when the cows come home.

Slow, Fast:
High-tailing it – running fast.
Fast as a rabbit.
Like green corn through the new maid.

Stop your complaining:
Well it's better than a kick in the arse with a frozen boot!
Well, it's better than a poke in the eye with a blunt stick!
It's better than a sharp stick in the eye.
Want in one hand, spit in the other, and see which one gets full first – reply to someone that wants something.

Poor, Rich, Money:
I don't have a pot to piss in or a window to throw it out of.
I don't have one penny to rub against another one.
I don't have two pennies to rub together.
Poor as a church mouse.
He may be good looking, but good looking won't put food on the table.
You've got champagne taste with a beer pocketbook – expensive taste, but no money.
Champagne taste on a beer budget – expensive taste, but no money.
Tighter than bark on a tree – not generous.
He's got enough money to burn a wet mule.
Filthy rich.
Dirt poor.

Dishonest:
He's so dishonest that he'd rather piss in the wind than tell the truth.
He knows more ways to take your money than a roomful of lawyers.
You can tell a lawyer's lying when his lips are moving.

Eat, Drinking and Cooking:
Wetting your whistle – getting a drink.
Gooder than candy and better than snuff – grandma's cooking.
He eats like a pin in a swallow.
Stump water – weak coffee.
Don't swallow watermelon seeds or you'll wake up one morning with vines.
Growing out of your ears.
Tad, smidgen, dab – Granny's cooking measurements.
Tough as shoe leather.
Grub's on.

How You Doing?:
Oh, I'm circling the drain.
Fair to middling – I am told that this has to do with grading cotton.
If I had a tail, it'd be wagging.
Well, better 'n getting poked in the eye, I suppose.

Telling Someone to Get Lost:
Take a long walk off a short pier.
Go away and boil your head.

Yes, No, Maybe, Never:
I might could do that – maybe.
When pigs fly – never.

If the good Lord is willing and the creek don't rise – when asked about the
likelihood of just about anything happening.
Does a bear shit in the woods? – yes.

Loud:
You kids are noisier than a fox in the henhouse.
You're so loud you could wake the dead.
Speak up, I think that mountain goat in Tibet did not hear you!

Cursing around children:
Son of a gosh darned sassafras root!

Acknowledgements

The English poet John Donne has famously written: "No man is an Island, entire of itself." We wish to thank the many contributors to the present work. Very little in it is original. Rather, it relies almost entirely on the contributions of many people who have been encountered throughout the years. Each has contributed to the jokes in this book.

We cannot begin to enumerate the people who have contributed to this volume. Among the many contributors are clients and members of the staff of Worldwide Chain Store Systems. Staff members include Dick Oksanen (who used to have a sense of humor before he began to take himself too seriously), Jim Meese, Jim Jones, Dave Gibson, Barry Grange in England, Gary Stephenson, Mukundan Shivaram, Marty Abt, Skip Passonno, Mike Beane, Jim Horton, Jim Schneider, Jim Moseley, Ken Mead, John Bailey, Don Vehlhaber, Mike Dirmeikis, Carol Larson, Linda Crombie, Nancy Martino, Marcie Cootware, Judy Parrot, Nancy Spicer and Ed Phillips, Chris and Cheryl Miller, Elie DeCassis, Tom Bielanski, Michelle Dudzik, Pat Gallagher, Ellary Kahan, Rick Phillips, John Knepper, John Kurach, Karen Landon, Juan Perez, Sam Little, Tom McDermott, Al Gregor, Tom Ramsey, Marilyn Rohn, Paul Hallyburton, Grover Shepherd, Rob Sommer, Don Whittemore, Julie Batts, David Burbank, Charlie Walte, Ron Clement in Australia, Clive Wiggett in England, Jose and Maria Bravo, President Charlie Fitzmorris and many others too numerous to mention.

Anyone who decides to self publish relies heavily on on-line publishers. We wish to thank the staff of iUniverse for this privilege. Particularly, we want to thank Laura Witkowski, Mara Rockey and everyone else who have been so helpful. Particular thanks are due to my Editorial Consultant, George Nedeff, and for the counsel and advice he has provided. Particular thanks are also due to my Publishing Services associate, Jesse Loudenbarger.